DIRECTING THE FLOW OF PRODUCT

A Guide to Improving Supply Chain Planning

JEFFREY H. SCHUTT, PH.D.

THE EDUCATIONAL SOCIETY
FOR RESOURCE MANAGEMENT

Copyright ©2004 by Jeffrey H. Schutt

ISBN 1-932159-19-3

Printed and bound in the U.S.A. Printed on acid-free paper
10 9 8 7 6 5 4 3 2 1

Library of Congress Cataloging-in-Publication Data

Schutt, Jeffrey H., 1950-
  Directing the flow of product : a guide to improving supply chain
planning / Jeffrey H. Schutt.
      p.   cm.
Includes bibliographical references.
    ISBN 1-932159-19-3
  1. Business logistics. 2. Production management. 3. Strategic
planning. I. Title.
   HD38.5.S39 2004
   658.7—dc22
                                    2003027451

Phone: (561) 869-3900
Fax: (561) 892-0700
Web: www.jrosspub.com

CONTENTS

PREFACE

This is a book about how to construct effective planning approaches for managing product flow. Planning the movement of product through manufacturing and distribution has been a concern for businesses for more than a century, but doing it truly well remains a worthy challenge for us.

The typical book about planning is either a textbook that teaches a broad variety of generally accepted techniques or an explication of a particular planning technique that is "just what you need to solve your problems." This book is a bit different. It includes a high-level survey of planning approaches, but it is focused on helping the reader understand those techniques in a new light, understand certain principles that are requirements for good planning system design, and learn a methodology for designing the right planning system for a given enterprise. This book is intended primarily for practitioners who already have considerable background in the planning field, although it can also be used as supplemental reading for advanced courses in operations management or supply chain planning.

Product flow planning is a vast subject and could easily fill a multivolume tome. Instead, this book has been consciously kept to a reasonable size because:

- Anyone thinking seriously about how to plan operations is a busy person, and we respect the reader's time.
- We have tried to not duplicate topics that are covered well elsewhere, and we provide many references to other material.
- We are far too lazy to create and manage a massive book!

We have attempted to maintain a light touch and sense of humor throughout this volume. Product flow planning is a complex and subtle subject, leading to mistakes that can seem absurd in retrospect. We hope that the reader's understanding is increased rather than lessened by our attempts at levity. The book is written in a very informal style, although we have retained one feature of more formal tomes: frequent references to other published work. Again, because we do not attempt to actually teach the techniques referenced here, we want to let the reader know where to find more detail.

THE AUTHOR

Jeffrey H. Schutt consults on supply chain planning and execution for Menlo Worldwide's Professional Services Group. He has taught in the Management Department at the University of Texas and served as a Partner in the Supply Chain Solutions practice of CSC Consulting. He is also an alumnus of optimization pioneers Analysis, Research and Computation, Inc. and of the seminal logistics firm Cleveland Consulting Associates.

Dr. Schutt holds bachelor's, master's, and Ph.D. degrees from Stanford University. His unique insights on supply chain planning are based on over twenty years of experience approaching it from multiple perspectives. He has led consulting projects to create new planning processes in the consumer goods, industrial products, automotive, paper, aerospace, high-tech, and distribution industries. He has designed and created custom planning systems for clients. He has led the design and development of packaged planning software and implemented software suites from other providers. He has performed postmortem evaluations of the effectiveness of new planning techniques.

This body of work has given him a unique perspective on the challenges businesses face in improving their planning, and led to this book.

ACKNOWLEDGMENTS

This book is dedicated to my loving wife June, son Robert, and daughter Katherine, who have supported me through many long nights and weekends of work on it.

I would like to thank numerous colleagues who have helped to develop the understandings presented here, contributed ideas, or reviewed the draft: Jim Kilpatrick, Dr. Bob Carlson, Atul Garg, Mike Ledyard, Tom Moore, Roger Kallock, Jeff Benesch, Steve Simco, Steve Goble, James Fehlberg, and Brad Scheller. I must, in particular, thank Dr. G. Terry Ross, whose brilliance has often influenced me.

ABOUT APICS

APICS — The Educational Society for Resource Management is a not-for-profit international educational organization recognized as the global leader and premier provider of resource management education and information. APICS is respected throughout the world for its education and professional certification programs. With more than 60,000 individual and corporate members in 20,000 companies worldwide, APICS is dedicated to providing education to improve an organization's bottom line. No matter what your title or need, by tapping into the APICS community you will find the education necessary for success.

APICS is recognized globally as:

- The source of knowledge and expertise for manufacturing and service industries across the entire supply chain
- The leading provider of high-quality, cutting-edge educational programs that advance organizational success in a changing, competitive marketplace
- A successful developer of two internationally recognized certification programs, Certified in Production and Inventory Management (CPIM) and Certified in Integrated Resource Management (CIRM)
- A source of solutions, support, and networking for manufacturing and service professionals

For more information about APICS programs, services, or membership, visit www.apics.org or contact APICS Customer Support at (800) 444-2742 or (703) 354-8851.

Free value-added materials available from
the Download Resource Center at www.jrosspub.com

At J. Ross Publishing we are committed to providing today's professional with practical, hands-on tools that enhance the learning experience and give readers an opportunity to apply what they have learned. That is why we offer free ancillary materials available for download on this book and all participating Web Added Value™ publications. These online resources may include interactive versions of material that appears in the book or supplemental templates, worksheets, models, plans, case studies, proposals, spreadsheets and assessment tools, among other things. Whenever you see the WAV™ symbol in any of our publications, it means bonus materials accompany the book and are available from the Web Added Value Download Resource Center at www.jrosspub.com.

Downloads available for *Directing the Flow of Product: A Guide to Improving Supply Chain Planning* consist of an exploration of leanness with agility, an illustration of the intellectual process of redesigning planning, a man–machine planning template, an analysis of the simplicity/accuracy trade-offs in planning, and the Conservation of Flow.

INTRODUCTION TO PRODUCT FLOW PLANNING: DEFINING OUR CONTEXT AND SOME KEY CONCEPTS

> *There was much attention to partial insights, but the effects*
> *on other parts of the system or other objectives were overlooked.*
>
> Jan Riezebos[1]

This book explores how enterprises can do a better job of planning the flow of goods. It is thus directed toward businesses for which material flow is important: basic materials producers, manufacturers, distributors, and retailers of physical goods. Our objective is to illuminate the fundamental issues of product flow planning in a comprehensive way, to consider both the fundamental challenges and the context in which planning is performed. We will take an unusually broad view of *all* the types of industries that produce and distribute physical products: consumer goods, industrial goods, high-technology products, chemicals, and so on.

Rather than being a textbook, this is a guide for the advanced practitioner or graduate student who is ready to hone his or her knowledge of how to design and implement better planning approaches. We do not teach the basic concepts here or the details of various techniques. Rather, we try to provide perspective on what planning techniques work well, under what circumstances, and teach how to design a comprehensive planning approach for an enterprise.

This book is also an attempt to persuade the reader about the truth of certain propositions. Not being coy, we can introduce the most important of those propositions now:

- Planning should be an integrative function of the enterprise, and hence the operations planning processes need to be considered as a whole — at least occasionally — and rationalized. We advocate beginning with a comprehensive supply chain view of the scope of planning, and then letting the most natural way to plan a specific business drive us toward the particular kinds of plans that may be necessary for manufacturing, order promising, physical distribution, inbound materials management, and so on. The need for a unifying map or vision of planning is a theme that we will return to repeatedly, and we will present various ways to express that vision, such as the backbone diagram introduced in Chapter 4.
- With modern computing and data communication capabilities, there are few remaining technical limitations on what we can do. There are, however, practical trade-offs we must make on how much planning we should perform and appropriate levels of expenditure on systems and staff. More planning is not necessarily better planning. Unlike aerobic exercise, having everyone plan for an hour every day does not necessarily improve our health.
- While good planning often requires powerful software, the core of better planning is *process improvement* driven by professionals who feel strongly that there is a better way to plan in their environment. This fact implies a different approach to improvement than the software sales-driven approach that has predominated in recent years.
- The best approach to planning for a specific business is highly dependent on the nature of that business. Indeed, finding the right approach to planning its operations is part of the way a business should differentiate itself from its competitors and achieve competitive advantage.
- Most comparisons of planning approaches, e.g., the MRP (material requirements planning) versus JIT (just-in-time) discussions of the last twenty-five years, are far too narrow and neglect important types of planning. We will introduce and compare more of the range here.
- Planning is performed primarily to make decisions, and a methodology of planning design that considers what decisions we have to make and

how those decisions interrelate in a particular business is a good way to rationalize how we plan. We believe that in practice it is fundamentally simpler to begin from the decision-requirement perspective than to try to begin from the vast array of "best practice" planning methodologies offered to us.

The book's title refers to "directing the flow of product" because they are the best words we have found to describe the challenge of planning the complete movement of materials and finished goods. We have chosen to de-emphasize the more common name "supply chain planning" because:

1. Manufacturing-oriented professionals sometimes feel excluded by that term and planning production is a very important part of what we will discuss here.
2. We do not want to overemphasize the word "planning" because we are not selling more planning; sometimes less planning is better.
3. Some commentators prefer the use of "demand chain" over "supply chain" to emphasize the importance of product "pull" over product "push" in contemporary thinking, or prefer "value chain" to emphasize the importance of value creation or outsourcing opportunities at each stage, or advocate other terms that emphasize specific strategies.

So we have employed a somewhat unique title that, we hope, carries little baggage. We do emphasize the term "flow," which is a very powerful theme in contemporary thinking about supply chains and manufacturing. We will also occasionally use the term "operations planning" as a synonym for product flow directing/planning, recognizing that to some people operations means manufacturing and to others in, say, service industries it does not refer to product flow at all.

Perhaps the hottest topic in planning the last few years has been collaborative planning, particularly collaboration between enterprises using the Internet. One of our objectives in writing this volume has been to make collaboration a fundamental part of how we present the product flow planning discipline, rather than something exotic or separate from the rest of planning. Similarly, the event management–based "planning" that occurs in near-real time to decide on the best immediate response to new information about operations is fundamental to our approach.

After this introductory Chapter 1, we will devote Chapter 2 to a high-level summary of some of the most important operations planning techniques that have been developed over the last century, with the objective of trying to develop some perspective on those techniques. Chapter 3 offers a set of principles and understandings that we believe are the essential foundation for effective product flow planning. Chapter 4 introduces some specific logical structures for planning that we have found very helpful in our work. In Chapter 5, we go fairly deeply into how different philosophies of operations underlie various planning approaches. Chapter 6 presents a specific methodology for designing and implementing supply chain planning systems. In Chapter 7, we present four case studies that illustrate the application or violation of our principles. Recognizing that computer software and data communications are the foundation for implementing many types of planning, we (finally) discuss their use explicitly in Chapter 8, and then conclude with a brief Chapter 9 that summarizes our most important themes and introduces a few additional ideas.

While this volume is to some degree sequential, the reader should not hesitate to jump around and explore interesting topics wherever he or she finds them. There are quite a number of concepts introduced here, and even if you read it from front to back, you will likely find yourself returning to earlier sections to review ideas.

THE SUPPLY CHAIN AND SUPPLY NETWORK

Since first identified by Keith Oliver of Booz Allen Hamilton in 1982, the concept of the supply chain has become widely accepted. It is the mechanism by which goods are moved and transformed from raw materials to delivery of value to the final customer. Figure 1.1 is a classic picture of the supply chain, showing the flow of product from left to right, the flow of payment from right to left, and the integrating movement of information and control in both directions to make it all work. "Directing product flow" is, of course, part of the information and control realm.

The basic supply chain concept of links stretching from raw materials to end users is accepted and pervasive today; it is the foundation for how most of us now think about goods-oriented operations. Supply chain management is the process of managing multiple steps along the path from raw materials to final consumers in an integrative way that helps achieve an enterprise's objectives. Its focus may be upstream from the enterprise, downstream, internal, or all of those flows.

A concept implicit in our supply chain is the *systems approach*, viewing a complex system as being composed of many related modules, with the performance of the entire system depending not only on the performance of each component, but also on the effectiveness of the interactions among the components. Systems thinking is, of course, much older than the supply chain concept,

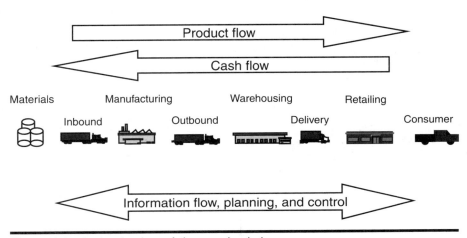

Figure 1.1   A classic view of the supply chain.

but quite relevant today given our interest in coupling the multiple enterprises that compose the supply chain. Furthermore, in spite of decades of talk about breaking down the walls of the functional "silos" in enterprises, organizations today are mostly managed as a set of silos (purchasing, manufacturing, distribution, sales, etc.). Achieving the highest performance of the supply chain system as a whole (or even of one enterprise in the supply chain) requires a thoughtful trade-off of letting system components make and execute their own planning decisions, versus loose integration, versus "global" optimization.

As thinking about product and information flow has matured over the last decade, we have realized that supply chains are really parts of much larger networks. Figure 1.2 shows a supply network consisting of multiple material providers, manufacturers, contract manufacturers, logistics providers, distributors, retailers, etc. Indeed, an entire industry can be typically diagrammed as one supply network. Manufacturers buy production materials from a largely shared set of suppliers; they often sell to a shared set of distributors or retailers and may rely on the same logistics providers. The supply network consists not only of an enterprise's customers and suppliers, but of its *direct competitors* as well. This diagram helps us to understand that when we talk about a supply chain, we are really focusing on one path through a quite complex network. Many, many supply chains are active at any one time in the supply network of most industries. (For the sake of intellectual completeness, it is also worth pointing out that you also participate in the supply chains of other industries. For example, you are a customer in the supply chain of your office equipment provider, even though you probably do not think of your business very often

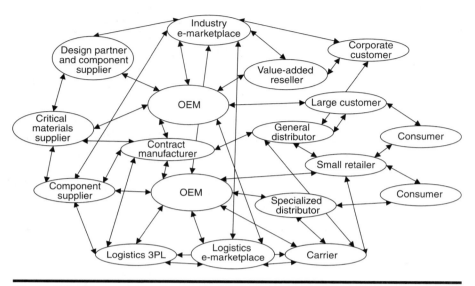

Figure 1.2   The supply network of an industry.

as being in that supply chain. In this volume, we will focus on the primary industry that an enterprise is part of from its perspective.)

Recognizing supply networks has also led to the promotion of some new variations on supply chain themes, such as the "Adaptive Supply Chain." Adaptive Supply Chain thinking emphasizes the need for flexibility and willingness to work with new supply chain partners, reliance on information rather than inventory, decentralization, and demand-driven flow.

In this volume, we will rely mostly on diagrams like Figure 1.3 to support our discussion of product flow planning. It is neither the simplistic traditional linear view of the supply chain, nor the full network view that implies perhaps hundreds of entities to plan among. Instead, we diagram one of each major type of entity that we might work with in a complex environment. No enterprise's supply chain has all of these features. For example, if you are a distributor of product, the in-house manufacturing boxes do not apply to you. But the first- and second-tier suppliers, the distribution network, and possibly some contract manufacturing may all apply.

Notice in Figure 1.3 that we have decomposed manufacturing into some of its typical major steps by separating parts fabrication (or product formulation) from assembly (or packaging) and also showing a separate manufacturing location. For product flow planning purposes, we need to be ready to think about how different parts of manufacturing — purchased inventories, fabrication or

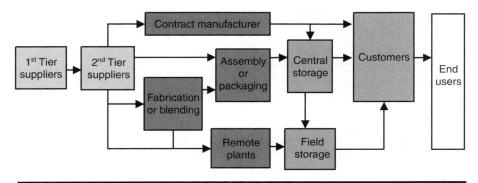

Figure 1.3 Simplified supply system for flow planning.

processing steps, work-in-process inventory, assembly, packaging, etc. — interact with the supply chain as a whole. For example, in part of the paper industry it is quite common to schedule expensive papermaking machines to manufacture (to inventory) master rolls of paper very efficiently and then, on demand from customers, to "convert" that inventory into the needed finished goods. The way that we control production inside an integrated paper mill is fundamentally a part of how we choose to interact with customers, at what stage we decide to inventory product, and, in short, how we have decided to manage product flow in the whole supply chain. Our diagramming approach is designed to keep reminding us of that fact, rather than the customary implicit assumption that what goes on inside the plant is somehow separate from the outside.

While manufacturing issues historically have dominated the development of planning concepts, contemporary thinking often places manufacturing in the context of serving customers. It is certainly time to close the gap that has been allowed to exist for too long between manufacturing planning and nonproduction supply chain planning. Manufacturing is very much a part of the supply chain. It is often the most expensive, complex, time-consuming part of the supply chain — its dynamics may even dictate the structure of the entire supply chain — but ultimately it is performed because of its supply chain function.

WHAT IS PLANNING?

In the product flow realm, planning can be defined as the process of deciding how we will use all the kinds of resources that ultimately provide product to end customers: manufacturing resources, labor, supplier commitments, multiple levels of inventories, transportation, warehousing facilities, and so on. Some of

- Economic order quantity (EOQ)
- Safety stock/cycle stock/reorder point
- Production planning
- Material requirements planning
- Master production scheduling (MPS)
- Master planning
- Final assembly scheduling
- Lot sizing
- Shop floor scheduling
- Finite capacity scheduling (FCS)
- Rough cut capacity planning
- Capacity requirements planning
- Supply management
- Demand planning
- Demand-based management
- Distribution requirements planning
- Inventory deployment
- Adaptive supply chain networks
- Advanced planning and scheduling (APS)
- Order profitability
- Order sourcing
- Hierarchical planning
- Strategic planning
- Tactical planning
- Sales & operations planning
- Workforce planning
- Supply planning
- Collaborative planning (and CPFR)
- Operational planning/scheduling
- Shop floor control
- Warehouse management
- Pick wave optimization
- Available to promise/capable to promise
- Toyota Production System
- Just-in-time
- Kanban
- Zero Inventories
- Drum-buffer-rope scheduling (Theory of Constraints)
- Pull versus push inventory management
- Transportation management
- Load building
- Carrier assignment
- Routing
- Vendor-managed inventory/continuous replenishment

Figure 1.4 Some of the techniques for operations planning.

the techniques for operations planning are listed in Figure 1.4. Planning has been a very active subject for research and experimentation for the last century (see the excellent history in Hopp and Spearman[2]). Indeed, one of the challenges we face today is the surfeit of philosophies, technologies, and methodologies for planning — that every student of this subject must invest the time to learn. One of our objectives for this book is to approach planning in a way that is unified, comprehensive, and ultimately easier to understand.

When planning is not being performed well, there are symptoms. Some typical ones are:

- Too much or too little inventory; short-lived product growing old
- Mediocre results in customer service surveys
- Many customer service calls per sale
- Lengthy cycle times for customers or for our own inventory replenishment
- Knowing we are not a low-cost provider — high manufacturing or logistics costs
- Poor utilization of labor
- Frequent last-minute changes to schedules
- Facility capacity utilization too low or too high
- Inconsistent material availability

■ Complaints from suppliers
■ Harried operations management — constant reacting or firefighting

Of course, most of these symptoms can be produced by other problems in the business as well. Data analysis, judgment, and perhaps a formal "root cause" analysis are required to determine what is causing what.

While the details will vary based on specific business circumstances, in general the objectives of product flow planning are to help the enterprise and its primary supply chain(s):

■ Provide the customer service required by their business strategy.
■ Maintain an appropriate speed of product flow that encourages sales by having product to market in a timely fashion and also minimizes product obsolescence and shelf-life expiration costs.
■ Have a minimum cost of procurement, manufacturing, and physical distribution.
■ Employ the minimum quantities of assets, both fixed assets like plants and distribution centers and working assets like inventory.

Some might argue that the role of product flow planning is also to deliver high-quality product, and we have worked in several environments where the key argument in favor of long production runs (and the huge impact they have on product flow) was that they were essential to maintaining high product quality. We will stay away from the product quality/flow planning subject in this volume because it dilutes the primary responsibilities of product engineering, manufacturing, and supplier management for achieving high product quality.

The role of product flow planning can be best understood through Figure 1.5. The operations of the supply chain can be diagrammed in the axes of time horizon and material flow. This diagram is similar to one first used by Dr. G. Terry Ross in the mid 1980s. The time horizon is diagrammed from left to right, from real-time execution to short- to longer-range planning and finally to the strategic business issues that go well beyond material flow. The division of planning into three time horizons — operational, tactical, and strategic — is generally considered to have been originated by Anthony[3] and has been followed by many others since. The flow of material through the supply chain is shown from top to bottom, from materials to manufacturing to distribution. We will focus on the middle portion of the diagram in this book, that is, on short- to intermediate-range planning rather than execution of strategic planning. However, we are not going to expend a lot of effort making planning horizon distinctions, because the scope of actual planning processes should vary considerably in practice based on specific needs.

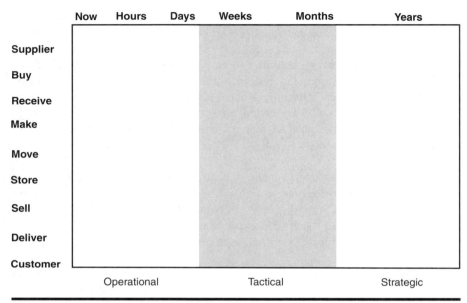

Figure 1.5   Matrixing the planning horizon and the supply chain.

PLANNING IN THE CONTEXT OF OPERATIONS PHILOSOPHY AND STRATEGY

Decisions about a product flow planning approach are heavily dependent on decisions made by the enterprise about business strategy, supply chain strategy, and operations philosophy, the area to the right side of Figure 1.5. Enterprises make distribution channel decisions about who to sell to, strategic decisions about whether to in- or outsource manufacturing, and philosophical decisions like "committing to Lean operations" or "building an adaptive supply chain." The combination of these decisions and philosophies significantly impacts which approaches to planning make the most sense, as we will discuss in more detail in Chapters 5 and 6.

For example, if we are aggressively converting our operations to a complete Toyota Production System–style of manufacturing including its principles, appropriate factory layout, and staff management approach, we will probably be much more focused on pulling material through the plant with kanbans (cards) than we are with building a more elaborate MRP II planning system (although we may well choose to incorporate elements of both). If we are intent on creating a "virtual enterprise" with several of our core processes outsourced to other firms, then the planning approach must recognize the degree of decentralization and collaboration inherent in our business strategy.

In this book, we do not attempt to evaluate the major philosophies of operations and pass judgment on them. Instead, we focus on planning and try to illuminate the relationships between each planning technique and various philosophies of operations, to give the reader a foundation for trying to answer hard questions like: "If I want to be basically Lean, but I know I have to carry some finished goods inventory, do I need to use a sophisticated master scheduling technique to smooth production and manage inventory?"

PLANNING IN THE CONTEXT OF PROCESS EXECUTION SKILLS

There is an analogous issue with the relationship between planning and process execution. To get much value from good plans, an enterprise must be able to execute its business processes reliably. For example, to execute a master production schedule, a business must be able to both:

- Make quality product most of the time, so that shippable product is produced in approximately the quantity scheduled.
- Produce product at a reliable rate, so that the products scheduled can be built in the time period planned and consume a predictable amount of machine resources.

In other words, if creating and maintaining a master schedule is to be more than a waste of time, an enterprise must actually be able to make product reliably. Michael George[4] gives us a good example of this effect in his book describing the symbiotic relationship between Lean operations and Six Sigma quality programs. Quality production is absolutely critical in a Lean environment.

Similarly, distribution functions must have their processes under control to be able to plan. A major industrial products distributor recently tried to implement a new facilities network that collapsed inventory storage from two echelons to one. Inbound products from manufacturers were cross-docked by a third-party logistics provider and shipped to the regional distribution centers. It took considerable effort to get the transportation/cross-docking process to work reliably, and then it was determined that the distribution centers were still not able to provide the projected service levels to customers. Part of the problem turned out to be that some of the distribution center managers were keeping a two- to ten-day backlog of unloaded vans in their parking lots in order to always have plenty of work for their unloading/put-away staff to perform and hence get maximum utilization out of that staff. But, of course, this unpredictable unloading queue played havoc with in-stock performance of the distribution centers. And if distribution center safety stocks were set high enough to compensate for this effect, there would be too much inventory to physically fit in the new distribution centers and the expected inventory reduction aspect of the new strategy would be largely undone. Execution of a reliable, short-cycle receiving/put-away process was an initially unrecognized but, in fact, fundamental part of the new strategy.

In this book, we do not address directly the issues of effective business process execution. We do not discuss how to operate a distribution center or run a manufacturing plant, nor how to organize quality circles or how to motivate salaried or hourly employees. In sidestepping these issues, we do not mean to imply that execution is easy or unimportant — indeed, effective execution is fundamental both to daily operations and to change. But this is a book about product flow planning.

THE NEW CHALLENGE IN OPERATIONS PLANNING

As businesses grew large and geographically extended in the late nineteenth century (the railroads, for example), growing bureaucracies divided and delegated the planning and operations. Relatively simple planning processes that relied on telegraphic communication had to suffice. There was no way to construct a "brain" big enough to plan the operations of the industrial beasts that had been created. In a later period, as the U.S. sought to win World War II by marshalling resources of unprecedented size across global geography, it had to rely on relatively ad hoc planning and control mechanisms to manage its supply chains. The confusion that resulted led to the classic slang acronyms "fubar" and "snafu."

Businesses operated during the twentieth century with similar challenges, having to rely on breaking tough problems into pieces and solving them sequentially, because that was the only way they could be solved reasonably. For example, in classic MRP II methodology, the master production schedule is generated assuming infinite production capacity and material availability. Material and capacity availability is compared with the requirements generated, and the master schedule is corrected to become realistic. While MRP is computer based, it was designed in the 1960s, very much for an era of limited computer and communication resources.

Today in business, for the first time, we no longer face such technical planning limitations. Extremely fast computers have become inexpensive, and powerful algorithms for planning are available. The Internet and other communication platforms are available to tie operations together, both within and between enterprises. *We are now in a position to construct as much "brain" for both the enterprise and interenterprise supply chain as we believe will be acceptable to the participants, effective, and cost justified.*

With this freedom, the burden falls on the planning process designers to decide what kind of planning really needs to be performed, the degree of integration among plans, and how much development effort (or software license fee) we can justify. *There are no more easy excuses for why operations are not effectively and efficiently planned.*

The range of planning options open to us is enormous. For example, a new order promising system was recently implemented at a major meatpacking firm in the Midwest. It provides capable-to-promise (or CTP, see the review in Chapter 2) logic with dynamic rescheduling of manufacturing on a massive scale:

> The system uses a total of 55 optimization models running on 14 multiprocessor servers. The largest of the models contains approximately 250,000 constraints and 300,000 variables, and are run more than 1,000 times per day. These individual CTP optimization runs typically take anywhere from 3 to 15 seconds. An average day sees roughly 4,000 optimization runs and 15,000 order-line-item transactions. There are approximately 1.2 billion average calculations per sales order to solve for availability. Today, approximately 7 schedulers and 40 salesmen use the system daily.[5,*]

This is quite an impressive system for a problem that generally was not recognized as a significant issue for product flow planning until about fifteen years ago! On the other hand, we have some advocates of Lean supply chains advocating virtually computer-less operations, arguing that information systems inherently add complexity and cost and divert attention from the real issue of refining processes to deliver the greatest value at the least cost.

There is no formula to tell us how much to invest in planning capabilities, or which decisions need to be made simultaneously, or what sorts of planning will work best in any particular business. We have to develop the judgment to make good decisions about planning processes and systems.

DIVERSITY OF PLANNING NEEDS

Product flow planning is certainly not just for manufacturers. Every participant in the supply network who has responsibility for controlling the flow of goods

---

* Reprinted with permission from *APICS—The Performance Advantage.*

is responsible for at least one planning process. Retailers typically have significant planning tasks, and of course Wal-Mart is famous for making material planning one of its competitive advantages as a retailer.

Consider the case of a specialized retailer that sells calendars primarily through temporary kiosks and stores located in malls during the autumn and holiday season. It faces a complex planning problem to schedule receipt of material into its distribution center, prepick the initial load of product for each of its retail locations, ship those materials at the last moment, replenish the retail locations as they sell product, and coordinate replenishment of the distribution center from manufacturers as they discover which items will be the biggest sellers this season. This retailer must plan a delicate dance each year between distribution center storage capacity, receiving, and shipping capacities to meet the store needs, while living within the order cycle times of on- and offshore calendar manufacturers. To do that successfully, it has developed an elaborate forecasting and planning process and custom systems that support it.

Distributors have great incentive to plan material flow if they are responsible for inventorying product, since their skill at managing that inventory has a huge impact on their profitability. Manufacturers can have some of the most complex planning problems because they have to plan based on both manufacturing and nonmanufacturing criteria. Tough planning problems are often associated with extended multiplant processes, bottleneck resources at multiple points in production, random-routing job shops, product innovation and rapidly changing product lines, and responsibility for optimizing finished goods inventories (FGIs) at multiple locations in the field in direct coordination with manufacturing.

As the above examples suggest, each player in the supply network faces a different planning problem. Even comparable companies in the same industry have different planning problems because their businesses have a different mix of products and they have chosen to operate by different business strategies and policies. For example, do you suppose that Dell's personal computer business, with its finely honed custom production for individual orders, would use the same planning approach as a more traditional personal computer business selling through retailers? Or that, say, a high-tech business that designs and manages the manufacturing of modems for communication carriers would need similar planning processes? No, even within one supply chain stage of one industry there is great diversity of operations strategy and great variation of planning needs.

We will discuss several examples of effective approaches to planning, but we will not attempt to define a standard "correct" planning approach for every participant in the supply network — there are too many subtle choices that depend on the specifics of a business. We will, of course, try to elucidate many of the relationships between business approach and appropriate planning.

It takes knowledge of planning tools, understanding of the enterprise and its context, imagination, and persistence to design and evolve good planning approaches. It is no coincidence that some of the best thinkers in the operations field have stressed thinking skills. Eli Goldratt[6] invented his Evaporating Clouds technique to improve the way problems are defined and attacked, and Shigeo Shingo[7] stresses the discipline of thinking through his Scientific Thinking Mechanism. Figuring out how to plan better is hard intellectual work and also fascinating work.

THE OBJECTIVE

Our objective is to design, operate, and refine the best planning approach for each enterprise. The "best" planning approach for an organization will probably continue to change, both because it will evolve as we try to perfect it and because it will need to be adapted (and occasionally rethought from top to bottom) as the business changes. For example, a shift from primarily North American suppliers to East Asian suppliers creates an entirely different planning problem because of the very different lead times involved. And a shift of some production from those East Asian suppliers to suppliers in Mexico (to, say, shorten lead times) can shift planning requirements yet again.

In the larger enterprise, we face a significant challenge in achieving the right balance between centralization and decentralization. And in any enterprise, we face the challenge of how to best collaborate with customers and suppliers, given our current and potential relationships with them.

So the challenge for each enterprise, and the supply chains in which it participates, is to decide on the right kind of planning processes and associated systems, data, and organization.

Value in Humans Internalizing the Plan

One of our goals for planning is to have our plans internalized and accepted by planners and management. By and large, humans are responsible for executing plans, and they will only execute effectively what they understand and are enthusiastic about.

The best planning decision support systems develop most of a plan but require the planner to do the rest, so that he or she internalizes it and can fully explain and sell it to management. Similarly, while plans should be up-to-date, preferably real time or near real time, we really do not want plans to change too quickly. That interferes with the human's ability to understand and internalize the plan. In other words, if we have the option of constructing a planning environment that creates plans that change significantly every hour as data are updated, but typical improvements are only 0.00001 percent, that may not be a good trade-off.

PLANNING IS INESCAPABLE

If the resources that we need to create and deliver product would always, spontaneously, be available for immediate use, we would have little planning to do. If manufacturing capability was always ready for our use, if the right number of production operators spontaneously walked in the door every day, if materials magically appeared when we needed them, if FGI was somehow always ready when a customer needed product right now, we would not have to plan. But reality is such that for all those activities to happen smoothly requires planning, working through all the logical relationships in material flow and resource utilization based on actual or expected requirements for product.

Most of us hate planning. It is psychologically uncomfortable for us to go through a process with as many issues as planning. We hate the effort that will be wasted when something changes and plans have to be revised. We hate the time spent planning when we could be "doing" and actually producing something of substance. We hate the time spent maintaining data that are required to support planning. Like the classic truism that "the forecast is always wrong," we know that a plan, based in part on a forecast, will be just as wrong. We hate that a plan is actually a model of future operations, and as such leaves out a lot of detail that the people doing the work will ultimately have to deal with. We hate the intellectual effort of working in the abstract space that a plan represents. But we cannot escape planning.

Product flow planning is not optional. If an enterprise conducts operations with physical goods, it will, one way or another, make decisions (i.e., plans) about how to direct the flow of that product, based on some expectations for the future. The organization must make this choice: Will it plan poorly or well? Does the organization want to take planning seriously enough to think through how it will plan and who will have responsibility for managing what sort of planning? If it chooses not to organize its planning processes consciously, it will plan, but it will do so in ad hoc ways in isolated pockets of the organization. In this book, we strongly endorse enterprises that comprehensively think through how they plan product flow.

The more difficult decisions an organization must make concern just how much to spend on planning, both expenses to incur for planning staff and investments in information technology. Depending on the complexity of the operations being planned, the size of the operations (and hence the operations volume base over which planning cost is amortized), and the operating philosophy of the organization (all we want in our company is JIT flow), a case can be made for keeping planning simple or spending substantial sums on staff and systems. An organization much first decide what it must do to plan effectively and then cost-justify staff and systems in relation to that objective. If we believe that we have a very challenging business that can benefit from very sophisticated and data-intense techniques (consider the meatpacking example referenced above), the key step is to persuade management to expend the substantial resources required to develop and/or implement a state-of-the-art approach. On the other hand, if simple techniques will serve the right planning process for a given enterprise, they may truly be the best solution.

GOOD PLANNING IS VALUABLE AND WORTHY OF RESOURCES

Good planning is planning that:

- Uses all the available information and uses it in a timely way (some of it near real time) from a comprehensive view of the data available to the enterprise; that is, it is fully integrated from customer through manufacturing (or other product source) to supplier.
- Quickly works out all the logical relationships correctly (see Chapter 3), including correctly making trade-offs across the supply chain among costs, asset requirements, and service.
- Creates plans that reflect those logical relationships and trade-offs, plus takes account of uncertainty and risks.
- Is internalized by planners and the organization as a whole.
- Does not waste elapsed time or planning resources; planning itself needs to be an efficient business process — we may be advocating "Lean planning" here.

Good planning is a very high-leverage activity for the organization. In other words, it produces great benefits in increased product flow, improved customer service, and/or reduced capital requirements and operating costs — relative to the modest resources actually devoted to planning.

For example, a soft drink bottler with three bottling plants and approximately $500 million in annual sales was able, in about five months, to increase customer order fill rates from 96 percent case fill to over 99 percent case fill, while simultaneously reducing material inventories by 36 percent, FGI investment by 12 percent, and operating expense by 12 percent — simply by better planning. Its incremental planning effort required three relatively inexpensive staff members, three personal computers connected with a local area network, and some moderately priced planning software interfaced to transactions systems to obtain a few key types of data.

This kind of economic leverage from good planning is not a surprise. In this example we are, after all, talking about the key short- to intermediate-range decision-making function for operations to support $500 million dollars of sales per year. This particular business is moderately difficult to manage because of the seasonal, holiday, and promotion-driven peaks and valleys in sales and the high utilization expected for processing, transport, and storage facilities in this business. Does it not make sense that performing planning well, rather than poorly, will easily pay for itself here?

A.T. Kearney[8] found, in its Global Excellence in Operations program in 2001, that of the five businesses selected as global leaders for general operational excellence, *100 percent reported that payback from their investments in production planning had met or exceeded expectations.* Doing planning well is one of the highest leverage, and hence highest return on investment, activities on which the typical organization can focus. Several people who plan effectively, supported by the right systems, and work with senior managers whose jobs are partly devoted to planning (e.g., via participation in Sales & Operations Planning) can make a huge difference in the cost effectiveness of operations.

On the other hand, it is quite a challenge to generate a positive return on investment from a truly massive investment in planning systems (millions of dollars in license fees, tens of millions more in implementation), although we present one case in Chapter 7 where it is successfully accomplished. Certainly, product flow planning does not drive the biggest decisions an organization must make (that would be strategic planning). To not do operations planning well is simply stupid. To do it more expensively than is necessary to plan well is wasteful.

Given all the advances in understanding the supply chain and its manufacturing "kernels" over the last few decades, and the fact that good planning is a high-leverage activity, organizations should take the time to think comprehensively about how their product flow operations are planned. There is much to be gained from looking at the totality of operations, from thinking about how decisions can best be made, and from creating a planning approach that will produce good decisions in each unique business. This thesis underlies this book — our primary purpose is to provide the tools to go about this comprehensive thinking process.

This thinking does not have to be an extremely laborious or expensive undertaking. As described in Chapter 6, an organization should be able to perform the core of it rather quickly and then move on to the larger task of turning the vision into reality.

We conclude with a press release from i2 Technologies that, while focusing on proprietary software rather than the planning process, is illustrative of the kinds of quantifiable benefits that solid improvements in planning can achieve.

Siemens EMC reveals business improvements achieved with i2 Factory Planner

DALLAS – August 4, 2003 – i2 Technologies, Inc. (OTC: ITWO), a leading provider of end-to-end supply chain management solutions, and Siemens Electronics Manufacturing Center (EMC) today published figures confirming the business improvements that can be achieved with i2 Factory Planner.

A business unit of Siemens Energy and Automation Inc., Siemens EMC calculates that it has:

■ Increased customer on-time delivery from 81 percent to 98 percent
■ Increased work order on-time delivery from 34 percent to 74 percent
■ Increased inventory turns by more than 50 percent
■ Reduced the manufacturing cycle time by more than 20 percent

These improvements have had a noticeable impact on Siemens EMC's customer satisfaction, as evidenced in a customer loyalty survey carried out by independent researchers in February 2003 and reported to Siemens EMC last month. The survey noted that Siemens had overcome schedule flexibility challenges, and for the first time in the five-year history of the survey, customers ranked Siemens EMC at the top of the category.

"We have a commitment to helping our customers succeed in their businesses," says Louise Stump, Siemens EMC Materials and Logistics Manager. "We are therefore focused on providing them with the highest standards of product quality and service at the lowest total cost of ownership. The implementation of i2 Factory Planner has enabled us to deliver on time, respond quickly to customer requirements and enhance production efficiency."

Part of the i2 Supply Chain Management solution suite, i2 Factory Planner is designed to simultaneously manage material and capacity constraints and to develop feasible operating plans for plants, departments, production lines or work centers. The solution was first implemented at Siemens EMC two years ago and rolled out in a phased approach across two manufacturing facilities in Tennessee and Ohio, USA.

Using i2 Factory Planner, Siemens EMC reports that it is able to:

- Generate material requirement plans in 15 minutes, rather than the weekly regeneration associated with a legacy system
- Provide customers with accurate delivery dates by the end of the day, not the end of the week
- Accept customer changes, view material and scheduling issues, respond to capacity needs and revise the production plan — all in one day
- Manage the large numbers of different parts required for low to medium volume, high product mix manufacturing
- Analyze capacity and view performance percentages daily to monitor productivity and customer service
- Reduce operating costs by realizing efficiencies in material and capacity planning

2

OUR HERITAGE OF PLANNING TECHNIQUES: THE TOOLS IN OUR TOOLBOX

> *...nothing is as impractical as a good theory of inventory. I will explain why what has been truly good inventory research for more than 35 years has not done much to advance the practice of industrial inventory control.*
>
> Harvey M. Wagner[9]

To be able to design effective planning approaches for unique enterprises and supply chains, we need to understand a significant fraction of the vast body of operations planning techniques that has been created over the last century. We are fortunate to be the beneficiaries of a great deal of thoughtful work by practitioners and academics and also of the software that has been developed and packaged.

While we need to build the best planning solution for our unique problems, we are not likely to create entirely new ways to plan product flow — we are not smart enough to do that, we do not have enough time to do that, and we probably cannot afford to create a custom set of tools from scratch to implement a completely novel approach. But by being more educated about the diversity of techniques, we are less likely to naively espouse the first approach we were ever taught and more likely to assemble an effective approach that draws from multiple sources.

We will base our work primarily on these rich traditions:

- On the early operations models that led to statistically based techniques for inventory control
- On the applied techniques that gave us MRP II, distribution resource planning, the Theory of Constraints, just in time, and Lean
- On the academic tradition that has given us a universe of Operations Research–based techniques including mathematical programming and search algorithms, expert systems, and complexity science–based techniques.

Obviously, we cannot hope to cover this material in any depth in a chapter or even one brief book. There are a multitude of excellent textbooks that cover these materials, several of which we will reference. And since some of this material is quite challenging, most students who need to truly understand these subjects will want to undertake formal coursework to master them, in addition to reading.

Our goal for this chapter is to discuss these techniques from a very high level and to provide some historical comparison and commentary on them. If you are quite familiar with the field of operations management and planning, you may want to skip this chapter. However, a note before you do so: The majority of these techniques have been developed for use in a manufacturing environment. We have much less wealth of historical practice in the nonmanufacturing supply chain space.

CLASSIC TECHNIQUES: INVENTORY CONTROL AND PROBABILITY MODELS

As discussed in Chapter 1, organizations that process or move materials have always had to plan. That was true of eighteenth century shipping companies, early manufacturers, and nineteenth century railroads. Many authors (see, for example, Hopp and Spearman[2]) date the beginning of mathematical methods for managing operations to Ford W. Harris's economic order quantity (EOQ) model of about 1913. Harris was one of the first to explicitly recognize the trade-off between the fixed cost associated with configuring machinery to make a specific part and the cost of holding inventory of that part, and then to turn that trade-off into a mathematical model: a lot size formula.

What is perhaps most noteworthy for our purposes is the realization we have come to over the last several decades that this model has very limited applicability in manufacturing. With its assumption of setup cost being associated only with the part at hand (and thus its unawareness of sequencing issues of other parts to be made on that machinery), its assumption of instantaneous production, its assumption that you want to inventory the part at all, and its neglect of load on the factory (and hence any concept of how much the capacity of production machines is "worth" to the business at any given point in time), the EOQ formula result is usually far from the best production quantity at any given time. The model actually applies much better in many distributor environments, where the decisions on quantity to reorder usually fit these assumptions more closely. It is also applicable for ordering indirect materials, or low-volume/low-cost direct materials, where the assumptions also apply and more powerful techniques are not worth using.

Thus, with the very beginning of modeling material flows, we also began a tradition of having to *re-examine our models and the assumptions that underlie them* to see what is really valid, to see what captures enough of our complex reality to produce reasonably "correct" answers, and to see whether a technique pioneered in one milieu is the best technique in a different context. (A common problem is for a model to be appropriate in the context for which it was invented and then to be misapplied elsewhere.) The domain of operations planning is a slippery place. We must be constant skeptics to confirm that what we are doing is valid, that we are using good models and techniques for our problems, and that we have not been sold something that sounds plausible but actually violates common sense.

For example, twenty years ago we had to watch a hair care industry client (consumer packaged goods manufacturer) adopt a large-scale material requirements planning (MRP) system that had been designed for complex assembled products. This manufacturer was mixing a few ingredients of significant value (the balance of ingredients like fragrance and color were used in tiny quantities and could be kept in stock at little cost) and putting them in bottles and then in cases and on pallets. We saw this manufacturer perform a major software implementation, adopt manufacturing orders and the accounting that went with them, and learn to manage a complex piece of software for its bill of materials (BOM). What it needed was a simple and quick way to allocate capacity to demand and a computerized one-level BOM. It was truly sad.

Inventory theory has grown from that first EOQ model to a large family of models with various assumptions about whether demand is deterministic or random, constant or dynamic multiperiod (i.e., varying by period) demand, backordering or lost sales, periodic review of inventory or continuous review, and so on (see Hadley and Whitin[10] for perhaps the most classic work on inventory and Silver et al.[11] for a more recent summary). The inventory models that include dealing with uncertain demand (based on probability theory) determine both reorder quantity and safety stock levels, so that a planned fraction of demand can be met successfully from inventory (e.g., a 98.5 percent case fill rate or a 95 percent order fill rate).

This inventory theory for uncertain demand situations, mostly developed during the 1950s, makes fundamental assumptions about the knowability of demand and lead time probability distributions that are absolutely not achievable in practice, given that actual demand probability distributions are nonstationary (how do you know the actual *current* demand probability distribution for a given item, given that a product's position in its life cycle and relative to the competition are usually changing), that unmet demand is seldom captured by sales systems, and there are numerous other problems with "dirty" data (see Wagner[9]).

Most inventory modeling is for a single stage of inventory. Recognizing that many real production and distribution systems must manage multiple echelons of inventory, a fair amount of work has been done on multiechelon systems (Clark and Scarf[12] is a classic reference). It turns out that if you are managing two or more levels of inventory, one inventory feeding another, then you know more than if multiple levels of inventory are each being managed independently. The right multiechelon inventory policies can achieve the desired fill rate with less total inventory. But the mathematics of multiechelon inventory theory quickly become intractable, and it was not a very attractive area of research for years.

Recently, several specialty software providers have implemented new systems (based on new research) that attempt to optimize multiechelon inventory. They report, as they should, improved overall inventory performance (service versus inventory required), but the jury is still out on which planning environments can justify the greater complexity.

Inventory theory today remains a key foundational element of product flow planning. Numerous types of products remain controlled by inventory formulas: finished goods stocked to quickly meet orders, spare parts to be consumed when a component fails, manufacturing direct materials used by many products or of low value (such as fasteners) or very low usage volume, as well as manufacturing safety stocks that are set by inventory theory for items that are replenished based mostly on dependent, time-phased demand (see MRP II below).

Good practice with inventory systems requires that we calibrate our inventory control logic to see what service levels a given set of control parameter values will produce, i.e., if we ask the system to deliver 98 percent case fill on a set of products and set our inventory policies at the suggested levels, and it actually delivers 95 percent case fill, we have to change the parameters. We have the choice of doing some of this calibration by simulating an inventory policy against actual historical demands, or we can calibrate in real operations by simply trying a set of parameter values, and then changing them based on the performance achieved. Either way, we get around one of the fundamental problems with inventory theory (and with its implementation in supply chain management software): trying to estimate probability distributions of demand and lead times.

BIG PLANNING AROUND THE PLANT: MRP II, DRP, JIT, AND THE THEORY OF CONSTRAINTS

As computers became powerful, reliable, and cost effective enough during the 1960s to be applied directly to operations, manufacturing planners realized that relying on probabilistic models (inventory theory) to maintain reorder point systems for work-in-process inventory and for purchased material was no longer necessary. There was now enough computational horsepower to support maintaining an accurate BOM for each product manufactured, including all the layers of components back to raw materials, and accurate inventory records for finished goods, work in process, and materials. We could regularly "explode" that BOM by multiplying it by the entries in a production schedule to compute time-phased, consolidated material requirements across all the products scheduled and net those requirements against current inventories to identify the need for additional subassembly and parts fabrication and for additional material purchases. This logic could be applied recursively down through as many levels of the BOM as appropriate, each time applying a "lead time" offset representing how much time should be allowed to produce or acquire each particular material in that next lower BOM level. These computations are the heart of MRP.

We now had a more powerful technique for planning "dependent" material requirements, that is, direct materials that depend on a production schedule we control, rather than relying on the statistical techniques that were still generally the best way to manage supply to meet "independent" demand, demand over which we have no control. The technique thus is an example of the principle of taking advantage of real knowledge we have about the future to plan more effectively than we could if we had no knowledge (see Chapter 3).

Users of simple MRP quickly discovered that they needed to have the right processes and systems in place around the core MRP calculations to make the technique generally workable. MRP with these additional modules was dubbed

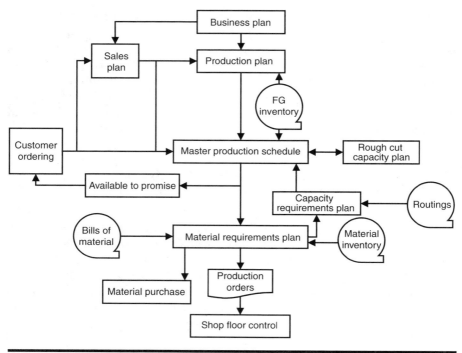

Figure 2.1   One version of the MRP II system structure.

Manufacturing Resource Planning, or MRP II. Figure 2.1 shows one version of the MRP II planning approach.

Perhaps the simplest form of MRP can exist in a pure make-to-order environment where the business only makes to customer order and customer order lead times are sufficiently long that all materials planning can be performed strictly from known orders (e.g., classic custom furniture manufacturing, with its fifteen- to twenty-week customer order quotations). However, many businesses accept customer orders for delivery in less time than their own material order lead times and thus need to plan materials based on forecasted sales. Hence a good forecasting or sales planning process is also needed in most environments. A "resource planning" function needs to be added to plan medium- to long-term changes in production capacity and labor levels. And a "production plan" needs to be added to plan production levels for various groups of products in the intermediate term.

A "master production schedule" is needed to drive the MRP logic, because it has enough detail (by individual item, by time of production completion) to get down to planning specific material needs and to drive the detailed depart-ment-by-department work lists that really control the plant. But master produc-tion schedules need to be feasible; they need to be valid in the sense of being producible with the actual resources available (capacity, labor, and materials that can actually be made available in each period of the master schedule). Hence another module, often called "rough-cut capacity planning," is necessary to test a proposed master schedule against actual plant capacity, and feedback is also expected from material planning on whether materials would actually be available — and the expectation set that the master schedule would need to be quickly changed if it were found to be infeasible.

Master production scheduling represents something of a conceptual break-through from the production schedules that preceded it because in performing it, planners realized that many of the product flow operations of the enterprise came together in this one place. It reconciled orders from customers and fore-casted demand further in the future, finished goods replenishment needs for stocked items, production capacity, and the costs associated with either building inventory to smooth production or varying production rates frequently (and suffering either labor underutilization or the cost associated with a highly variable workforce). The master production schedule's existence explicitly separated what we planned to produce in each period from what we planned to sell (the sales plan), a very important logical distinction given the traditional predilection in some businesses to "manufacture the forecast."

While master production scheduling is often performed at the level of fin-ished goods, there are manufacturing environments where it should be per-formed elsewhere, for example at the level of major components production, with a final assembly schedule used for a less significant final assembly step. Plossl[13] provides a nice discussion of how to determine the manufacturing level at which to master schedule.

MRP II represents the most precisely defined "universal" structure for prod-uct flow planning that has ever been created. It was advocated by most experts and was the basis for the "MRP Crusade" promoted by the American Production and Inventory Control Society in the 1970s and 1980s. Much packaged software was created by many providers to implement this standard specification (the earliest MRP software had generally been custom coded by an enterprise's own information technology group). These MRP II software packages grew to in-clude the software to track inventory and manage customer orders as well, that is, to perform some of the core day-to-day transactions by which the business was executed — not just planning anymore.

By the early 1980s, the software was being extended to add distribution resource planning (DRP) capabilities (see Martin[14]). The DRP modules recog-nized that for products that must be stocked in many locations (for example, food and many other consumer goods), the demand the master production schedule saw was not really independent (customer order or forecast) demand. The demand was actually dependent demand that could be netted up from current inventories in those multiple locations and expected depletion of those field inventories by forecasts or orders. And there was another set of decisions that needed to be made about when and with how much product to replenish those field inventories, what we now call inventory deployment. Just as with manufacturing materials requirements, some simple time-phased calculations could produce better demand numbers to drive the master schedule and plan deployment shipments to the field locations.

The MRP family of software grew in the 1990s to become enterprise resource planning (ERP), including largely separate software modules to cover the major nonoperations portions of a business: human resources and financial management. ERP had become the complete system with which to run a business, and true planning was a relatively small part of it. There were obvious reasons to tie operations to accounting, for example, for a software system to be able to take the completion of a manufacturing order and immediately increment the value of inventory on the firm's general ledger. As the twenty-first century was beginning, ERP providers were adding Internet-based modules for customer relationship management (CRM), to better manage customers and the sales force, and supplier relationship management (SRM), to better manage procurement and suppliers. This extended ERP was in some cases called ERP II.

Thus MRP not only structured much of our thinking about operations planning, but also ended up forming the core of integrated systems that could serve most of an enterprise's transaction needs! MRP/ERP is a tribute to the power of simple but logical concepts and dedicated promotion over a period of decades.

As MRP usage experience increased, however, it became clear that MRP was not the definitive planning approach for many environments. Many of its problems are due to logic that does not adequately address manufacturing capacity or material constraints. The master production schedule as initially generated is based on the assumption that there is infinite production capacity available, and multiple passes between the master production schedule, rough-cut capacity planning, material requirements, capacity requirements planning, and sometimes finite scheduling logic (for individual departments or machines) are usually necessary to generate a truly feasible master production schedule. But in real operations, there is typically little time for these multiple passes, and plants would often try to execute master schedules that were not feasible.

Interestingly, while the master production schedule assumed infinite capacity, the material requirements logic tried to acknowledge shop capacity in a roundabout way through its material lead time parameters. In other words, MRP implementers had to put material lead times into the systems that assumed some unchanging delay to have that material be available (due to competition from other work). The lead time for subassembly A might be assumed to be two weeks. But this is always "wrong," because if there is no competition for making subassembly A, it can probably be assembled tomorrow, and if the plant is extremely busy and your particular manufacturing order is of low priority, you might not be able to get any of subassembly A for two months! Again, the inability of MRP scheduling to truly understand capacity relative to demand (the dynamic supply/demand balance) makes it very difficult to produce valid schedules, and, of course, it is impossible to stay on invalid schedules.

The use of substantial material lead times to try to deal with capacity constraints led to a guarantee that total lead times for finished goods would be long (even when the plant was not in fact very busy). Process variability could produce even longer production times. Thus MRP-controlled plants tended to have manufacturing orders sit in the plant for a very long period. This tendency, of course, both drove manufacturing costs up and created unhappy customers.

In addition to these logical problems inherent in MRP, MRP systems were often applied in small environments where planning needs were in fact very simple, resulting in significant system and process waste. For example, MRP systems institutionalized the concept of the manufacturing order, e.g., the authorization to acquire materials and begin production of a particular run. While manufacturing orders had been used in many industries prior to the creation of MRP as a way to collect the cost of materials and labor, in most process industries they had not been utilized. Manufacturers in those industries tended to make product to a schedule and perhaps run some type of simple materials explosion program. Introducing manufacturing orders increased the complexity and cost of manufacturing control without adding value. Manufacturing orders also made it easy to create a backlog of unmanufactured product, product that was supposed to be produced, but had not yet been, but for which time had now passed in the master schedule.

Just in Time

As Japanese manufacturers overtook U.S. and European manufacturers in many manufactured goods sectors during the 1970s and 1980s, manufacturing control experts often blamed the poor planning techniques and poor execution of Western manufacturers for their poor competitive performance. Some of the efforts that resulted went in the direction of improved quality and ultimately the Total

Quality Management and Six Sigma program techniques, and some went toward just-in-time (JIT) material delivery and ultimately Lean manufacturing techniques.

The Toyota Production System used kanbans (cards) to implement a type of pull operation on the plant floor. Consumption of a small batch of parts at one stage of production initiated production of a small batch of the parts at an upstream production stage. The technique worked extremely well when many external controls were in place (for example, approximately level production of each group of products) and when the plant was organized into manufacturing cells. It is easy to imagine Toyota building cars in Japan in the 1970s for the U.S. market that were so attractively priced that it could quickly sell every one that arrived at a dealership. Toyota was able to talk easily about the flowing stream of manufacturing and delivery because it had such control of ultimate sales. Concepts like lowering inventory flow to expose rocks (problems) made sense with that constant stream of demand.

North American manufacturers scrambled to implement a similar approach and used it with modest success. Given the greater physical distance between assemblers and component suppliers, implementation of JIT for components to be delivered directly to the assembly line often required offsite material storage hubs to feed the plants as needed. When special offsite staging was required to implement JIT, it often led to a debate about the actual supply chain economic effectiveness of JIT: whether it actually reduced total cost or just transferred costs to suppliers.

But JIT has survived in many North American industries, including those where considerable scheduling effort is required to get suppliers' products delivered from outside the plant to manufacturing lines just as needed. For example, in many types of food processing and beverage filling, packaging materials (glass bottles, aluminum cans, boxes) are delivered directly to packaging lines very efficiently for both the manufacturer and supplier.

By the 1990s, our Western understanding of JIT had grown to appreciate that it was part of a much larger Lean philosophy of manufacturing and operations, which was quite powerful and flexible (see Womack and Jones[15]). Lean is designed to eliminate waste at every step of product flow. We will discuss the implications of the Lean philosophy for planning in some detail in Chapter 5.

Vendor-Managed Inventory

Vendor-managed inventory (VMI) is an operations and planning approach that is closely associated with JIT and sometimes confused with it. The roots of VMI go back decades, certainly including traditional supplier responsibility for keeping inventory topped up: "I use solvent from that tank over there, and once a week Charlie comes around in his truck, fills it up, and charges me for what I used." In the late 1980s, there was a burst of enthusiasm in consumer goods industries for "continuous replenishment," based on utilizing new computer and communication technologies, to have suppliers manage inventories at their customers based on a continuous flow of information. For example, a manufacturer might be given daily data from a retailer on consumption of each SKU (stockkeeping unit) and current distribution center inventory and agree to take responsibility for replenishing that inventory multiple times per week, essentially guaranteeing that the retailer would not run out of stock. Better yet, if the manufacturer were given point-of-sale data as well, it could understand even more about how product should be replenished.

This movement led to a general recognition of the power of VMI in a new era where information about consumption and need could easily be transmitted to suppliers. There are some theoretical advantages to suppliers managing inventories of their products at customers: They can manage replenishment more efficiently by adjusting replenishment quantities to fill trucks, and they can reduce inventories slightly at many customers' locations when availability is a bit short, thus working through the shortage with no one running out of stock. By essentially guaranteeing to keep the customer in stock, they can maximize sales for the customer and themselves. VMI programs were often proven effective through documented increases in sales.

VMI was also considered a way to force greater supply chain efficiency by forcing everyday low pricing into consumer goods channels. It essentially makes it impossible for a retailer to play the game of buying product from the manufacturer only when it is promotionally priced and eliminates the manufacturer's incentive to use price promotions at the manufacturer/retailer echelon of the channel.

But in practice there are problems as well. In consumer goods, VMI is often demanded by retailers as a way to help reduce their inventories and is only grudgingly provided by manufacturers. Suppliers, in spite of contractual promises, are sometimes tempted to load customers up with product when they needed the additional quick sales. Customers often feel vulnerable when they do not have direct control over key product supplies. Customers may have special information about consumption plans that they do not want to pass back to the supplier, causing replenishment problems.

To deal with these issues, many forms of VMI have been devised. We call the pure form, where a supplier replenishes a customer completely at its discretion, "hard" VMI. But often "soft" VMI is more comfortable. In a typical soft VMI, the supplier tracks consumption and initiates the replenishment process, but the customer either must confirm the replenishment or has the option to cancel or change the replenishment if it chooses to. There is also the consignment version of VMI, where the goods remain the property of the supplier until actually "consumed" in some way by the customer (which is obviously less attractive financially to the supplier).

A few years ago, we worked with a truck manufacturer to design a VMI process for maintenance parts being supplied to dealers. Dealers are independent businesses and can buy parts however and from whomever they choose. Dealers sometimes buy non-original-equipment-manufacturer parts and frequently fail to do a good job of staying in stock on parts, thus leading to poor sales performance and unhappy truck maintenance customers and reflecting poorly on both the dealer and the manufacturer. The manufacturer in this case chose to propose a soft VMI approach that involved its own management of the process, but gave dealers the right to modify orders or not participate in the program at all. This approach preserved dealer independence while giving the manufacturer the primary things it wanted: increased parts sales (by displacing aftermarket purchases) and more consistently applied inventory replenishment logic for dealer parts stocks.

VMI operations require somewhat specialized planning tools. In addition to the considerable data communication necessary to keep the supplier informed of consumption and inventory, the supplier typically must have some type of short-range forecasting software (often with only a seven- to fourteen-day horizon, by day, of course) and then logic for making replenishment decisions. Because VMI has remained a minority of business for most manufacturers, many have failed to integrate their VMI replenishment process with their "mainstream" planning systems. They have also often neglected to install the kind of sophisticated logic mentioned above, to actually optimize the combination of transportation, inventory, and manufacturing savings.

While VMI is a key part of many supply chain operations today and often very efficient, it has failed to become the norm in most industries. JIT between supplier and customers has had a greater impact in most industries, because it retains the traditional customer/supplier roles and responsibilities while still permitting smaller-than-traditional inventories on the customer side. As suppliers' manufacturing and distribution sophistication has grown, they have become more adept at meeting JIT service requirements.

Theory of Constraints

Over the course of the 1980s, Goldratt[6] and Goldratt and Cox[16] introduced a powerful set of concepts called the Theory of Constraints, often abbreviated to TOC. The theory represents a philosophy of operations management, a management system, and a set of tools/principles to improve operations. Initially,

TOC promotion focused around the fact that most manufacturing operations have a few bottleneck steps that limit the throughput of the plant under typical product mixes. The goal of planning, then, should be to schedule these bottleneck steps efficiently so as to achieve maximum throughput, to schedule steps before and after the bottlenecks in order to best support the bottlenecks, and to "elevate" the constraint by adding capacity there and thus shifting the binding constraints elsewhere in the system. The drum-buffer-rope scheduling methodology (see Schragenheim and Dettmer[17]) was invented to support plant operations to "exploit" constraints to the maximum possible (get maximum throughput through them) and "subordinate" other manufacturing steps to the constrained ones.

As TOC evolved, greater emphasis was placed on the fact that the principles apply not just to manufacturing, but to supply chain operations as a whole, and even to non-supply chain activities like project management. These principles led to a universal five-step methodology for business improvement (Goldratt[6]):

1. Identify the system's constraints.
2. Decide how to exploit the system's constraints.
3. Subordinate everything else to the above decision.
4. Elevate the system's constraints.
5. If in the previous steps a constraint has been broken, go back to step 1.

TOC has helped raise the level of discourse substantially in product flow planning because it focuses on elements that MRP neglects. Whereas MRP tries to downplay the importance of capacity constraints, TOC points out correctly that planning product flow is, in fact, all about managing around constraints. Constraints are a fundamental part of operations not only for the rather pedantic reason sometimes quoted in the TOC literature that "any system that did not have a constraint would have runaway volume," but also for the more practical reason that real businesses have to achieve good asset utilization in order to compete economically, and hence simply buying plenty of capacity so that constraints do not impact operations is seldom a feasible strategy.

TOC has also helped us to recognize that while well-managed supply chains operate with less inventory than poorly managed ones, systems that have significant process variability (which is to say almost all operations systems) must plan to operate with some inventory. Corollary concepts that TOC has given us are that not all processes should be fully utilized (we have to leave slack in some steps so that we can focus on a few bottlenecks), that manufacturing lead times cannot be modeled statically and are truly dynamic, that economic order quantities are seldom useful in a manufacturing environment, and that transfer batch sizes (between workstations) can be much smaller than reasonable fabrication batch sizes — thus improving flow and reducing work-in-process inventory. TOC's emphasis on always increasing throughput has remained more controversial, as has the fact that it disputes decision making based on traditional cost accounting.

PLANNING HEURISTICS: I NEED A GOOD DECISION RIGHT NOW

Planners have always needed to make decisions quickly and have created a vast number of rules and techniques to support that decision making. Heuristics are decision rules or algorithms that produce good, workable decisions without attempting to truly optimize a model of operations.

Traditionally, heuristics were manual rules of thumb. "Since I know that product A is my fastest seller and it runs the best on machine 1, I always start scheduling by putting product A on machine 1 and figure that I will run products B and C, which run about the same on all machines, on machine 2. Of course, sometimes I can't make enough of them on 2, and I have to take some machine 1 time for B or C." Simple problem, simple logic, possibly even optimal schedules in this case!

With computer technology, more complex heuristics could be programmed and solutions quickly generated. For example, some of the best-known early finite capacity scheduling tools offered the plant scheduler a menu of heuristics to apply. One heuristic was: Improve the sequence of jobs to be run on this machine by selecting adjacent pairs of jobs in the current candidate schedule, reversing their sequence, and seeing if overall changeover cost is reduced while still meeting all due dates. This particular heuristic, repeated hundreds of times, is actually quite effective. Users were invited to construct compound heuristic solutions of their own by "programming" a sequence of simple heuristics, i.e., perform this heuristic two hundred times, then perform this step fifty times, and so on. Of course, the resulting proposed schedule is highly dependent on the path taken by the solver, on the heuristic logic itself, but that is a typical characteristic of heuristics, as opposed to true optimization techniques that are solution path independent.

Numerous heuristics are in use today. They are still utilized heavily in scheduling and planning systems. But perhaps the best known is the Silver–Meal heuristic (see Silver and Meal[18]) for quickly computing a recommended production lot size for each item in a master schedule.

Good heuristics are usually intuitive and easy to explain to planner/users, are very useful in producing recommended decisions quickly, and can recommend high-quality solutions to problems too difficult to solve optimally. But they also have some dangers. The classic danger is that it is very difficult to perform sensitivity analysis on a problem that is being solved heuristically. If we add a week of overtime on resource 2 and we generate a schedule that costs 7 percent less, is it because the extra week of overtime is really worth that or because the different data sent the algorithm down a different path that found a better solution?

In our experience, a more important problem is that constructing a heuristic to solve a very large, complex planning problem can lead to the creation of a logical "monster," a beast that is very difficult to work with. It is difficult to tune to produce the best performance (see the section on tuning in Chapter 8) because the sequence-dependent nature of the logic means that when "you push in here" with one control parameter, the solution does not necessarily "pop out there" where you expected it to pop out. Related to this is the difficulty of transferring maintenance from the original developer of a complex heuristic to his or her successor or to the successor's successor. The developer's insights into how this monster is supposed to work are usually lost, and ultimately the system is abandoned as unmaintainable. Unfortunately, this latter problem also applies to the more mathematically elegant systems discussed below.

POWERFUL ALGORITHMS FROM MATHEMATICAL RESEARCHERS

With the first significant use of operations research during World War II, academic researchers were eager to begin tackling corporate operations problems in the late 1940s and 1950s. There were immediate gains in better theories for inventory management (see the section on inventory above), scheduling algorithms, and mathematical programming approaches to operations planning (see Manne[19]).

Mathematical Programming

A mathematical program is a formally structured mathematical problem in which an "objective function" of many variables and their coefficients is to be minimized (if we want to minimize, say, cost) or maximized (if we want to maximize profit) subject to "constraints" that are also composed of many variables and their coefficients. These problems have true mathematically optimal solutions: There is no lower cost solution (or higher profit) than the optimal solution. In "linear programs," all of the terms in both the objective function and constraints are simply sums of the individual variables times their coefficients, with no variables squared or cubed and no variables multiplied times each other. Linear program variables can typically take on any positive value, whole numbers or fractions. Integer programs restrict variable values to integers (whole numbers) and are often used as switches to indicate that you will or will not undertake a certain activity (I will make some of a product this week and incur the entire setup cost for it, or I will not). Mixed integer linear programs restrict some variables in a problem to integer values, but not most of the variables. Nonlinear programs have variables taken to other powers (squared, for example, in a quadratic problem) or multiplied times each other.

Much of the "power" of operations research is due to the development in the 1940s, even before there were any computers, of very efficient algorithms for solving linear programs with hundreds of variables. With late 1950s and 1960s computer technology, problems with thousands of variables could be optimized, and with current technology, problems with hundreds of thousand to millions of variables optimized. Integer programming and mixed integer problems are usually much harder to solve, with much less efficient algorithms available for many of them. Consequently, even problems that are formulated as mathematical programming problems are not solved all the way to optimality when they contain many integer variables.

There are many techniques that are considered part of the operations research field that are not mathematical programming: queuing theory, game theory, Markov chains, etc., and the inventory theory and heuristics discussed above. But we will not spend more time here on them (see Hillier and Lieberman[20] for a good introductory textbook). Mathematical programming techniques first became well known in operations management by solving refinery planning/ blending problems, and by the 1960s every major oil and petrochemical company had an operations research department. They became important for operations planning in other companies as well — Procter and Gamble's operations research group was a well-known route for bright, young, quantitatively minded professionals to be prepared for the P&G management ranks.

Formal mathematical optimization models of production and supply chain operations began to have some significant impacts in the 1960s and 1970s. For example, Lasdon and Terjung's[21] work on optimizing "multi-item scheduling" of tire production led to a new comprehensive planning system at Kelly-Springfield Tire (see King and Love[22]). In the late 1970s, some significant advances were made in solving extremely large network models — a specialized type of linear program that is both easier to understand because it can be diagrammed as a network of arcs and nodes and is much faster to optimize than a general linear program. These advances led directly to the formulation and solution of the first useful integrated "production/distribution/inventory" model that simultaneously optimized a multilocation production planning, inventory positioning, and transportation problem, looking about one year into the future, for an agricultural chemical fertilizer company (Glover et al.,[23] repeated in Miller[24]). If you are curious as to why such advanced mathematics was first applied to something as "down to earth" as fertilizer, you just need to recognize that demand for fertilizer is extremely seasonal as it is mostly applied in the spring, leading to great benefit from planning its production, distribution, and storage in a time-phased fashion for each annual cycle.

Hierarchical Production Planning

One of the important planning structures that came out of operations research work in the 1970s and early 1980s was the hierarchical production planning (HPP) approach, developed by Arnoldo Hax and many colleagues (see Hax and Candea[25]). As shown in Figure 2.2, this approach focuses on planning at the product type level (the broadest category), then at the family level of disaggregation based on decisions already made at the type level, and finally at the item level based on type and family decisions. Its hierarchy is analogous to that of the MRP II structure (production planning, master scheduling, shop floor scheduling), but differs significantly in that each level of planning is performed by a mathematical technique that takes capacity and material constraints directly

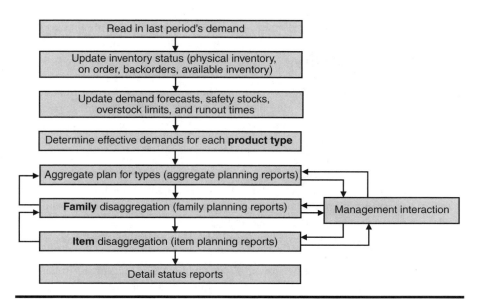

Figure 2.2 Hierarchical production planning. From *Production and Inventory Management* by Hax/Candea, © Reprinted by permission of Pearson Education, Inc., Upper Saddle River, NJ.

into account in the initial solution. Perhaps most significantly, it demonstrated that one could, if desired, completely plan a manufacturing operation with optimizing, capacity-cognizant techniques, although its hierarchical decomposition of planning does not deliver a true "global" optimum.

Operations research conducted on a custom basis had limited impact on most enterprises, however. Not only did it require some very technically powerful people to build the models and their solution algorithms, but supporting these creations often took someone with the equivalent of a master's degree in operations research to maintain them as the business evolved. It also took significant computational resources (relative to computing power in the 1970s), tended to require very time-consuming solver runs to produce answers, and required a stream of input data that were not readily available from the business execution systems of the 1970s.

While a few operations researchers attacked these comprehensive product flow planning problems (see Johnson and Montgomery[26] and Shapiro[27] for comprehensive reviews of supply chain models), the majority of researchers labored on finding better mathematical formulations and solution algorithms for small, very specific problems, such as particular types of scheduling for one or two machines (see Graves[28]). These problems fit more easily into a scope that individual researchers could successfully address, and could lead to a steady stream of publications for those researchers, but seemed esoteric and irrelevant to most people in business. Optimization-oriented tools tended to be very specific to the particular problem structure addressed, making it difficult to use one algorithm for a range of problems or adapt the tool as the business changed.

But work continued on the more comprehensive problems as well. A recent operations research–based standard structure for product flow planning is shown in Figure 2.3 (see Shapiro,[27] based on Tayur et al.[29]). Note that this example is more comprehensive than the MRP II or HPP structures, because it addresses the planning issues of logistics and distribution just as fully as it covers production. It also reflects the current expectation that an ERP system will provide the base of transactional data from which to create plans. Like HPP, it proposes that the bulk of the planning work be performed by mathematical optimization models at three levels: strategy, planning, and scheduling. Also like HPP, this is a general template, not a fully specified planning machine like MRP II with the logic all fully defined.

Mathematical programming–based planning has mostly remained in the "big gun" category of planning tools. Most planning tools that use linear programs are solving large problems, which usually require many minutes, if not several hours, of computer time to complete. Interestingly, this is more the result of how

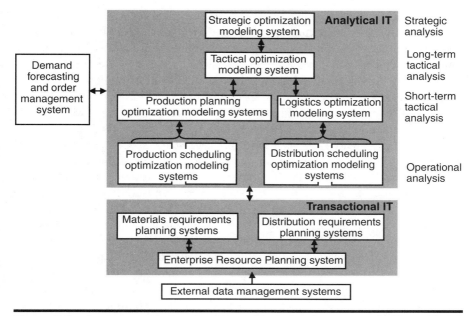

Figure 2.3   A more comprehensive hierarchical planning approach. From *Modeling the Supply Chain* 1st edition by Shapiro, © 2001. Reprinted with permission of Brooks/Cole, a division of Thomson Learning: www.thomsonrights.com. Fax 800 730-2215.

we have chosen to implement math programs, by building ever larger and more elaborate models that better reflect reality or letting them run a long time to achieve optimality or near optimality, than a characteristic of math programming logic itself. If we formulate relatively small problems and solve them with efficient software, we can produce answers in seconds that can be used, for example, for event response. There is no technical reason why a truck's route cannot be reoptimized every time its position is reported; there is no reason why a master schedule cannot be reoptimized every ten minutes (the value of doing either of these is, of course, a different question).

Dynamic Event Simulation

While manufacturing planners in the 1960s realized that readily available computing power meant they could compute dependent demand (MRP), researchers in universities and industry realized it also meant that they could easily simulate the interaction of the individual operations of enterprises (the arrival of an order, the completion of a manufacturing run, the release of a truckload of product) and develop better rules for planning and execution. Discrete event simulation quickly developed a significant number of disciples and was used more heavily to study operations than the continuous system simulation technology that Forrester used for studying industrial dynamics.[30]

Discrete event simulation languages were created, including IBM's General Purpose Simulation System (GPSS) (see Gordon[31]). By the 1970s, Don Bowersox and colleagues at Michigan State built the large-scale, special purpose LREPS simulator for logistics. Alan Pritsker and associates created the GASP IV and later Factor/AIM system for simulating production systems and scheduling rules, providing a combination of discrete event and continuous simulation capability.

Simulation permits much more detailed modeling of operations than any other technique because it permits any type of logical relationship between variables. What it does not do, of course, is determine optimal plans. It does provide a way to test the results of any type of planning rule or optimization technology that is embedded in the simulation. Most simulations are of the Monte Carlo type, meaning that what happens in them is based to some degree on chance interactions between the events; their results must be carefully analyzed statistically, based on multiple simulation runs.

Simulation technology has progressed continuously over the last four decades and excellent tools are available commercially today. A key advance in the 1980s was the development of visual displays for simulation, so that the user could watch the simulation (and interact with it) as an animation.

But simulation remains a labor-intensive type of modeling. By its very nature, simulation requires a lot of different types of data about operations to describe the behavior of each of the model elements. These data must be collected and refined, and the model built (and maintained) with them. While all types of models of operations have to be tested, tuned, and validated to make sure that the models produce "correct" results, this validation is particularly challenging for simulation because of the large number of data elements.

Over the years, we have worked with many clients on the question of how to set inventory levels. Often we categorize the choices as:

1. Inventory theory formulas (as discussed above)
2. Simulation
3. Incremental experimentation with the enterprise ("Is our service good enough? It is? OK, let's cut our inventory 10 percent. Is our service still good enough? OK, repeat the exercise.")

Sadly, in most situations, clients opt for alternatives 1 or 3. Simulation is usually viewed as just too much trouble or expense for merely setting inventory policy parameters.

Simulation with Intelligent Agents

A new form of simulation has emerged from the "chaos theory" research of the 1980s and the "complexity science" of the 1990s. This approach models complex systems through the interaction of multiple intelligent agents. The "emergent behavior" of the system as a whole often leads to new understandings of the fundamental dynamics of the system and new ways to manage it.

A supply network is certainly a multiagent system (with the intelligence of each agent perhaps debatable) and thus amenable to these types of simulations. Plate and Perrott[32] discuss the application of this type of simulation to a Procter and Gamble transportation problem to identify which system parameters had the most impact — such as the number of trucks available to redistribute product among stores versus a rule requiring full truckload shipments.

Murthy et al.[33] describe an elaborate system for the integrated scheduling of paper production and distribution. At its core is a team of separate software agents, called the asynchronous team or A-team, that cooperate to solve problems.

Search Heuristics

Since early in the use of computers to support operations planning, researchers have recognized that mathematical programming techniques were "particular" about problem formulation, and simulation did not directly find the best plan. There had to be another way, and there is. If one can describe a planning problem precisely enough to be able to compute the objective function value for any combination of variable value, one can use the brute computational power of the computer to search for the best solution, the combination of variable values producing the best objective function value (see, for example, "Search Decision Rules" in Buffa and Taubert[34]).

Searching is inherently inefficient, but it has become more practical as computers have become much faster and cheaper and as search algorithms have improved. A significant algorithmic improvement was achieved with the Tabu search (see Glover[35] and Glover et al.[36]). The search begins with a coarse examination of the solution space, and then proceeds to search for local optima in detail, while being careful not to visit solutions already investigated. It is a search heuristic. Note that while we use the term heuristic again here, just as we did in an earlier section, we are now discussing the optimization of the search logic itself, not, as we were before, rules for directly specifying a solution to the planning we are trying to solve.

Another contemporary search approach is the use of "ant algorithms" (again based on complexity science, as discussed above in connection with intelligent agent simulation) that find good solutions to problems with very complex structures. Ant algorithms use a colony of artificial ants to explore paths, reinforce the best ones, and ultimately find very good solutions. Lloyd[37] reports on the successful use of an ant algorithm at Unilever to find the best locations for and movement between storage tanks, mixers, and packaging lines in a plant.

Better search heuristics are making it possible to solve problems that have a very complex structure or little structure, unlike the well-structured problems solved by linear programming algorithms.

Artificial Intelligence

In addition to the intelligent agent simulations described above, which are sometimes categorized as part of the world of artificial intelligence, two technologies developed by artificial intelligence researchers have been promoted over the last two decades for product flow planning: expert systems and artificial neural networks.

Expert Systems

Expert systems are systems that use rules adapted from human experts to perform diagnoses or make decisions. The systems are typically architected so that they are in two parts: the rules database, which must be constructed for each implementation of an expert system, and the inference engine, which applies the rules and can be generic. There are various forward and backward chaining techniques for applying rules, but relatively little decision "power" in this technology compared with, say, the simplex algorithm for linear programming (although this comparison is unfair in that you would seldom see expert system technology and linear programming competing to solve the same problem).

Expert systems have made their mark in other applications such as medical diagnosis and complex product configuration, but do not seem to have had a lasting impact on product flow planning. The concept of "business rules" that can be turned on or off is widespread in packaged applications for product flow execution and planning and is clearly important to controlling these applications, but business rules are much simpler and more direct than the typical rule set on which expert systems rely.

Artificial Neural Networks

Artificial neural networks (called artificial, because the real ones exist in living biological creatures) have some very interesting characteristics. They are self-learning systems composed of multiple layers of artificial neurons that can remember whether a given response to stimuli from other neurons produced a correct or incorrect result. Thus, a neural network can be trained by showing it various scenarios and telling it whether a given outcome is desirable or not. The networks then can produce good solutions to problems that are subtly different from those they have seen before. While specialized neural network processors have been designed and sold (neural networks on silicon), most neural networks are implemented through software simulators that run on conventional computers (that are then, of course, simulated artificial neural networks, which somehow strikes us as a bit amusing in their multiple layers of abstraction).

Neural networks have proven valuable in process control, where their ability to respond quickly to poorly structured problems is important, and in other fields unrelated to product flow planning. But for most product flow problems, which can typically be given a lot of structure by the modeler, they are not as powerful as other techniques described here.

GETTING THE ORGANIZATION TO DANCE TOGETHER: SALES & OPERATIONS PLANNING

Most of this chapter focuses on planning technology, not on management of the planning processes. One of the key conceptual breakthroughs of the 1980s was the recognition that enterprises needed a specific process to get the functional silos to talk to each other at the vice presidential (more or less) level. Ling and Goddard's 1988 book[38] brought attention to this area, and the Sales & Operations Planning (S&OP) process it introduced and named has become broadly accepted, if not always successfully implemented.

The core of the S&OP concept is that a business unit general manager and many of his or her direct reports (generally sales, manufacturing, marketing, engineering, finance, and perhaps procurement and human resources) should meet approximately once each month to:

- Review recent sales, production (or purchases if you are not a manufacturer), and inventory.
- Review customer service issues.

- Review updated aggregate operating plans for the short to intermediate horizon.
- Make decisions that need to be made at this level of management and accepted across all functional departments. These decisions might be, for example, major changes in production rate based on recent sales and revised forecasts, agreement that certain products may have to be shorted to provide capacity for other products that marketing and sales want to push harder, and so on. The management team may also need to make decisions that should be resolved at a lower level, but for some reason are too difficult or politically sensitive to have been resolved there.

To make the S&OP management meeting effective, there must be a significant effort each month to crystallize the plans of each department (particularly an updated demand plan from marketing or sales and an updated supply plan from manufacturing or operations), compare them, and combine them into a plan/presentation deck that top managers can digest.

S&OP is often depicted as the apex of a basically top-down planning process in which S&OP drives the detailed sales plan and master schedule, but that is not fundamental to the concept.

Having quite a bit of experience implementing optimization-based tactical planning tools that combined sales plans, planned production, and inventory at a fairly detailed (sometimes SKU) level, we have seen the S&OP communication process supported very effectively with an aggregation of the detailed plan. In other words, the planning staff develops a detailed plan and discusses the problems in it with the sales, manufacturing, and distribution folks, and then it is presented to the management team as a rolled-up set of numbers and the specific decisions that still need to be made. In this approach, there is a big component of bottom-up planning, as well as specific decisions that come out of the S&OP meeting and are imposed top down. Of course, the aggregate and detailed plans must be kept synchronized.[38]

In our experience, we have seen benefits from S&OP not only through improved integration of plans across the functional departments of an enterprise and forcing functional heads to explicitly agree on a plan, but also from the mere fact of getting high-level managers to devote a couple of hours per month to thinking about product flow! Many managers at this level tend to avoid involvement in product flow decisions and in the absence of an S&OP process often abdicate important responsibilities. Indeed, we have seen S&OP implementation fail in a situation where senior managers stoutly refuse to be involved in product flow planning. But the much more common reason for implementation difficulties is an inadequate preparation process that does not create a short, insightful briefing for senior managers or succinctly present decisions for them to make, i.e., crude attempts at S&OP that do not fully respect top managers' time.

PACKAGED SUPPLY CHAIN PLANNING SOFTWARE MEETS THE ENTERPRISE RESOURCE PLANNING ESTABLISHMENT

By the early 1980s, research on production scheduling had arrived at the point that general purpose software could be written to solve a family of problems and do it on an inexpensive small computer. Perhaps the best-known early packaged tool was Schedulex from Numetrix, Inc. (now part of PeopleSoft). It could address several types of finite capacity scheduling problems (as well as dealing with the management of one inventory for each item), and it offered a broad range of heuristic scheduling techniques that had been developed by industrial researchers.

Meanwhile, a production/distribution/inventory solver was being offered as semi-packaged software (by Analysis, Research, & Computation, Inc.) and later evolved into packaged software to solve the general problem of integrated tactical planning. Other techniques were developed. For example, by combining a decision-making heuristic with a network linear program, certain types of finite capacity master schedules could be created very quickly on a personal computer (Cleveland Consulting Associates). Other heuristics were developed to combine finite scheduling of the plant with MRP-type BOM explosions and material availability constraints to permit more realistic planning of complex plants (i2 Technologies).

As we entered the 1990s, all of these techniques achieved a degree of commercial success for many packaged software providers and began to impact how companies planned product flow. They became known as advanced planning systems or advanced planning and scheduling (APS either way) and later as supply chain planning (SCP) systems — the planning subset (as opposed to the execution subset) of supply chain management software. Different tools were interfaced (to a greater or lesser degree by their respective software developers) to provide integrated planning tool kits that grew to support, as the 1990s progressed:

■ Sales forecasting
■ Logistics network strategic design
■ Tactical planning or supply planning (the direct successors of the production/distribution/inventory optimizer, and almost always solved with a linear programming solver)

- Finite capacity detailed production scheduling
- Integrated plant planning of both materials and production resources
- Available-to-promise (ATP) logic
- Master production scheduling
- Detailed production scheduling
- Field inventory replenishment and VMI planning, sometimes using DRP and sometimes a more capacity-cognizant approach
- Transportation planning, load planning, and carrier assignment
- Capable to promise (CTP), a much more complex concept than simple ATP
- Order profitability calculation: Will I make money on a proposed customer order given all its impacts on my system; should I accept it?

By the mid-1990s a considerable cadre of APS/SCP vendors had developed, basically offering supply-chain-focused tools as best-of-breed add-ons to the ERP vendors' offerings. In addition to those named above, they included Manugistics, Chesapeake Decision Systems (acquired by AspenTech), Logility, Synquest (which later joined with Viewlocity), Paragon/Adexa, OTG, Red Pepper, Caps Logistics, and many others.

The APS software was initially revolutionary in the marketplace because it represented a direct philosophical break with the MRP II structure of planning. The MRP II/ERP software vendors were still selling planning approaches that relied exclusively on basically infinite capacity MRP and DRP technology. The planning technology philosophy gap was bridged over the course of the 1990s as the mid-sized ERP providers bought APS vendors and the largest launched into their own development programs, often based on the C-Plex commercial mathematical programming package from ILOG. Thus they were able to add SCP capabilities to their manufacturing-only planning cores and add capacity constraints and optimization to planning processes:

- PeopleSoft bought Red Pepper (1996) and announced redevelopment of tools in 2003.
- JD Edwards bought Numetrix (1999) and PeopleSoft bought JD Edwards in 2003.
- Baan bought Caps Logistics (and in 2003 SSA bought Baan).
- SAP developed its own planning tool set (APO).
- Oracle developed its own planning tools.

Currently, even some of the "mid-market" ERP providers claim advanced planning capabilities in addition to providing their traditional business execution and MRP functions. In general, with their installed base of transaction systems, which their licensees were dependent on to even do business, the ERP vendors weathered the down cycle of 2000–2003 much better than the independent planning software providers. As the ERP providers' planning capabilities matured, they were able to win a substantial fraction of product flow planning software licenses over the independents. They had fundamental advantages in the nominal preintegration of their planning tools with their transaction systems and the freedom to price their planning software licenses very "flexibly" to keep competitors out.

Two other technologies significantly impacted product flow planning as we turned the corner into the new millennium: event management and ATP/CTP.

EVENT MANAGEMENT AND ORDER PROMISING

With warehouse management systems in many distribution centers providing real-time information, and more transportation carriers able to provide constant information about where shipments are currently located (and in some cases revised estimated arrival times), logistics managers recognized that they could construct systems to provide essentially real-time "visibility" of what is going on in the supply chain. Packaged systems to provide just this kind of visibility are available today. Note, however, that in general these systems provide visibility of the nonmanufacturing supply chain, i.e., of transportation, inventory, and orders, but not of manufacturing events that may delay or accelerate production.

With this visibility comes the obvious question: If an exception occurs that disrupts our product flow plan, can we do something about it immediately before it cascades into broader problems requiring more reaction? Are there near-real-time decisions we can make that nip the problem in the bud? If an inbound material shipment for production is going to be late, can we move a different product not requiring that material into that production time slot, or can we conserve existing stocks of that material by not making a product just now that is not critical, or perhaps find some of the material that we can borrow nearby?

Making these kinds of near-real-time decisions is usually called event management. Several of the software systems that provide visibility also claim decision-making capabilities, although these capabilities vary considerably. Usually there are parameters as to what adjustments to let the system make on its own, versus which decisions require human approval or overrides. Some of the decisions that can be made with such a system are (from Viewlocity[39]):

- Shipment expediting
- Finding an alternate shipping location, which has the inventory on hand to meet an order

- Diversion of inventory currently in transit
- Substitution of functionally equivalent product for that originally ordered

These capabilities have lent greater weight to the case for some decision-making power to be decentralized, so that the systems and staff that are close to the problem can make an adjustment in operations as quickly as possible. However, it can also be argued that making the kind of decisions in the list above requires the same information and much of the same logic as the main-stream short-term planning processes that are part of order management, order sourcing, and inventory replenishment, and that supply chain event management must either duplicate this data access and logic or make poor decisions. We will talk about this more in Chapter 4.

Certainly, event management has pulled the center of gravity of planning closer to execution. A good example of this is what has happened in recent years to ATP logic. The classic approach to order promising, ATP, was a natural outgrowth of the MRP world and master production scheduling (MPS). Indeed the basic ATP calculation can be performed on an MRP-MPS time-phased spreadsheet (see Vollman et al.[40]), but as better information systems for tracking transportation and inventory developed in the 1990s to provide continuous visibility, it was realized that certain types of order promising can be better performed by combining real-time logistics information with the production schedule.

For example, if a product is made in the Far East and shipped in ocean containers to the U.S., order promising may logically be made from these multiple categories:

- Currently in transit to customer, expected to arrive at time xx
- In stock in the U.S.
- In transit to the U.S., expected to be at the U.S. port at time xx
- In stock in country of manufacture, expected to ship at time xx and arrive in U.S. at time yy
- Scheduled to be produced at time xx

In this kind of a supply chain, there is so much information about the status of product already produced, and such a significant time from production to arrival at the customer, that much of the ATP "action" naturally shifts from manufacturing to distribution, and ATP becomes distribution centric rather than manufacturing centric.

The issues around CTP are a bit different. The logic required to decide whether and when a supply chain system can deliver product that has not yet been scheduled for production is complex — particularly given that it must be reliable enough to support promises to customers. We have not yet worked with a system that attempts to do that automatically in real time based on up-to-the-minute manufacturing and logistics information (although software is available that promises to do essentially that).

Given the range of ways to implement ATP/CTP, one software provider offers four alternative modules for order promising to try to meet the diversity of client needs.

FORECASTING AND DEMAND MANAGEMENT

The sales forecasting discipline has advanced steadily over the last several decades in tandem with planning. While we view forecasting as a separate field from planning and do not really cover it in this volume, we must speak to the relationship between forecasting and planning. Good forecasts significantly improve operations efficiency. For example, a classic rule of thumb is that reducing forecast error by half allows a one-sixth reduction in supply chain inventory. Because we will not be returning to forecasting in this volume, our description in this section will be more oriented toward contemporary best practice and less historical than most of this chapter has been.

One of the subtlest and most often confused aspects of planning product flow is its relationship to forecasting and demand management. Figure 2.4 is a brazen attempt to impose order here and to diagram some of the relationships we need to discuss, in particular that sales forecasting, sales planning, and product flow planning are distinct activities. While the reader will likely react "I don't think about these things in this way," bear with us and we will try to illuminate a few points.

We have shown five traditional functional organizations here in heavy rect-angles. Conceptually above them are the ideas of supply chain management, demand management, and supply management. Marketing and sales are clus-tered under demand management, while distribution, production, and procure-ment are under supply. Key planning processes are then located in this orga-nizational space: promotion planning, sales planning, and product flow planning (with S&OP artificially broken out since we have discussed it in detail and it is broader than most of product flow planning). Supply chain execution and product allocation processes are also identified. Finally, we have added sales forecasting, which provides data to several of the functions.

Note that our use of the "demand management" terminology is different here than the APICS definition (see Cox and Blackstone[41]): We assert that demand management is primarily the activities that marketing and sales perform to stimulate demand — branding, promotional activity, sales calls. It is euphemis-

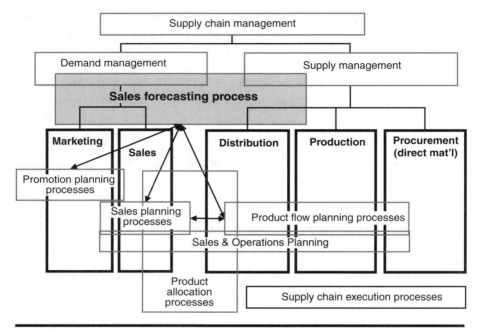

Figure 2.4   Forecasting process located in the supply chain conceptual "organization chart."

tic to refer to the usually minor activities that customer service and operations
groups do to (slightly) shape demand so that they can better meet sales, e.g.,
specific promise dates for orders, product substitutions, allocation of scarce
product, and so on, as demand management. Typically the sales organization
determines the policies under which these perturbations of demand are executed
anyway.

The sales forecast is a projection into the future of expected sales, given a
stated set of environmental conditions. What kinds of constraints on sales are
incorporated in it is up to the enterprise to decide, but they need to be explicit.
The sales plan is, of course, the targets that the sales organization intends to
measure itself against and the set of managerial actions it intends to take to
deliver the planned sales. The promotion plan is an outline of marketing's
intentions, which impacts the sales forecast and is impacted by it.

Forecasting is a data-development process rather than a planning activity
because it does not make decisions (see Chapter 3). A good forecast is a critical
asset for the whole of enterprise management: It is used not only by the several
supply chain planning processes diagrammed in Figure 2.4, but also by non-

operating functions, such as finance's use of it to prepare a financial plan. Good forecasting takes considerable effort and is normally led by a full-time forecaster or forecasting core team. Traditionally, they reside in the marketing function (because there they are close to the folks driving demand and because forecasting logically begins on the demand management side of the house). If the forecasting core team is in marketing, operations usually has responsibility for breaking down the aggregate forecast that interests marketing to the SKU/location level needed by operations.

Indeed, for VMI and internal inventory replenishment purposes, operations need extremely detailed forecasts of sales by SKU/location/day. This level of forecasting is far below the level of detail that humans want to be involved or can probably add value (with the exception of key date-specific bits of sales knowledge which are not yet reflected in customer orders). These most detailed forms of the forecast represent enormous quantities of data and are usually generated by computer breakdown of aggregate forecasts, using location profiles of demand, SKU profiles (to break out SKU sales from product family), and daily profiles (to break out sales by day within the week). This is as it must be, and operations planners must generally be content with little human oversight of the forecast at the most detailed level.

Let us summarize some of the key points for managing forecasts:

- It is important to keep forecasting logically distinct from planning. Forecasting requires a different mindset than planning: "What is our best, unbiased view of the future?" for the forecaster versus the planner's "How do I make decisions now given an uncertain future?" It typically requires a different kind of professional to do it. The plan names that we used in Figure 2.4 are, of course, just archetypes. An enterprise defines the specific processes and plan types that are appropriate for it. The key requirement is that a business knows what the forecast represents and what each plan represents, knows what to use each for, knows what is required to get from one plan to another, and does not get them confused. Many enterprises, in fact, have trouble keeping these plans sorted out.
- After much debate over the last forty years, there appears to be some consensus that an organization should operate from one sales forecast. That forecast has to be comprehensive because so many different constituencies must use it. If a central forecasting process is not meeting all the organization's needs, "pirate" forecasting will often spring up to meet some of those needs.
- Twenty-five years ago, it was a bit of a conceptual breakthrough when software vendors first presented an aggregation triangle, with SKU/

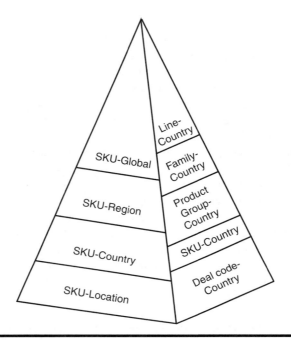

Figure 2.5   Pyramid of forecasting views.

locations at the bottom and highly aggregated product groups at the top — and the ability to manually edit the forecast at any level and have the software automatically aggregate or disaggregate up or down from there. Now we view the forecast as a pyramid with multiple faces, and hence multiple triangles with a different product aggregation scheme on each face for some constituency (Figure 2.5 is an example).

■   The forecast should not be "aligned" with any particular plan, of course, since the forecast supports all kinds of plans. On the other hand, most planning processes will begin with some type of forecast transformation logic to format the forecast for input to that process or software module.

■   The science of forecasting is well developed with a literature comparable in size to that of product flow planning, from classic time series methods to modern "business analytics" that attempt to go deeply into causal modeling of sales.

■   Statistical techniques for sales forecasting are well established and are usually used as a starting point. There are multiple mathematical models available, e.g., exponential smoothing, and software tools designed to figure out the best models to use for each part of the product line. The most intuitive, easily understood forecasting models are of the Winters type, which break the components of a forecast into base, trend, and seasonal components (to which adjustments for planned promotions are then added [or subtracted] by the software for businesses with sales promotion). Good forecasting software packages typically have time series–type logic to estimate trend and seasonality and regression logic of some type to separate the impact of specific "events" such as promotions or price changes. The profile of event impact is then added into future forecasts when a similar event is planned.

■ The statistically generated model should normally just be the starting point for a forecasting process that incorporates manual adjustment from members of the organization who have specific information to contribute. Defining this human adjustment process requires a fair amount of thought about where knowledge resides in the organization and can be efficiently applied to the forecast, and sometimes recognition that part of the organization is too biased to make accurate contributions to the forecast. It also requires a full-time forecasting process management staff that not only attends the statistical tools and manages the data, but also supervises the human revision process. Sometimes it requires the use of collaborative planning software to support interaction between a field sales force and central forecasters. Indeed, an enterprise may appropriately spend as much dedicated staff time on forecasting as it does on planning. *Forecasting is more about creating and maintaining a rational forecasting process that assembles all the knowledge than it is about specific statistical techniques or software packages.*

■ Mature forecasting processes carefully measure forecast accuracy. Understanding our errors and whether we have systematic error such as bias high or low in the forecast or a forecast adjustment process that increases error instead of reducing it are usually the keys to more accurate forecasting. We are particularly interested in forecast accuracy metrics to support product flow planning, because some of the decisions we have to make, such as inventory safety stocks, depend directly on forecast accuracy.

■ Advanced forecasting approaches will likely track sales for each individual major customer, and then forecast sales by those individual customers (and often in collaboration with those customers). Historic sales information is becoming an increasing part of contemporary customer relationship management systems, and these systems track sales by customer. These forecasts must of course then be correctly combined with more aggregate forecasts for "all the other customers." This kind

of customer-specific forecasting has been used for some time by consumer goods companies, and they have had considerable success with
it.

■ Collaborative planning, forecasting, and replenishment (CPFR) was
   introduced several years ago by the VICS manufacturer–retailer consor-
   tium (Voluntary Inter-Industry Commerce Standards Association). It
   includes a specific methodology for collaborative planning and forecasting. Its greatest successes have come in collaborative forecasting, which
   has proven particularly valuable in the industry where CPFR was invented: consumer goods manufacturing and retailing. Part of the reason
   for this is that in this industry, promotions are originated at both the
   retailer and manufacturer levels, and to really create an accurate forecast
   the promotion impacts must be combined. While collaborative forecasting has achieved documented successes in increasing supply chain
   efficiency, it is quite difficult to take to scale, that is to a large number
   of SKU/locations, because of the fairly manual way it has generally
   been implemented.

While some planning approaches attempt to minimize their dependency on
forecasting by focusing on quick reaction to changes in operations, it is impossible to eliminate the need for forecasting. However, in situations where there
is very little real information to drive a forecast — particularly very short-term
forecasts over the next few weeks of sales— it may be appropriate for operations planning to assume a constant average rate of demand rather than try to
guess about essentially random ups and downs. It should also be noted that in
forecasting, like planning, the enterprise chooses how much money it wants to
spend to do it well. Not every organization can afford to spend a lot on it, and
smaller enterprises may find that an elaborate forecasting process is not cost
effective.

THE SHAPE OF PLANNING TECHNOLOGY TODAY

In the product flow planning field today, we enjoy the fruit of some of the best
mathematical and practical minds (and some that are both) of the twentieth
century. Every one of the technologies discussed in this chapter is valid in its
appropriate context, and most are fully supported today in packaged, licensable
software and services.

We have achieved what feels like a certain stability of planning technology
here at the beginning of the twenty-first century. The underlying computer
architectures continue to face new questions (see Chapter 8): Should planning

tools really be thin-client, web browser–based applications? Will web services fundamentally change how applications are integrated? But most of the planning concepts and functional technology that we work with (the kinds of things we have reviewed in this chapter) are fairly mature at this point from a logical perspective. That is not to say that they will not change further as new concepts are invented, but we have a much better foundation today than we did, say, twenty-five years ago.

One of the theses of this volume is that our planning options are no longer severely limited by communication or computational power. Do we have the technology today to take all known data and instantly generate a globally optimal plan (assuming that we would want such a thing)? No, but we have the technology to solve most of the problems we might care to solve. We know what simulation, heuristic, and optimization-based solvers can do for us. We know what inventory theory can do, what MRP does, and where JIT processes can help us.

The first challenge we face, then, is to figure out what we are trying to accomplish with our planning: Who is going to make what sorts of decisions; what data need to be incorporated in making good decisions? We are going to present some principles in Chapter 3 to help us answer those questions, some planning approach design structures in Chapter 4, and then come back and cover some of these planning technologies again in Chapter 5 under the banner of the different supply–demand strategies they represent.

With that under our belt, we will be in a position in Chapter 6 to launch into the process of actually selecting the right combination of planning techniques to meet our needs.

3

PRINCIPLES OF PRODUCT FLOW PLANNING: THE FOUNDATION ON WHICH WE BUILD

The practice of solving problems by importing best practices is not a best practice.

Michael Schrage[42]

While this volume is not constructed in any sort of formal logical hierarchy, a lot of the points we emphasize can be traced back to some key core principles. These principles come from many sources: the business and operations literature, experience by the author, and, in a few cases, simple logic. In this chapter we will make them explicit, so that it is easy to refer to them as we make the case in later chapters for consciously and carefully building planning structures in the enterprise.

PLANNING IS PERFORMED TO MAKE DECISIONS

Planning is only worthwhile if we use it to actually make decisions about resources, to commit or uncommit them to a given task, to increase or decrease them, to accept orders, or try to delay them. Indeed, this is the first principle we introduce, that:

> **1. Planning is performed primarily to make decisions that commit resources, and secondarily to coordinate activities among multiple participants.**

The decision might be to increase the staffing level by a shift, to make a certain amount of an item next week, to replenish field inventory at a stocking location by a certain amount. But they are all decisions, and once made and acted on, there is a significant cost to reversing them. Identifying the decisions that have to be made is a key step in our methodology for rethinking planning processes.

Most of the value in better product flow planning does not come from something associated with the plans themselves, but from better decisions about operations — better order "acceptance" decisions, better inventory replenishments, better capacity investments, and so on. It is the capability to make better decisions that justifies significant staff salaries and systems investments for planning.

The world is not quite as simple as the first part of this principle implies. Plans also create a sense of direction in an organization and help the different parts of an organization move in a coordinated way in that direction. For example, a plan to shift customer order sourcing to a new distribution center as of a certain date will result in a whole set of coordinated activities by warehouse managers, inventory managers, customer order management staff, information technology support staff, and so on.

A more subtle example of coordination through planning would be a tactical planning process that results in a plan to build ahead of the sales forecast by 200,000 cases of product to meet next summer's demand peak. It may not result in any immediate decisions and may never be executed exactly as initially planned. By the time we get to next spring, when the inventory build would nominally begin, demand higher or lower than our "plan" will probably result in a different prebuild decision. But the existence of the plan has helped us share expectations throughout the organization and perhaps with suppliers or customers. Thus there is also some value in planning that produces "planning bogies," planning that does not immediately lead to a decision.

Budgets are another type of plan that is key to managing an enterprise and that has some impact on product flow, but typically indirectly. Budgets certainly affect decisions on capacity resources, such as operator staffing levels.

In general, when we have to allocate resources to planning processes, we should consider the critical product flow decisions that need to be made and let them guide where we allocate our time. In most situations it is not cost effective to devote resources to creating separate, nondecision-oriented plans, to plans that exist mostly because certain managers are more comfortable if they have a plan.

The "decisions as our driver" principle for planning may seem trivial or academic, but it is actually important to recognize. As we shall see, focusing on the decisions we need to make will help us to find the simplest, least expensive way to create good plans.

It will also help us to avoid significant mistakes as we design planning processes, such as allowing redundant planning processes that cover the same operations area. For example, it is not unusual for headquarters planners to generate schedules of what they think their manufacturing plant should produce in each of the next several weeks, when in fact the plant is generating its own production schedules from the bottom up based on its own forecasts and customer orders. Can you guess which plan actually gets executed in these situations? Which planning process is probably a waste of time and systems? In general, we see redundant planning going on because different departments have not agreed on who is really responsible for making certain decisions.

Plans can be far more detailed than they need to be. We once worked with a paper company that used a planning system that computed how much of each finished goods stockkeeping unit (SKU) was going to be slit and packaged each day, one year into the future. This was, or course, an absurdity. Beyond two to three weeks into the future, the business had no idea what finished products were going to be produced on any given day, nor were there any item-day-related decisions to be made for production 365 days from now. But the company had implemented software that made that computation, and it executed it and printed reports with that information on it. While the human planners did not spend much time looking at these detailed plans for distant periods, the fact of their creation wasted computer time, paper, a little planner time, and in general reduced the credibility, speed, and efficiency of planning.

We also see unnecessary planning being done because a manager thinks it is a good idea to regularly generate a plan for his or her area, even though it is not clear what decisions are to be made from the plan. In another example, a manufacturing company decided that it had too much finished goods inventory and created an inventory manager position (plus staff) to do something about it. The manager initiated a monthly inventory planning process, failing to recognize that inventory was created by executing a production schedule (which he did not have control over) and consumed by sales (which he also did not have control over). The primary place where he needed new processes was, in fact, the regular identification of old inventory as obsolete and its disposal (which management was loathe to do because of the impact on short-term profits). The planning process he created and tried to execute mostly invaded other managers' areas of responsibility and was largely unnecessary.

While good planning is high leverage, unnecessary planning is very low leverage — maybe of negative value. Good planning has a significant cost. It usually requires more than some part-time work with a spreadsheet program. It requires good management, good staff, systems, data, and support for those data and systems. We do not want to waste resources by overplanning or create confusion by having competing plans.

By this criterion of being decision oriented, sales forecasting is not planning! As was mentioned in Chapter 2, forecasting is a data-generation process that supports many parts of the organization: operations planning, sales planning, marketing program development, management budgeting, financial planning, and so on.

WHAT IS THE ESSENCE OF GOOD PLANNING?

> **2. Good planning is the process of taking all relevant information about the current state of operations and real information about the future, quickly working out the logical implications, and making decisions about product flow.**

There are a lot of key words in this principle. First of all, good planning requires using all the relevant information. For example, if you are a successful manufacturer who is planning how sales will be met over the next year and where the product you need will come from, you must take your manufacturing capacity into account as a fundamental part of the process. You will need to take existing customer orders into account. And for most businesses, you will also need to base it on a forecast of the coming year's sales by month or week.

Forecasting is always a difficult issue, but most organizations have some information about what they are going to sell. This is real information, not random guesses. For example, if we forecast that an established product (e.g., twenty-four-ounce boxes of corn flakes) is going to sell 800,000 cases per month for the next year, we are providing real information to the planning process. We may sell 900,000 cases or 650,000, but we will not sell 100 cases or a billion cases. Much as we hate to use "incorrect" forecast data, we cannot avoid relying on forecasts to some degree.

Planning logic needs to be correct. Surprising at it may seem, it is not unusual to discover significant simple errors in planning tools: inappropriate or misprogrammed safety stock logic, interfaces between planning steps that are not valid, spreadsheets that do not enforce the law of conservation of product flow (product out does not equal product in), and so on. Invalid plans are no basis for good decision making.

Logical implications need to be worked out quickly so that new decisions can be made before avoidable problems occur. And decisions need to be made quickly so that they do not waste people's time or give them incentive to skip replanning or bypass the formal planning system. One of the hotter topics of recent years has been "real-time" planning, the efforts to reduce replanning lags to virtually zero.

What is adequately quick varies with the type of plan. A "plan" for where to store the next pallet of product to come off a truck should take no more than a second, regeneration of a tactical plan for production and inventory no more than a couple of minutes to recompute (although probably much longer to review), and a strategic plan no more than an hour to recompute. These time recommendations are often not met in practice, either because planning software executes slowly or considerable human intervention is required to manage a "run." A planning manager may think: "So what if it takes my staff a few days to recrunch a strategic plan; we only do it once a year." Wrong. Planning is a highly iterative process; one does it again and again as new data arrive and as managers figure out "what ifs" that need to be investigated.

It has been said that product flow planning is the "balancing of supply with demand." That is a pretty good way to think about our goal and to evaluate how good our planning process is. If we are able to balance supply and demand effectively each day and each week, to meet demand while keeping costs down, inventory down, and not wasting assets, we are doing a very good job.

THERE IS NO ONE BEST WAY TO PLAN

Figure 3.1 illustrates the diversity of the planning areas in which various types of organizations must make decisions. Because of differences in operations, operating philosophy, and management goals among organizations, each enterprise is essentially unique in the decisions it must make. These different plan-

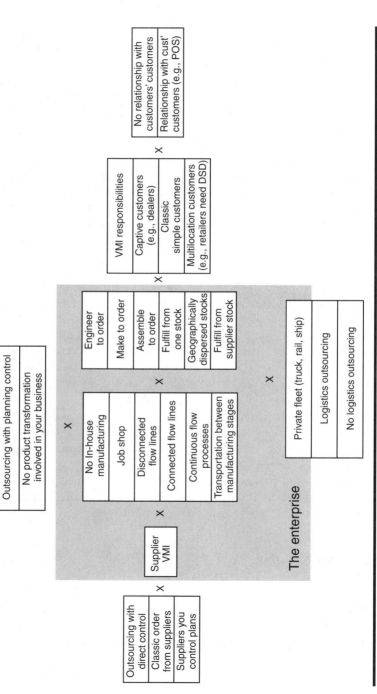

Figure 3.1 Planning needs vary greatly based on differences in operations.

ning "requirements" should lead to different, at least moderately unique, planning approaches.

> **3. There are many ways to plan, depending on the circumstances of the enterprise. There is no one best way to plan for all businesses and supply chains.**

Another way to look at this principle is that "best practices" are of limited value in the planning sphere. Of course, we should understand what leading enterprises are doing, perhaps including direct competitors. Of course, we need to understand all the techniques referenced in Chapter 2. Of course, we need to understand what is available in packaged software. But ultimately, we must decide for ourselves the best way to plan our product flow, based on the particular business we are in, the strategies by which we are pursuing that business, our culture, and the investments we have already made (e.g., a commitment to a particular enterprise resource planning software environment).

WHEN DO WE NOT PLAN?

Good planning takes time and expense, and hence we need to do it as efficiently as we can and limit the total amount of planning we perform. Indeed, much of the conceptual work that has been done over the last couple of decades is figuring out when to not plan or how to plan less. For example, the Theory of Constraints (see Goldratt[6]) has correctly pointed out that minimal planning is sufficient for nonbottleneck resources, resources that have plenty of capacity anyway.

Some forms of Lean operations require that product be pulled through the supply chain, with some planning at the tactical level, but none required at the manufacturing lot level. Making this approach operate successfully requires many enterprise attributes that broadly affect operations: smoothing of demand, maintenance of surge capacity, reasonable cycle times for fulfilling customer orders.

Note that the system characteristics that have reduced planning requirements in this Lean example are not short- or mid-range product flow planning decisions! They are decisions at the strategy and policy levels of the business, because this approach requires that all aspects of the business be aligned to work well. More precisely, we should say that the decisions we make at strategic and policy levels determine the decisions we will make at the short to intermediate level, and hence the types of planning necessary to support them.

4. When there is little real information on which to base a plan, little variation to plan for, or no decisions to make, it may make sense to not plan.

If we are going to operate as a make-to-stock food processor with finished goods inventory at five locations around the country to support mixed-product truckload shipments from any of the distribution locations to customers within forty-eight hours of order receipt, those decisions have a lot of implications for our product flow planning. They imply a lot about how we must coordinate manufacturing and distribution, how we should schedule production, how much ingredient material we keep at the plants, how much packaging material we keep at the plants, and why we can provide 99 percent customer order case fill rates while maintaining 90 percent capacity utilization at plants. We get point-of-sale information from our mostly very large customers and plan product promotions with them several months into the future. We have chosen to operate a fairly "planful" business. But after attempting to plan ingredient inventories carefully, we gave up on the ingredients that are widely used across our products and, for example, contracted to have Cargill just send us a rail car of high-fructose corn syrup every four days, based on our aggregate production rate. We chose not to plan a major material in detail.

If we have little information about the future, we may choose to polish our skills at reacting rather than planning. If we make a custom industrial product, never perform final assembly until an order is received, promise one week order-to-ship cycles, and have a large number of customers, we have a set of critical planning decisions to make about subassembly inventories, fabrication capacity, and final assembly capacity — but not about finished goods inventories. We have chosen to plan very differently than our cousin in the food industry, and we maintain substantially more idle production capacity and subassembly inventory to make it work.

PLANNING IS A PROCESS, BUT REQUIRES ORGANIZATION, DATA, AND SOFTWARE

5. Planning is a set of business processes that are supported by organization, data, and software. Planning is not primarily about implementing or using software.

A process is a series of actions with a clearly defined goal. That planning is primarily a process should come as no surprise to anyone who has ever planned operations. But it is identified as a principle here because during the 1990s many managers developed the misconception that by licensing planning software, the challenges of planning could be easily solved. The marketing messages of the planning software companies of that era implied that this was true, and the information technology–oriented analyst community implicitly supported that message by focusing its reports on the acquisition and implementation of software.

One of the key themes of this volume is that a "software first" approach is naïve and backwards. Well-managed enterprises first figure out how they want to run their businesses, then configure software to support their planning and execution. We will discuss this in more depth in Chapter 6 on methodology, including the point that it is equally naïve to design planning structures without understanding the capabilities of today's software.

PLANNING IS REALLY REPLANNING

> **6. Developing a totally new plan is a rare activity. Replanning is the norm, and our skill and speed at doing that will significantly determine the quality of our results.**

The fact that product flow planning is normally replanning makes it different from most of the kinds of planning that businesses and individuals do. Mostly we plan projects or other events that we do not expect to immediately repeat: new offices, product introductions, weddings, a vacation trip. Product flow planning goes on and on, again and again, day after day, week after week, revising the plans that we revised yesterday or last week.

Because we replan, good planning is based on rolling schedules. An example of rolling plans is shown in Figure 3.2. The upper bar in the diagram shows actual days of operations divided into weeks. Our planning horizon is seven weeks, of which we consider the near-term portion "frozen," only to be changed if absolutely necessary; the next portion, which we would prefer not to change, "chilled"; and the most distant portion completely flexible. Of course, a plan might have more or fewer zones than this example.

It is quite reasonable, by the way, to restrict the amount of change in the near-term portion of the schedule. Change itself becomes a significant cost in the near term: changes in planned staffing levels, restaging of materials that

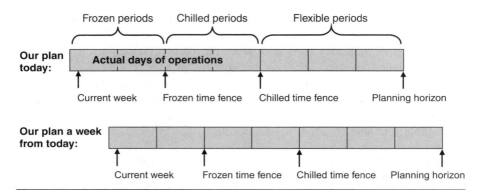

Figure 3.2 Planning is the management of rolling schedules.

have already been staged, and management and staff time to recommunicate what we are going to do. Furthermore, if decision making is less than excellent, emergency decisions may result in a net decline in schedule effectiveness. Example: "We jammed this product that one customer really wanted into tomorrow's schedule and didn't produce three other products that we were committed to shipping the day after tomorrow." That said, in a typical operations environment, sometimes the biggest obstacle to near-term schedule change is scheduler resistance to having to take their own time and energy to rework the schedule once again — sheer schedule inertia. Good scheduling tools and processes should largely overcome this effect.

If an enterprise does not view a plan as a kind of rolling plan or schedule, it may be because it fails to develop preliminary plans for the outlying periods. It may also be that it does develop planning bogies for those outlying periods, but calls them another type of plan. For example, a master production schedule might extend out only eight weeks, but an associated production plan extends to six months. We will talk more below about the relationship of these kinds of hierarchical plans.

Only the time periods transitioning from flexible to frozen (or perhaps from flexible to chilled to frozen) actually represent decisions (see the arrows extending from "our plan today" to "our plan a week from today" in Figure 3.3). We also make decisions when we violate the "frozenness" of the very near term by making emergency changes.

The direction of progress in product flow planning has been to steadily reduce the length of chilled and frozen horizons and permit more changes so that our supply chain is more flexible, or "adaptable" to use a currently popular term.

Having good planning processes and tools that let us go through the replanning cycle easily and quickly is very valuable (as we first alluded to in the

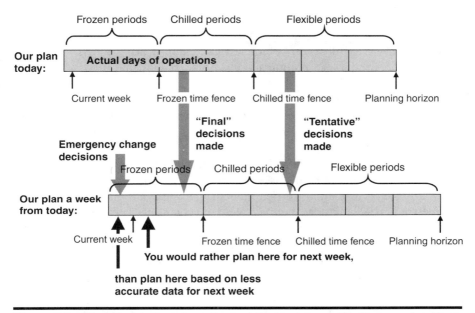

Figure 3.3   Decisions are made at the transition points and in the very near term.

section on the essence of good planning above). Time that we can reduce in the replanning cycle is a wonderful resource. Unlike inventory or production resources, reductions we can make in cycle time improve performance at little cost. Think of it this way: If we can do a weekly replanning cycle in four hours, including communication with the operating folks and any preparation they need to do, we can use finished goods inventory and customer orders as of 7:00 a.m. Friday (or perhaps 7:00 a.m. Saturday if we are really hard core) to finalize the plan for next week. If it takes us four days to replan, we must use inventory and order data as of 7:00 a.m. Tuesday of this week, at which point we have a far less accurate picture of what real starting conditions for next week's operations are going to be. That increased uncertainty due to the larger planning time offset means extra safety stock we need to hold, or larger contingencies built into material arrival times, or whatever — it costs money (see the lowest annotations in Figure 3.3).

WE ALWAYS PLAN FOR AN UNCERTAIN FUTURE

By its very nature, planning is about decisions we make now to be ready to execute operations in the future. But the future is uncertain; we base our plans on our expectations for the future. Plans made on the basis of sales forecasts are not based on solid ground and must usually be revised and/or the consequences of "wrong" decisions ultimately accepted. Make-to-order operations are often espoused as a solution to this problem, but they do not solve it. Organizations that take orders for delivery well into the future typically experience considerable change in the orders as time progresses. If there is currently a shortage of capacity in their industry, customers may well place orders for several times as much as they need, canceling the extra supply as the delivery dates draw near.

In early 2002, Intel (the leading manufacturer of microprocessors) decided to quit reporting orders to the U.S. Commerce Department. The *Wall Street Journal* reported that Intel justified this change by saying that "...the number of orders was misleading and not indicative of actual sales because many clients cancel their orders within weeks of when they are booked."[43] The mere fact that an order is on the books does not mean that a planning system can assume that order must or will be filled. Those who strictly advocate make-to-order operations sometimes forget that issue.

Shortening Cycle Times with a High-Velocity Supply Chain

Uncertainty about the future, whether due to forecasting or to soft customer orders, costs money because it leads to decisions that turn out to be incorrect — materials ordered inappropriately, the wrong product manufactured, and so on. The best way of reducing it is to increase the velocity of the supply chain, so that less time elapses from when an order is placed until when it is filled.

As shown in Figure 3.4, the supply chain is a peculiar kind of "time machine" in that as we move upstream in the time machine, we make materials that will go into finished goods delivered further and further into the future. Obviously, if we can build a supply chain with a minimum amount of time between creation of the first noncommodity components and delivery of finished goods, a supply chain with the greatest material velocity, we minimize the uncertainty and hence minimize the likelihood of making product flow mistakes. That is a major part of the argument for high-velocity supply chains and Lean in particular. But eliminating inventory completely by having the whole order-driven supply chain execute within a short finished goods customer order cycle time is very, very difficult to achieve, given the norms of most industries.

Cisco Systems is a designer and marketer of data routing and communication hardware, famous for being one of the earlier high-tech firms to outsource essentially all production. It had to suffer a $2.2 billion dollar write-down of inventory in 2001, the largest in history (see Kahla[44]). While Cisco was oper-

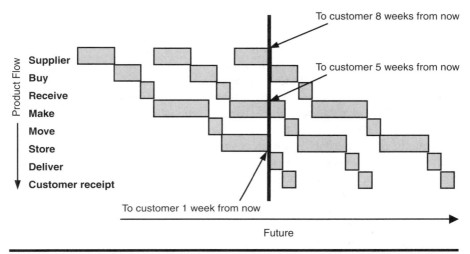

To customer 8 weeks from now

To customer 5 weeks from now

Product Flow

Supplier
Buy
Receive
Make
Move
Store
Deliver
Customer receipt

To customer 1 week from now

Future

Figure 3.4 The supply chain time machine.

ating an assemble-to-order business for its customers using contract manufacturers, it did have to take on considerable financial responsibility for component
inventory. In many cases, expensive components also had long lead times and
hence represented a large responsibility. This factor, combined with duplication
of finished goods orders from customers, produced the extra inventory. Part of
Cisco's solution to avoid this problem in the future is a system to provide
visibility of final demand to upstream component suppliers, based on a visibility
hub provided by an outside application service provider. That is, it plans to rely
on a higher visibility supply chain planning solution.[44]

> **7. We must design supply chains and planning systems to control
> and minimize risk from future changes in demand, but we can
> seldom eliminate it completely.**

GOOD PLANNING IS NOT A BAND-AID®
FOR POOR OPERATIONS

Several years ago we worked with a tire manufacturer that had very carefully
expanded one of its plants, adding just enough extruding capacity for certain
kinds of treads to keep up with expected demand, just enough fabric coating

capacity for each specialized type of ply that was used for certain classes of high-performance tires, just enough molds for each SKU to serve the average level of demand, and so on. The plant had arrived at a state in which there were about thirty active constraints on product mix based on various component fabrication capacities, in addition to the (normal) hundreds of individual SKU production constraints based on the limited number of molds available to cure each item. This plant presented the hardest scheduling problem we have ever encountered. The combination of these layers of capacity constraints, the significant changeovers to make different tires, and the demand from management that the plant make its capacity of 45,000 tires every week (which itself required a certain mix of tire types) made it virtually impossible to vary production to build the tires that were selling. Product shortages were rife, and surplus inventory of unneeded product was everywhere.

This was an extreme example of a situation we have seen many places, where conservation of investment capital, healthy sales, and corporate demand for high utilization of resources create an impossible-to-manage situation. This example certainly violated the Theory of Constraints tenet that active capacity constraints should be allowed to exist in only a few places. And the problems in this case were not the problems of material velocity found in poorly managed job shops — the plant could make its planned throughput and did not have large quantities of work in process; it was just a nightmare trying, and each week slightly failing, to both make that volume and make the products that were selling well.

Manufacturing and supply chain operations need to have facilities that are suited to the current business. Capacity needs to be flexible to meet changing market needs on a week-by-week basis, and expectations for facility utilization need to be realistic. When that kind of infrastructure is not built, the result is lost sales, distressed (suicidal?) planners and managers, and, if production is driven by financial targets, excess inventory. A trend in recent years towards operating plants 24/7 (Aeppel[45]) has reduced flexibility in manufacturing capacity and made production planning even more difficult.

We have also worked with more than a few manufacturers who argued that long production runs were necessary to achieve acceptable product quality, that it took them so long to get a production process under control after a changeover that they simply had to have long production runs to avoid wasting an unacceptable amount of production time and material making bad product after changeovers. While there is, of course, some legitimacy to this argument on a temporary basis, relying on it for years and decades represents an inappropriate use of planning (and inventory) as a Band-Aid® for weak manufacturing practice. Manufacturing processes need to be reasonably robust, whether in a Lean or conventional production environment.

Because of the flexibility of planning processes, it is all too tempting to use them to make jerry-rigged, Rube Goldberg kinds of operations work acceptably. But planning can never turn a poorly designed operation into one that is truly cost and service competitive. Good planning of a poorly conceived operation can mask problems that need fundamental solutions, not ever more skillful planning to try to cover for them.

> **8. Flexible planning is only effective in covering up facility and operational problems for brief periods; ultimately it is no substitute for well-designed strategies, facilities, and operating processes.**

4

PLANNING STRUCTURES: CONCEPTS UNDERLYING OUR DESIGN WORK

You yourself are actually a planning machine.

David Allen[46]

We are now ready to take the basic principles we identified in the previous chapter and apply them to changing how the product flow of an enterprise and its supply chain are planned. We will also define a few additional principles to guide us.

GETTING A HANDLE ON PLANNING DECISIONS

Since we believe that planning is performed primarily to make good decisions, we need to begin with those decisions. We have laid out some typical product flow decisions in Figure 4.1 on the same diagram we introduced in Chapter 1. From left to right, we work from decisions that are acted on right now, through tactical decisions that impact the next few weeks and months, to strategic

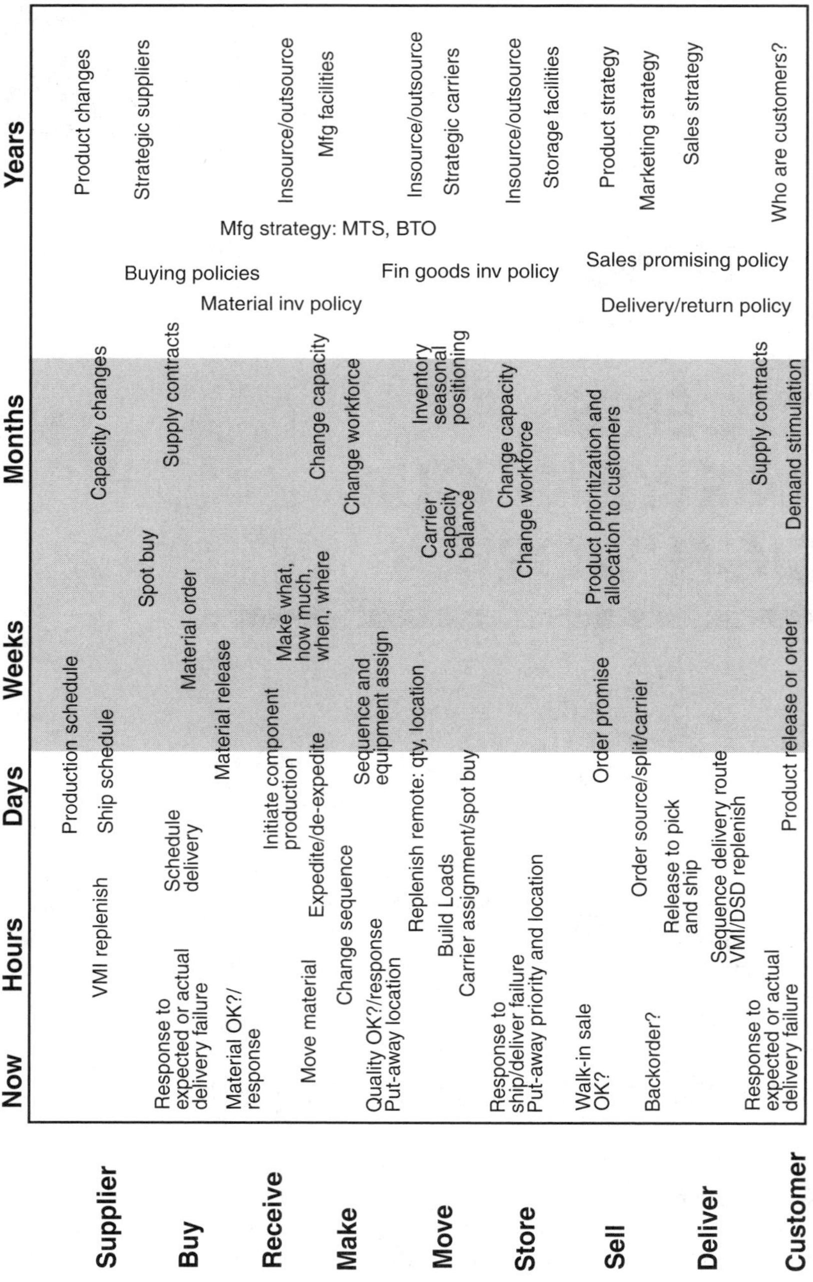

	Now	Hours	Days	Weeks	Months	Years
Supplier			Production schedule			Product changes / Strategic suppliers
Buy		VMI replenish	Ship schedule / Schedule delivery	Spot buy / Material order	Capacity changes / Supply contracts	Insource/outsource / Mfg facilities
Receive	Response to expected or actual delivery failure / Material OK?/ response	Move material / Expedite/de-expedite	Initiate component production / Material release	Make what, how much, when, where	Change capacity	
Make		Change sequence	Sequence and equipment assign		Change workforce	Insource/outsource / Strategic carriers
Move	Quality OK?/response / Put-away location	Replenish remote: qty, location / Build Loads / Carrier assignment/spot buy			Carrier capacity balance / Change capacity / Change workforce / Inventory seasonal positioning	Insource/outsource / Storage facilities
Store	Response to ship/deliver failure / Put-away priority and location		Order promise	Product prioritization and allocation to customers		Product strategy
Sell	Walk-in sale OK? / Backorder?	Release to pick and ship	Order source/split/carrier			Marketing strategy
Deliver		Sequence delivery route / VMI/DSD replenish	Product release or order		Supply contracts / Demand stimulation	Sales strategy
Customer	Response to expected or actual delivery failure					Who are customers?

Middle-band policies:

- Mfg strategy: MTS, BTO
- Buying policies
- Material inv policy
- Fin goods inv policy
- Sales promising policy
- Delivery/return policy

Bottom axis: Operational   Tactical   Strategic

Figure 4.1   Decision space for product flow planning.

decisions that may be implemented over a period of years. From top to bottom, we consider the various flows in the supply chain. At the top are decisions made primarily by our suppliers and at the bottom decisions made by our customers. We do not attempt to break out activity by our suppliers' suppliers or our customer's customers, although those decisions can be critical in some supply chains.

In Figure 4.1, we present a range of generic decisions that are made by a "universal" enterprise that performs most types of supply chain activity. There are certainly a large number of decisions shown in this diagram. There are many more decisions that could be added here if we looked in detail at a real enterprise, as well as some that could be deleted for any specific business. But rather than worry too much about whether we have exactly the right decisions in the diagram, we shall work through the different categories of decisions and get to know them a little better.

Enterprise Business Strategy and Philosophy

Figure 4.2 shows the strategic decisions, the ones that define what business we are really in. They range from what our products are, to whom we buy from, to whether we manufacture product ourselves, to whom we sell to. These decisions determine the business context for product flow planning, but they are not the subject of this book. Note that in this strategic decision category we have also included decisions like what manufacturing and distribution facilities (if any) we should have, which arguably represent operations strategy rather than true business strategy, but are certainly long-term financial commitments for the enterprise.

The business philosophy under which strategic decisions are made directly impacts product flow planning. Treacy and Wiersema[47] provide a very useful framework for understanding business priorities in *The Discipline of Market Leaders*. They argue that an enterprise should concentrate on one of three primary disciplines (while providing acceptable performance in the other two): operational excellence, product leadership, or customer intimacy. For example, a company that focuses on product leadership is likely to make expensive investments in research and development and perhaps in manufacturing technology. They argue that doing everything at an industry-leading level is too expensive to be competitive economically, and customers are likely to associate only one primary virtue with a supplier anyway.

Three of the heavily promoted directions in management philosophy over the last several years line up rather nicely with the three Treacy and Wiersema disciplines. Advocates of the Lean philosophy implicitly advocate designing the whole business to support operational excellence. Supporters of customer re-

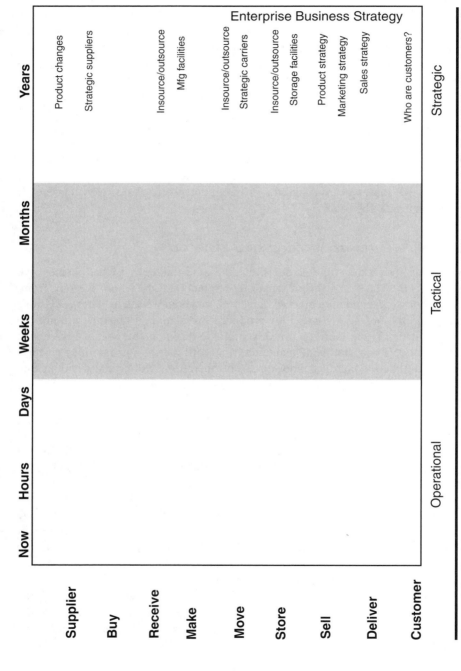

Figure 4.2 Decisions near business strategy.

lationship management, who argue that it is not just systems but rather a whole philosophy of customer-oriented management, are essentially making the case for customer intimacy. And the advocates of product life cycle management, who argue that it represents not just systems but a whole product-centric orientation for the enterprise, are doing much the same as advocating the product leadership strategy.

We make no such argument for planning — that businesses should all be transformed into "The Planning-Focused Enterprise." Rather, enterprises should take stock of what their business strategy is and develop the best planning approach that is logically consistent with that strategy and employs an appropriate quantity of resources.

An organization focused on operational excellence is likely to make investments that, for example, let it provide extremely high levels of on-time delivery service. It probably will want to invest in a more complex, unique, higher performance approach to planning than if it is content to be an adequate performer. Enterprises more focused on customer intimacy require elaborate processes for wooing customers, but perhaps less powerful product flow planning. And those focused on product leadership will be especially interested in where product flow planning and product life cycle management intersect: in planning new product introductions, scaling up volume, and carefully managing late-life scale-down, inventory sell-off and transition to new products.

As discussed in Chapter 1, every enterprise with product flow must plan operations, but the extent to which we invest capital and incur operating costs to perform better planning is very much a management decision. Of course, a decision to perform operations but not to be excellent operationally may be a mistake; if there is no commitment to excellence in operations, it may make more sense to outsource them as completely as possible and let someone else worry about them.

Unfortunately, most enterprises do not have statements of business strategy that can be translated into guidelines for operations planning. As covered by the methodology presented in Chapter 6, that usually means managers who want to improve planning have to begin with some working assumptions about the enterprise's priorities.

Supply–Demand Strategies

Even more relevant to defining how we want to plan are the supply chain and manufacturing policies that we have established for each of our families of products. Some typical policy areas are shown in our planning decision matrix, Figure 4.3, on the "near-term" side of strategy. Tom Wallace[48] provides an excellent description of this level of decision making: "These strategies spell

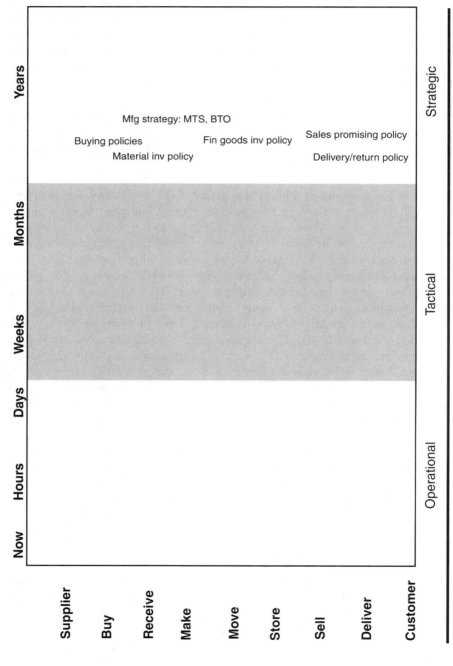

Figure 4.3   Product supply–demand strategies.

out whether the product family is make to stock or make to order, what the target customer service levels are, and what the desired level of finished goods inventory or customer order backlog is." This is a level of strategy that is seldom discussed, but is absolutely fundamental.

Have we decided that we will be a make-to-stock business in one product family and a make-to-order in another? Have we decided that we are going to produce all of our high-volume product at the Monterey, Mexico plant and all the low-volume product at the Indianapolis plant (even though either plant could produce all the product with minor investments in equipment)? Have we decided which products are going to be stocked at all of our distribution centers, versus which ones are only going to be stocked at a central distribution center, versus which ones will be shipped directly from our suppliers to our customers?

Here are the issues that are typically resolved at this level:

- Plant missions (what kinds of products will be produced for what kinds of customers)
- Distribution center missions
- Customer service levels (order cycle times, fill rates)
- Manufacturing philosophy for each class of products (make to stock versus make to order versus assemble to order, flow versus job shop)
- Workforce policy (retain versus layoff in downturns, use temps versus seasonal employees)

Many of these issues should be addressed periodically and reoptimized. Often supply chain design tools such as logistics network optimization software or multiechelon inventory optimization software can help. Some of the decisions end up being quite subjective, like determining the level of inventory in-stock performance we think is right or how we feel about varying our workforce levels and the labor climate that policy creates.

Product Flow Planning and Scheduling

In Figure 4.4, we see the decisions that are really the heart of product flow planning and what most practitioners think of as "planning and scheduling": decisions that affect action in the hours, days, weeks, and months of the future — what orders we will accept, what product we will make, where we will deploy it, and so on. We have included quite a number of relatively short-cycle decisions in this diagram, all the way down to operational details like product storage locations, because there is no natural line between these hourly/daily decisions and weekly/monthly decisions. For example, finite capacity scheduling tools usually perform Gantt chart–type line scheduling down to the minute-

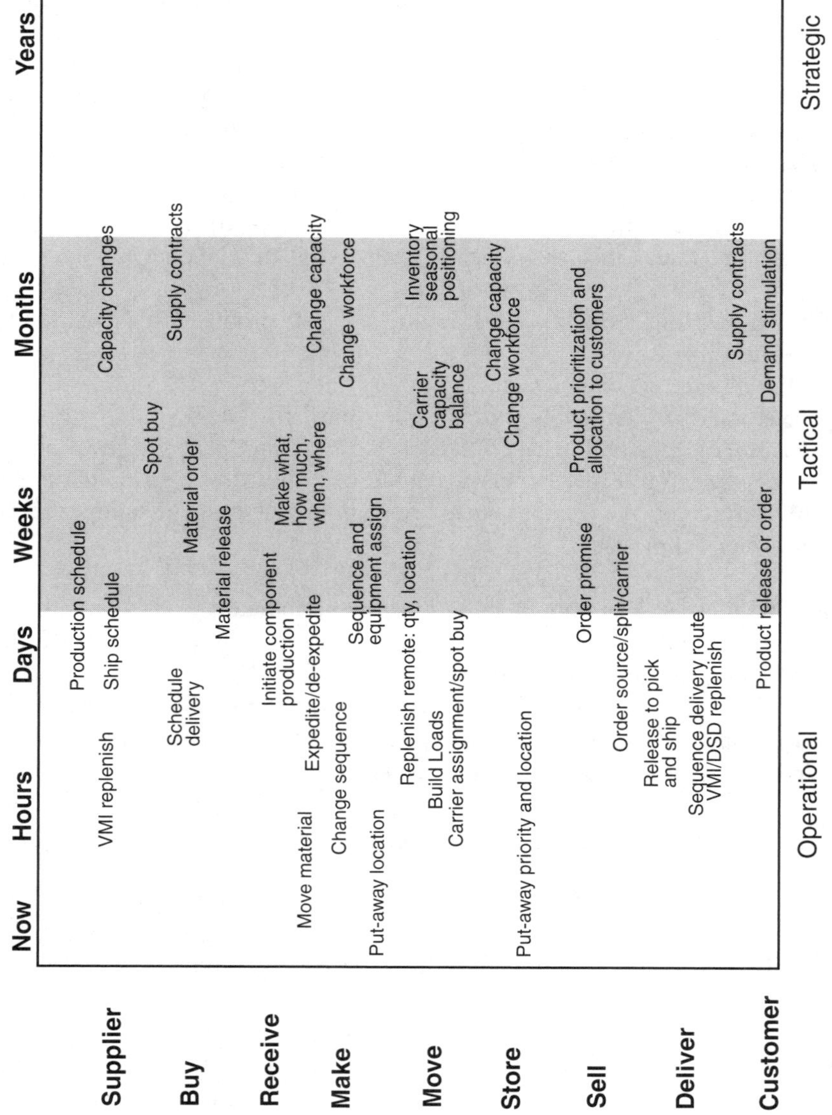

	Now	Hours	Days	Weeks	Months	Years
Supplier		VMI replenish	Production schedule / Ship schedule		Capacity changes / Supply contracts	
Buy		Schedule delivery	Material release	Material order	Spot buy	
Receive	Move material		Initiate component production / Expedite/de-expedite	Make what, how much, when, where	Change workforce	
Make	Put-away location	Change sequence	Sequence and equipment assign		Change workforce	
Move		Build Loads / Carrier assignment/spot buy	Replenish remote: qty, location		Carrier capacity balance / Change capacity / Change workforce	
Store	Put-away priority and location				Inventory seasonal positioning	
Sell			Order promise	Product prioritization and allocation to customers		
Deliver		Release to pick and ship / Sequence delivery route VMI/DSD replenish	Order source/split/carrier		Supply contracts	
Customer			Product release or order		Demand stimulation	
	Operational			**Tactical**		**Strategic**

Figure 4.4 The core decisions for product flow planning.

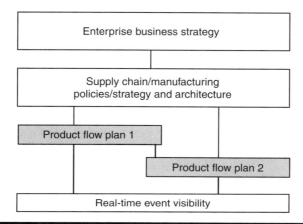

Figure 4.5   Hierarchy of planning.

by-minute level, but also look weeks into the future to balance inventory and help decide what to make. Recent systems from Moore & Associates to optimize warehouse operations operate at the minute/hour level, but also look days into the future.

The product flow scheduling processes, of course, depend on the higher level decisions about how the business will be run. It is helpful to think of the decisions as being organized as shown in Figure 4.5: business strategy drives supply–demand policy, which then determines what is required from flow planning.

While flow planning is certainly subservient to business strategy, it is not subservient to facility layout and equipment. One cannot effectively design a supply chain facility, be it a manufacturing plant or a distribution center, without simultaneously considering how the operations of that facility will be planned. Manufacturing cells, conveyer capabilities and locations, storage types, and so on can be consistent with the supply–demand strategy and planning policies, or they can inappropriate and ultimately less effective.

Event Management and Near-Real-Time Planning

One of the hottest issues in planning today is making optimal use of the availability of more information about product movement in the supply chain: transport, inventory, and manufacturing status (Figure 4.6). These data are available from better internal systems, from suppliers, customers, and service provider systems (such as transportation carriers). The Internet is often the preferred mechanism for communicating the data.

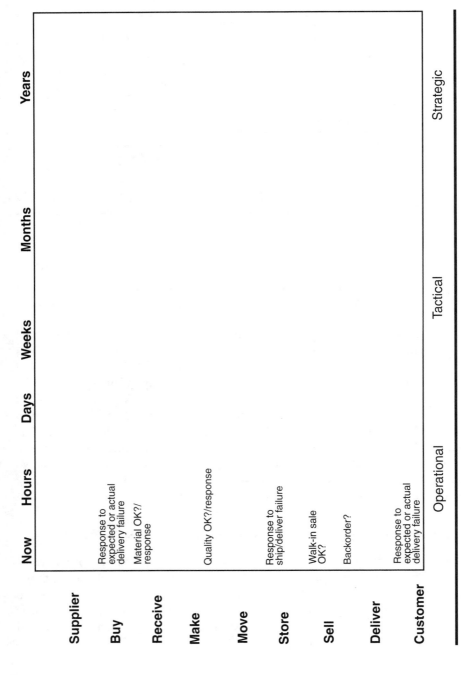

Figure 4.6 Event management decisions.

It is not particularly important to make hard distinctions between the activities of execution and monitoring in Figure 4.6 and true planning. Most managers do not care, a lot of software providers are not careful to make this distinction, and, frankly, this book is about how to figure out the best way for an enterprise to plan, not putting borders around planning. Certainly, software providers have been happy to combine them, most notably when one of the traditional advanced planning vendors (Synquest) combined with its neighbor in Atlanta, event management company Viewlocity, and adopted the Viewlocity name for the whole business.

One of the hardest planning challenges is to make intelligent decisions in near real time based on new data about operations and to integrate those decisions with the longer cycle planning processes. Let us use Figure 4.7 to contrast the difference between a pure visibility and event management approach and a near-real-time planning approach, using a transportation example.

In a traditional environment (situation "a" in Figure 4.7), each evening a shipper might take all the customer orders that are authorized to ship tomorrow (right side of the diagram), run them through the load-building and carrier assignment planning logic of its transportation management system, and produce the next day's first and second shift loading schedule (and tentative schedules a few days into the future, see Figure 3.2), dock-door assignments, and so on. Now suppose that a large rush order comes in during the morning the next day, and inventory is available to cover it. Traditionally, order management staff

a. Process orientation with separation between short-range planning and visibility/event management (Transportation example)

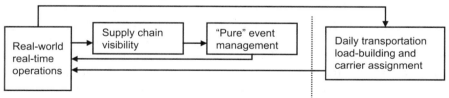

b. Integrated event management/planning process

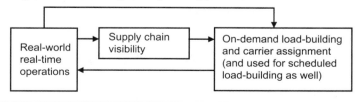

Figure 4.7   Integrated planning and event management.

would have called transportation dispatch to line up a vehicle for later that day, or, perhaps using visibility and event management systems, the need for rush transportation for a same-day order would be sent to dispatch as an alert. The customer is served, but at the cost of a separate shipment.

Contrast that with situation "b" in Figure 4.7, where the shipper reschedules transportation on demand as needed — subject to whatever "frozen" time constraints on carrier communication, bill-of-lading printing, distribution center work assignments, and so on might exist. When the rush order comes in, the shipper is able to replan today's loads and perhaps take advantage of the additional volume to fill a partially full truck, reroute a multidrop load for closer stops, or whatever. The shipper has achieved both a very high degree of customer responsiveness and has done it economically — perhaps at a lower shipping cost per pound than the original shipping schedule.

Of course, there are many types of nonplanning process issues that limit the organization's ability to respond both quickly and efficiently, but traditionally the planning cycle itself has been a key obstacle. In this example, by improving the planning process, we may have improved our operating efficiency significantly, and we have also simplified our processes by eliminating a separate "box" in our diagram for event management that uses different, more "quick and local" logic than our mainstream load-planning process. Analogously, inventory visibility data can be rolled into short-range inventory management logic and the results reflected in deployment plans almost immediately, within minutes — if it is appropriate in a particular operation.

Rethinking our planning processes to take advantage of real-time visibility from operating processes is a major current opportunity. An increasing amount of packaged planning software is configured for exactly this kind of near-real-time use. It is certainly a requirement that the process be able to go through the replanning cycle in a few minutes: data update, "solver" run (assuming that there is enough logic required to justify a solution algorithm), and manual review/blessing of the new decisions. A truly aggressive process might eliminate the need for human review altogether, at the risk of the planner then not internalizing the revised plan and not being able to be an advocate for it — but that is perhaps less critical for very short-term decisions that will be executed almost immediately. Planning software that is not able to support event-triggered, near-real-time planning is becoming obsolete.

ELEMENTS OF THE PLANNING APPROACH

As we think about planning decisions, the question naturally arises as to what "planning machinery" is required in an enterprise to make good decisions.

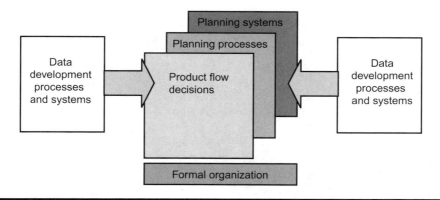

Figure 4.8 Elements of the planning approach: decisions, processes, systems, data, and organization.

Figure 4.8 shows the relationship of planning decisions, planning processes, and the formal organization that underlies them and also includes data development activity.

Planning Processes

Planning processes are at the heart of product flow planning. How do we pull data together to make good decisions? Who is responsible for doing what? What logic is used to suggest decisions? Do we need to collaborate with other planners inside or outside the enterprise? Process design has been a hot topic in management circles since the business re-engineering wave of the early 1990s. Formal process design is now a standard part of figuring out how to execute the daily transactions of operating a business.

Good planning processes are carefully thought out as well. Figure 4.9 is an example of one planning process diagrammed as a process map, also known as a "swim-lane" diagram. It lists each of the participants in the process from top to bottom, and then shows each process step in the appropriate lane (of who is responsible for that step) going across the diagram from left to right. We will talk more in Chapter 6 about when and how this kind of design is best done.

Data Development Processes

Data development can represent more cost and effort for the organization than performing planning itself. For example, figuring out what manufacturing changeover costs are is not a trivial exercise. Having good transaction process-

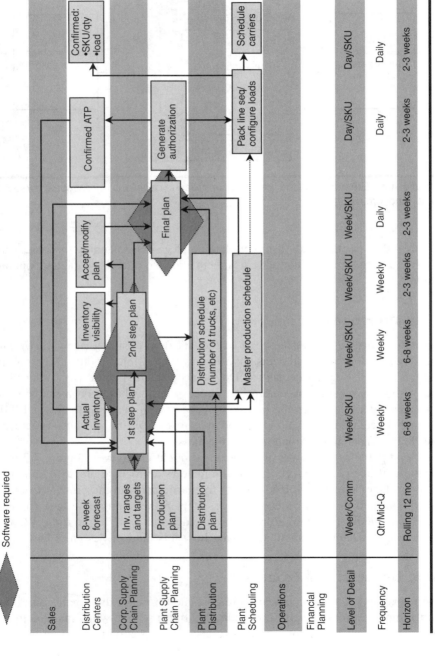

Figure 4.9 Example of a process map or swim-lane diagram.

ing systems in place that, for example, accurately track real-time inventory is not cheap. These kinds of systems, with their data collection points perhaps distributed across hundreds of locations, are large undertakings. Supporting planning effectively is one of their primary purposes (certainly the enterprise's accountants could get by with inventory records that were a couple of days old, as long as they were accurate).

The largest and perhaps most expensive of the data development efforts is sales forecasting. As we have discussed previously, forecasting does not make flow decisions and hence is not truly part of our operations planning — it supports many kinds of plans in the enterprise.

We are going to talk a lot more about the mechanics of managing planning data in Chapter 8.

Planning Systems

While processes may be the heart of product flow planning, systems are certainly the arms and legs of planning (and of data development). Most of what we can do today in planning that we did not do fifty years ago relies on the computational, user interface, and communication capabilities of modern information systems.

However, it is worth noting here that we view computer systems as tools for planning, not the core of it — which is the planning process. When we read the publications of the analyst community, which primarily tracks trends in software and systems, it is sometimes easy to get confused and begin to think that systems are somehow the essence of planning and other business functions. That is true for you only if you reside in an information technology group and your job is to provide good systems for the enterprise, not to actually plan operations or make product flow decisions.

Formal Organization

What kind of planning is performed where in the organization? Who does the planning? Who do they report to? While we have introduced planning organization here as part of our comprehensive planning structure, we are going to talk about it in depth in Chapter 6 as part of our planning approach change methodology.

DESIGNING PLANNING STRUCTURES

If we want to decide how a business should plan, we need to begin by defining the domain over which we can, realistically, take responsibility for planning. Let us suppose that we are a paper manufacturer that also creates a number of

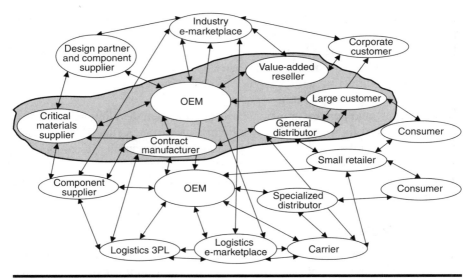

Figure 4.10   Defining the planning sphere.

value-added products. Figure 4.10 shows the "planning sphere" where we have some ability to lead the planning process. Of all the competitors, suppliers, distributors, end customers, and so on in the complete supply network, the portion of the network shaded here is the part where we can truly impact planning. ("Sphere of influence" is old terminology from international diplomacy. We have borrowed a little of that terminology here.) In some of this realm/sphere, we have complete control, and in some of it we can have only a collaborative relationship with other enterprises that have, naturally, retained responsibility for planning their own operations.

Figure 4.11 shows a cleaner version of the sphere, looking only at the interesting part of the network (similar to Figure 1.3). Organizations that are independent and will continue to have their own planning processes are shown connected by only a thin arrow representing collaboration. Note that in this example, to illustrate our point about limited control, we have assumed a perspective (say, we are located in a supply chain functional organization of our enterprise) in which we do not have direct responsibility for planning our own papermaking, but rather have a collaborative relationship with the manufacturing organization. We have greater direct control over a contract manufacturer and over a large customer for which we perform inventory management (vendor-managed inventory).

In light of some of the idealistic talk in the late 1990s about the virtual enterprise and "planning the complete supply chain," the concept here of care-

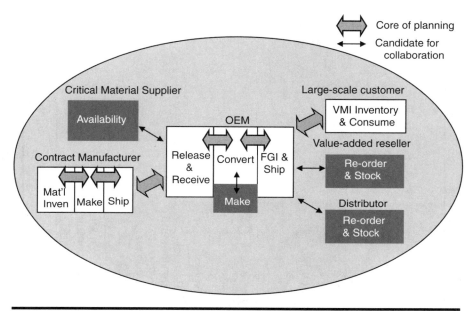

Figure 4.11   Refined picture of planning sphere.

fully determining the boundaries of what can be planned may seem reactionary. But we have found that being realistic about how much scope and how many participants we can include in the redesign of planning processes is a critical first step in being successful.

So how should an organization organize its product flow planning? The most successful way to answer that question is to begin with the most important decisions, the "backbone" decisions that are most fundamental in our product flow. Figure 4.12 is a "backbone diagram" for our papermaker/converter. We have looked at the scope of what we want to do and we have thought about which sets of decisions really provide leverage and prevent major inefficiencies (or more typically, we have thought about which decisions need to be brought together to save money that is currently being wasted). A good planning structure makes sure that things that are closely tied logically are planned together — the backbone shown here; multiple backbones in some situations — and that more peripheral decisions are not on the backbone. For this particular business (and common in the paper business), how we allocate our planned production to long-term commitments to customers is perhaps at the very center of our planning process, but key decisions on the backbone include short-term order promising, our own production scheduling, and the production schedule of the contract manufacturer we rely on for a lot of our product.

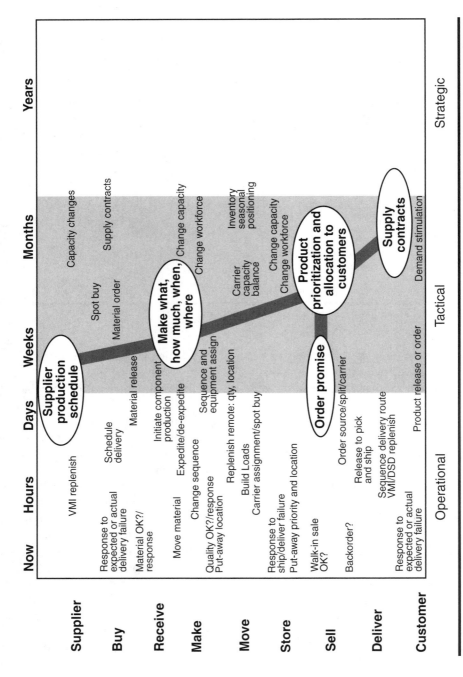

Figure 4.12 Backbone diagram.

Note that when we call a decision "peripheral," we are saying only that it is not as critical to making the product flow decisions in this enterprise that save or waste the most significant amounts of money or have the greatest impact on customer service. In some businesses, building full-truckload shipments is absolutely essential to the economics of the business; in others, it is a comparative afterthought. In those latter businesses, planning operations to build truckloads is not going to be part of the backbone. But even if not critical to the business as a whole, those decisions are important to someone, e.g., a transportation dispatcher tasked with doing that planning job well.

Consider another example, deciding how to perform order promising. As we discussed in Chapter 2, order promising can be manufacturing-centric or distribution-centric. If order promising is critical in a business, then it may be tied in the backbone to either manufacturing decision making or distribution decision making.

If we want to compare our thinking to a "best practice" model of how planning should work, the most complete is that provided by the Supply-Chain Council. It is a nonprofit corporate membership-based organization founded in 1996 that periodically updates its Supply-Chain Operations Reference (SCOR) model, a process model for supply chain management. This model is quite comprehensive and consists of five sections: Overall Plan, Source, Make, Deliver, and Return. The planning processes in SCOR are quite thorough and are intended to have applicability in every industry. They are an excellent reference for thinking about how to best plan in your enterprise and your supply network.

Designing a planning structure, using work tools like the process map and backbone diagram, is arguably the most creative and least formulaic step in the methodology we will discuss in Chapter 6. In many ways, it is at the center of what this book is about. The essence of it is to decide what is critical for better product flow planning and how the critical pieces need to connect to other pieces. Some of the elements that should drive this analysis are:

- Important bottlenecks that restrict throughput or degrade service (the Theory of Constraints is right, you have to plan to maximize them)
- Distributed inventory management needs (if you have to keep finished goods inventory at multiple locations, it requires some very sophisticated logic and processes to manage well)
- Manufacturing strategy (manufacturing dynamics always have a big impact on supply chain flow)
- Primary drivers of manufacturing efficiency (what really moves the cost numbers for these products)
- Primary drivers of transportation efficiency (transportation can make a huge difference in overall supply chain costs and service — do we actually need to optimize it?)

■ Purchased materials
■ Key determiners of customer service

For each of these areas, decide: How important are they to the business in terms of contribution to cost and contribution (or subtraction) from customer service? Where are their known inefficiencies, the "money left on the table," the "low-hanging fruit"? To what degree can better planning influence these areas? The combination of these two is *leverage*, that is, the combination of significant inefficiency and the ability to eliminate that inefficiency via planning defines a high-leverage opportunity.

Leverage Points

What are some typical high-leverage points in operations? That is a tough question to answer because it varies so much by business. However, we can provide some generic suggestions, based on experience:

■ Rule of thumb: "Larger scale" decisions have more of a profitability impact than smaller scale ones, i.e., strategic over tactical over operational; deciding to add a shift to production for three months has a bigger impact (good or bad) than deciding to take a changeover into a particular product group.

■ The master scheduling set of decisions — how much of which items are we going to make (or have made) when — dictate much of the rest of operations: inventory, customer service, what staff we really need in the plant, how much product we can distribute. They are truly a powerful set of decisions at the core of a manufacturer's operations.

■ Decisions that "hide in the cracks" between current functional organizations: How sales' allocation of product to customers impacts production, how end-of-quarter peaks are impacting operations.

■ Better forecasting: It may not be decision making, but a better forecast can have a huge beneficial effect on plans and hence on operations. But this only works if you were not forecasting very well previously. If you were already doing an excellent job relative to what is possible, spending substantially more resources may improve accuracy only slightly.

■ If any offsite warehousing is being used by shuttling product to and from that offsite location, any decisions you can make that let you end that shuttling have a big profit impact; offsite operations cost a lot more than most managers realize.

■ Inventory optimization is usually not a leverage point. If inventories are in the ballpark, the savings from optimizing them are usually fairly small. On the other hand, we have worked with many businesses that did such a poor job of setting inventory policy (or managing operations to that policy) that they were two blocks down the street from the ballpark.

You want to invest your time where the leverage is going to be the greatest. Be sure to get input at this stage not only from the project team working directly on this, but also sponsoring managers, champions, and politically sensitive others. With the factors above in mind, construct a couple of backbone diagrams. The idea here is to get the key elements down on paper and then show which ones need to be planned with which others.

Having done that, you are ready to formulate a planning approach for at least the portion of the planning sphere that is highest priority. What planning processes make the most sense in your company? What parts of the organization will participate in each process (draw a few process maps)? Do you need a software tool to support a given process, or will it be manual? How will the different planning processes relate to each other?

Compare your ideas to the standard MRP II (manufacturing resource planning) process diagram; compare it to what your existing operations software provider recommends (or can support). Compare it to other planning software available. Modify your concepts based on these inputs and think it through again.

So we now understand what the core is, what decisions we would like to make together — in some sense simultaneously or optimally — and we understand where the major collaborations need to occur to tie together separate planning processes.

MINIMUM NUMBER OF PLANS

> **9. Enterprises are best served by the minimum number of planning processes (and plans) that are adequate to cover the portion of the supply chain that can be planned (planning sphere). There should be only one plan "responsible" for each type of product flow decision to be made.**

Considering Chapter 2, it is pretty obvious that a very large number of standard planning problems and techniques have been defined over the years. In some sense, this very large number of planning techniques makes it more difficult and

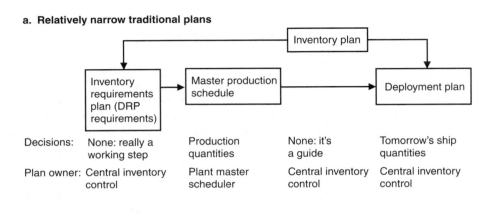

a. Relatively narrow traditional plans

Decisions:	None: really a working step	Production quantities	None: it's a guide	Tomorrow's ship quantities
Plan owner:	Central inventory control	Plant master scheduler	Central inventory control	Central inventory control

b. Simplified, integrated planning

Production and deployment plan

Decisions: Production quantities and tomorrow's ship quantities
Plan owner: Central inventory and production planning group

Figure 4.13   Broad plans often make more sense.

complex to actually plan an enterprise's operations. For example, if you have one group in the manufacturing organization generating "production plans" and a second one in logistics planning finished goods inventory, each is trying to solve two-thirds of one problem, and then they both have to deal with the challenge of reconciling their plans! Plossl[13] correctly points out that inventory control and production control cannot be separated. Figure 4.13 shows how four plans can be collapsed into one, in some settings, using contemporary technology. We are back to the issue of plan redundancy, but we have arrived at it from a different direction.

Keep in mind our guideline: We need to have the fewest number of plans and planning processes that will result in all of our decisions being well made. The traditional, overlapping way that the comprehensive product flow problem has been broken down can help us, because it identifies problems for which others have probably figured out solutions (and software). But we have to develop our own vision of how to best plan the operations of an enterprise, one that will perhaps utilize some traditional techniques and possibly new hybrids of traditional techniques. The best planning approaches have found ways to have each plan serve multiple objectives and drive many different decisions across various business functions. Figure 4.14 illustrates a number

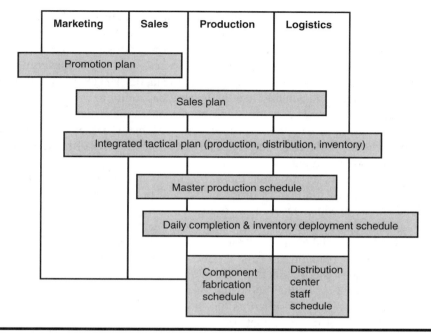

Figure 4.14 Good plans are cross-functional and serve multiple needs.

of typical plans and how broadly most of them impact the functional organizations of a simple enterprise, with a couple of plans at the bottom that are more narrow. Note that the boxes here are broader than in Figure 2.4 because the emphasis here is on usage of the plan, not on creation of it.

Complexity Created by Multiple Processes

In addition to the redundancy, confusion, and wasted time issues already discussed, breaking down the planning problem creates logical challenges that can be difficult to solve. A good example of that was stumbled over a few years ago by an aftermarket auto parts manufacturer that was attempting to implement two separate planning processes, one for managing inventory in the distribution network and the other for scheduling production. Each used a planning module from the same software provider. The module that performed the equivalent of distribution requirements planning (DRP) could do a good job of comparing current inventory to plan at each distribution center and adding in near-term orders and forecasts to generate product requirements, and the production scheduling system was ready to take requirements and schedule production. But because the manufacturer was far behind filling field inventory needs, near-term need for product far exceeded production capacity. The production scheduling process did not have the data or logic to decide how to make the right products in the near term to have enough of each item to keep a little stock everywhere and avoid losing sales — the best actual operating tactic. The DRP-type module was quite high tech and actually had the general capability to generate production capacity-constrained inventory requirements, but because many of the actual production constraints were item specific, it was unable to model and constrain capacity at the level of detail required. The parts manufacturer ultimately abandoned both software modules.

There are other ways to solve this problem, such as having the DRP-type tool create a priority gradient of different types of product demand and having the production scheduler know how to utilize these priorities to allocate near-term capacity appropriately. But the interesting fact is that the problem was *created* by the artificial boundary between the distribution planning process and the manufacturing planning process. Product replenishment needs in a distribution network and master production scheduling can be dealt with in one process, and software can support that approach. But because of traditional boundaries between manufacturing and distribution, most process designs and most software designs do not consider that option.

Working with shared plans reduces the likelihood of "hidden decisions" being made.[38] For example, if manufacturing decides to drop the second shift of work in a production department next month, it will likely impact both the human resources organization and sales (which may have been planning a big push on a new product made there). To the extent that everyone is working off the same plan (in this example a Sales & Operations Plan [S&OP]), the communication problem is largely solved.

During most of the twentieth century, planning problems essentially had to be broken down into small problems and the myriad of issues created by this bird's nest of planning processes had to be reconciled somehow. We no longer are truly limited in that way for most kinds of planning. The issue now is to strike the right balance between centralization and decentralization, to balance the complexity bundled into one process versus the complexity created by breaking planning into multiple processes, and then fitting the pieces back together. The best plans are usually joint plans; they are shared and a way is found for their users to collectively own them.

We can also view our objective as trying to minimize the total amount of complexity we are creating and managing, while also doing an excellent job of making all the decisions we need to make. Complexity always costs money, even if the cost is as indirect as the recurring costs of additional training and more errors in executing processes (forgetting for the moment costs like software licenses and computer support). Hence, in general, if we want to adopt a complex planning process to generate better plans and decisions, we need to make sure that we are getting substantial value from that complexity.

But how does an organization reduce the number of plans? Specific techniques for minimizing the number of plans and total complexity are:

- Establish the policy that groups, not individuals, own plans. It is a ground rule when you come to work here; you cannot have your own operations plan. You participate in group planning processes.
- Follow the methodology described here and in Chapter 6 for developing a comprehensive planning structure.
- Use telescoped time periods in a single plan, not separate plans. Figure 4.15 shows the three versions of the classic relationship between a production plan and a master production schedule. The first view takes the naïve position that we simply "impose" a production plan on a master schedule. The second view recognizes that there is a lot of decision making that must go on to convert from an aggregate production plan to a master schedule as the master schedule horizon advances in time. This view also recognizes that it is actually at the master

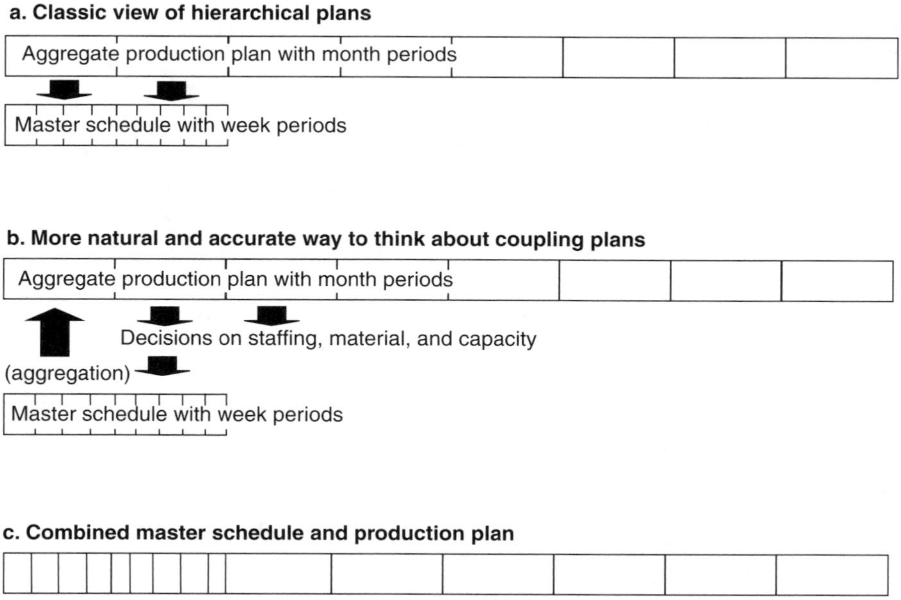

a. Classic view of hierarchical plans

b. More natural and accurate way to think about coupling plans

c. Combined master schedule and production plan

Figure 4.15   Example of coupling plans that are hierarchical and sequential.

schedule level that real decision making occurs in near-term periods, and the aggregated master schedule must be "imposed" on the production plan in those near-term periods or the production plan is quite inaccurate. The third view recognizes that, where it is technically and organizationally feasible, the simplest solution is to simply combine the two plans into one telescoped plan. We discuss this in more detail later in this chapter.

■   Plans developed at a fairly detailed level, and aggregated up for certain decision purposes, e.g., to provide S&OP support.

CENTRALIZATION AND DECENTRALIZATION IN THE ENTERPRISE

Thirty years ago some of us believed that, as it became technically possible, we would want to construct centralized planning systems that could see all events in an enterprise, revise plans almost instantaneously, and quickly broadcast changes. These systems would in effect become omnipresent, omnipotent (in terms of planning and control) planning centers for the business.

But with considerable experience in the use of integrated planning tools, many no longer believe that "simple" centralized planning is truly possible or would even be the most effective approach. There are three primary reasons for that:

1. For at least the next few decades, businesses will be operated mostly by humans. Humans need a sense of self-control, or at least a sense of having contributed to a joint plan, in order to be enthusiastic executors of that plan. Enthusiastic, committed execution is often more important to organizational success than a globally optimal plan.
2. The reality is that some business decisions can best be made "locally" in each part of the enterprise. Local resources know enough of the relevant information to make a good decision, and good decisions, made quickly, represent a better way of operating than "global optimization" that requires some degree of delay and the chaining of staff to data management tasks to support that type of system. Indeed, some planning software has been designed with decentralization specifically in mind.
3. Collaborative tools originally designed for use in the extended enterprise supply chain, such as tools for collaborative forecasting, have proven to be quite useful within the enterprise, such as between "outside" field sales staff and central forecasters.

However, the fundamental validity of bringing all the planning data together and making globally optimal decisions, and doing it continually in almost real time, is indisputable. So this dimension of solving the planning challenge comes down to creative trade-offs that hopefully capture the best of centralization and decentralization for the enterprise, and do it at an appropriate budget and level of sophistication.

> **10. Finding the right balance between centralization and decentralization is one of the subtlest challenges in planning system design and deserves specific attention. Centralization makes highly integrated and optimized decisions easier, but keeping responsibility for planning operations near the responsibility for action produces much more enthusiastic execution.**

Given all of the above arguments, the challenge we face, then, is to design product flow planning approaches with the right balance between centralization and decentralization for a given enterprise and business context and to be prepared to change that planning system fairly frequently as changes in the business and/or the enterprise change that balance. That is the consequence of the technical freedom we now have to create integrated planning systems.

PLANNING IS ALWAYS HIERARCHICAL

If you consider the various planning approaches reviewed in Chapter 2, you will see that all of the "complete" systems for planning have a hierarchy of plans: MRP II, hierarchical production planning (HPP), the Toyota Production System (where there are typically a couple layers of production plans before we get down to kanban tuning of flow), and so on. Indeed, all real-world approaches involve some degree of hierarchy, with more aggregate plans being used to make more general decisions, which impact more detailed plans (and vice versa). Whether a planning system designer chooses to emphasize the hierarchical nature of the system (e.g., with the HPP system) or ignore it, it exists nevertheless.

There are too many decisions to be made in an enterprise for all of them to be driven directly by one comprehensive but detailed monolithic plan.[24] Given that many of the decisions in an enterprise do in fact decouple rather easily from one other (where a pallet of work-in-process components is stored in the plant has nothing to do with how much finished product we are going to deploy to the Chicago warehouse next Thursday), no one advocates elimination of hierarchy from operations planning.

> **11. All practical, complete enterprise or supply chain planning systems involve some degree of hierarchical planning.**

While we argue for a minimal number of plans (see section above) and point out that some hierarchical relationships are not strictly hierarchies (see the section on sequential integration below), there is always an element of hierarchy in our approach.

DEGREE OF PLANNING INTEGRATION

One of the themes we will deal with repeatedly is the degree to which planning processes truly integrate and rationally reflect the relevant data. In other words, do the planning processes bring together all the information that should impact the plan perfectly to reflect what is known, or do the processes do something less than that? Figure 4.16 shows four approaches to integration that are a useful way to categorize the level of integration. (These concepts have evolved from those originally proposed by Steve Simco.)

Optimal (1)

The most integrated approach to planning develops optimal plans in a couple of senses of the word. The concept here is that there is a single planning process that brings together all the relevant data and creates a plan that simultaneously, rationally reflects all the information. This sense of optimization is consistent with the way that operations researchers have for years used the word "optimal" to mean that for a given set of quantifiable objectives, constraints, and costs, an optimal solution is the best solution that can exist. But, perhaps even more importantly, the word "optimize" implies one single planning process for the domain being considered in which all parties participate directly in making the best joint decisions. Needless to say, truly optimal planning processes that encompass broad scope are quite rare.

Sequential (2)

This is the degree of planning integration when some decisions are made as part of one process, and then those decisions limit the options for other planning

		Concept	Examples	
1	Optimize	• Take all data into account "simultaneously" to generate best plan; multiple processes combined into one • Ideally do it in real time as often as needed	• Build comprehensive tactical plan directly from a linear program that understands all demands, capacities, and costs	Requires Control and Trust
2	Constrain	• Make some decisions, use them to constrain other decisions • Minimum cycle time between plannng stages	• Regenerate a master schedule strictly within the bounds of the tactical plan • Limit production plan based on a supplier's plan to resupply	
3	Collaborate	• Attempt to have a consensus plan based on one or more iterations between planning units • Minimum cycle time between stages	• S&OP process • Manufacturer and a retailer agree on a forecast of sales	Requires Trust
4	Show	• Share planning data from one planning unit with another • Ideally real-time sharing of data and regeneration of each independent plan	• Manufacturing tells logistics what, when and how much they are going to build • OEM shares its master schedule with a supplier	

Figure 4.16   Levels of planning integration.

processes. We see sequential planning processes in many environments. We see them in hierarchical planning environments, the HPP introduced in Chapter 2, and in the case of a master schedule being developed and then detailed schedules created for each work cell to implement that master schedule. Is this as optimal as developing two levels simultaneously? Usually not, but it works well if the master schedule understands the constraints and economics of the cells, and, most importantly, it corresponds with the organizational hierarchy (see more discussion of this in Hax and Candea[25]).

We also see this form of schedule coupling in the external supply chain, such as an automotive original equipment manufacturer (OEM) changing its final assembly schedule and then parts suppliers scrambling to adjust their schedules to meet the changed requirements. Note that in this case the supplier's service agreements with the OEM effectively require the supplier to make its schedules subservient to the customer's schedules. And finally we see it in some heuristic solution algorithms for planning, in which certain decisions are made first, and then others are made to fit best with those initial decisions.

Coupling Plans Together (A Digression)

Note that in any of these sequential processes, as well as the less integrated processes below, there are multiple, distinct planning processes that are executed. This raises the issue of how plans are best coupled together. Usually this topic is given short shrift, e.g., "The master schedule is required to build the amount of product decided in the production plan" (per Figure 4.15a) and other similar kinds of statements. Is this issue really that simple? It is less an issue for the collaborative and visible approaches discussed below, where there is agreement that each party has its own plan and can ultimately do what it wants to with it.

Even in a sequential environment, directly "imposing" one plan on another is not necessarily appropriate. A case can be made that instead of arithmetically forcing one plan on another, plans should be coupled "naturally" through the real decisions about resources that have been made. For example (as shown in Figure 4.15b), rather than saying that "The master schedule must be made equal to the production plan," the more relevant guides in developing the master schedule may be "What levels of production of various products do we have the machine capacity for, the material for, and the staffing for (with and without extra-cost overtime)? Since we have purchased longer lead time materials and set staffing levels based on the production plan (made decisions about real resources), a good master schedule should be close to the production plan, but never equal to it.

Coming at the issue from another direction, how many master schedulers do you know who would say: "Well, we need to make 5,610 units next week to meet the orders we are supposed to ship, and we have the materials, capacity, and staff to make the mix we need, but the production plan says we only make 5,000 units each week this month, so that's all we will do!" The businesses I have worked with do not function that way and do not want to in the age of "agility." The issue is different when customer orders or finished goods inventory management only require 4,200 units against a plan of 5,000 — more of a business policy issue of "If we promised management we would make 5,000 units worth of 'profit' next week, we have to make it whether we need the product or not." This is less a coupling issue than an operating philosophy issue.

Carrying on with our master schedule/production planning example, let us consider the case of replanning the production plan for the next sixteen months. What is the correct value for the first month of the horizon, which we happen to be in the second week of right now? We know what we actually made the first week of the month and we know what we have in the master schedule for the second, third, and fourth weeks of the month (and our operating policy is that the first three weeks of the master schedule are inside the frozen time fence), so it seems like the first month of the most realistic production plan ought to be the sum of actual production and master schedule, not the value we used the last time we planned production! So now we have the master schedule dictating to the production plan in an arithmetic sense.

"Sequential planning" is a more complex concept than you might at first think. These kinds of coupling issues need to be carefully thought through wherever we maintain multiple plans. And of course, if we want to honor Principle 9 (minimum number of plans), and it is practical to do so in a particular environment, it is probably preferable to combine plans (Figure 4.15c).

Collaborative (3)

We see collaborative planning going on in many environments. S&OP is largely a collaborative process, generally occurring within a single enterprise. When a manufacturer and a retailer agree on a replenishment plan, they are collaborating between enterprises. The best collaborative processes provide the opportunity for multiple iterations so that the separate plans can converge to an appropriate degree. Whole scales of collaboration have been defined, an example of which is listed here:

- Joint decision making in unstructured environments
- Negotiations
- Definition and maintenance of common documents
- Bidirectional data sharing
- Unidirectional data sharing (essentially the same thing as "visible" below)

The classic MRP II planning structure has both sequential and collaborative aspects. Master schedulers are expected to live within the bounds of the production plan, but often have a collaborative relationship with material plans — ideally the master schedule drives material plans, but often must live within its constraints, and master schedulers often end up negotiating with materials buyer/planners for what they can get.

Visible (4)

When one planning process makes its input data or output plan visible to another planning process, we can think of it as showing or sharing its data and work with the other process. If a retailer passes its consumer promotion plan to a manufacturer, with no particular expectation of the manufacturer agreeing it can supply product to fulfill that plan or not, that is mere visibility. If the retailer makes its point-of-sale data available to manufacturers, that is visibility. If a manufacturing plant notes the master plan that is sent to it by the headquarters planner, but basically decides for itself what it is going to produce, that is visibility.

Note that every form of integration between planning processes (and between parts of planning algorithms) requires trust. The group supplying the data and/or plan must trust the recipients of it to use it in ways that positively support the enterprise or supply chain, to not give it to competitors, to not completely ignore it.

The two more integrated forms of planning involve more than trust; they involve control. The participants in an optimal process have agreed to operate from the single comprehensive plan; the downstream participants in a sequential process have agreed to abide by higher level decisions. Conversely, the participants in a collaborative process have agreed only to work together systematically, with the presumption but not the guarantee that they will always arrive at compatible plans. And the participants in a visible relationship have agreed to supply data and communicate, but nothing more.

Are more integrated planning processes *better* than less integrated processes? They are better suited to generating the "best" plans in the sense of the best logical result from all knowable information. But the reality of enterprises and supply chains often makes less integrated processes more appropriate. For example, the most obvious situation for collaboration is where planning processes exist in separate enterprises in the supply chain. They have no formal control over each other, just a shared desire to make the chain work to their mutual benefit. Even within a single enterprise, if management is completely decentralized, it may make good sense to have separate planning processes with an agreed level of control and collaboration among them, even if that means having more than the minimum number of plans.

There is an interesting parallel between levels 1 and 3 and between levels 2 and 4. Collaboration (3) can be viewed as an effort to achieve an optimal plan (1), but with the recognition that core processes have to be kept independent and hence we just collaborate as far toward global optimality as we can. Similarly, providing visibility (4) is analogous to sequential planning (2), but with no control: "Here's what we're doing — now we hope you take it into account in your plans."

As the Internet and other tools have made it easier to iterate rapidly between separate planning processes, it has been recognized that in many situations high-quality collaboration (3) can approximate optimization (1) and that collaboration is "good enough" in terms of the logic by which data are combined and much more practical where organizations legitimately have separate interests.

While we do not discuss planning speed in the above categories, the ability to execute all of them quickly is important to good planning. Visible, collaborative, and sequential approaches all work better if time delay can be wrung out of the steps of their collective processes. It is difficult to call a plan optimal, even if it is mathematically "optimal," unless the data updating and reoptimization of the plan can be done as quickly and as frequently as is of value.

It is worth pointing out that in defining these levels of integration as we have, we have consciously not based the categories on whether the planning processes are inside one enterprise or separated by multiple enterprises. Obviously, the more tightly integrated processes are easier to construct within an enterprise than with multienterprise planning domains, but the best process will depend on the situation. You may have noted that in the examples above, we have a case where an automotive assembler has sufficient control to essentially dictate a sequential process to a supplier, and another situation where central "planners" must tolerate making plans merely visible to plants in their own enterprise.

> **12. While the more integrated forms of planning have a fundamental advantage in meeting the goal of "taking all relevant information into account," each level of integration has its advantages and business situations where it is the best approach.**

COLLABORATIVE PLANNING IN THE SUPPLY CHAIN

Planning a supply chain is by its nature an exercise in influencing but not controlling the "sphere of influence" of the planner and enterprise. Why? Because a supply chain is part of a supply network, as shown in Figure 1.2, that includes not only your enterprise, your customers, and your suppliers, but that also includes all of your competitors. In most industries, those competitors are buying from the same suppliers and selling to many of the same customers. (There are, of course, exceptions: exclusive dealer networks, for example.) Since competitors buy from the same suppliers, they often compete for the same supplier capacity, and suppliers must jealously guard the control of that capacity.

Indeed, there are often legitimate concerns that in collaboratively planning capacity with you, your supplier implicitly gives away competitive information about what your competitors are doing. A food supplier that tells a retailer collaboratively "Sorry, I can't support a big promotion of this product that month" is often doing so because the supplier is already committed to another retailer's promotion.

In the early days of business-to-business transactions on the Internet, some commentators thought that if we could fully develop the technology of planning over the Internet, we could integrally plan the supply chain and wring considerable waste from it. To quote from Oliver et al.:[49] "...core elements of the central planner's Utopian dream live on in academic papers, in the business press, and in the sales brochures of uncounted software and technology vendors...Armed with more real-time data, a better algorithm, more connectivity, and a bigger information technology budget, managers (or their computers), the dreamers believe, could control their extended enterprise free of market imperfection."

With that technology largely in hand, but little integrated planning actually going on, we thought that perhaps if supply chain participants could just "develop enough trust" in each other, they could plan integrally. Perhaps third-party supply chain hubs could plan for us, from their perspective above daily operations. But this planning integration can happen to only a limited degree, because our suppliers and customers must maintain their relationships with our competitors as well. We must recognize that the collaborative planning in a supply chain can never be complete unification of planning.

We also cannot have complete trust with suppliers or customers because we compete with them — for the best price. We will continue to compete with them, and hence trust outside the enterprise will always be limited. For example, in recent years automobile assemblers have become famous for enormous pressures on their suppliers to cut costs. While they are happy to provide production schedules to their suppliers so that their suppliers can provide 100 percent service levels on a just-in-time basis at low cost, they ultimately cannot take responsibility for supplier operations planning. Put another way, many decades ago when Ford gave up the River Rouge "iron ore to automobiles" totally integrated operations approach in favor of using outside suppliers, it implicitly also accepted the idea that suppliers would plan their own operations and there would be some disconnect from Ford. While there is a cost associated with this disconnect, Ford believed it was better than operating steel mills itself. Virtually every other industry has come to the same decision as businesses have "perfected" the structure of capitalism.

Indeed, while the availability of Internet communication has greatly facilitated collaborative material flow planning and vendor-managed inventory, it has also provided support for business practices that run counter to collaboration. In particular, reverse auctions conducted by customers (or by third parties for customers) have become popular as a mechanism for obtaining the lowest price for some purchased goods, both commodity items and custom products. In general, suppliers react to a customer decision to procure via a reverse auction as a decision to not engage in long-term collaborative relationships. "Reverse auctions also wring such savings from the procurement process because they erase all relationship issues....Relationships get in the way when you are trying to have an objective negotiation process."[50]

Some customers explicitly attempt to maintain relationships with suppliers even though using reverse auctions to set prices.[51] While some suppliers are perhaps willing to plan collaboratively during the execution of a supply contract won through auction, they clearly have minimum incentive to engage in any kind of truly trust-based relationship. And they have maximum incentive to withhold information that might damage their positions in the next auction (or even to plant false information that might help their position in the next auction). Auctions implicitly say, "Our business together is a matter of perceived value in this one transaction, and we do not wish to invest in an extended partnership."

Another interesting area of contention around collaborative planning in the supply chain is the fight to control the process and the information itself. Since planning information has value, and that value is recognized by all the members of the supply chain, there is clear motivation to fight over who will control that information. In the North American automobile industry, for example, the automobile manufacturers created the Covisint hub in part to manage product flow planning information. Tier One suppliers to the OEMs were generally reluctant to commit fully to it, in part because it threatened their ability to exclusively manage the information from their own lower tier suppliers.[52] This fear appeared well justified, given the history of using information to extract price concessions.

Enterprises can only enthusiastically execute plans that they believe are in the best self-interest of the economic unit — their enterprise. Understanding the supply network, and the relationships of the participants in it, it is pretty obvious that planning product flow through a supply chain will remain a multicentered, largely decentralized set of processes. Few enterprises are going to cede primary planning responsibilities for their operations to other organizations — planning is too critical a part of most enterprises.

Oliver et al.[49] suggest the concept of "federated planning" as a realistic goal for planning in the supply chain. Planners and their managers within enterprises will maintain responsibility for advancing the causes of their enterprise, recognizing that they must function as an effective confederation of different interests in order to operate a competitively successful supply chain.

Thus far, collaboration in the supply chain has consisted mostly of:

1. A shared forecasting process (which is truly at the collaborative level [3] described above), in which the customer provides to the supplier his or her best estimate of what he or she will need, and the supplier reviews it and either
   - Accepts it and incorporates it in the customer-specific portion of his or her own forecast.

- Comes back to the customer with issues if the supplier believes that it is either not realistic (i.e., the customer has made some error in his or her thinking) or does not reflect the contractual sales quantities between the buyer and seller.
- Comes back to the customer because the supplier knows he or she cannot physically provide that quantity of product.

2. A sequential planning process (level 2 as described above) in which the customer provides his or her production material needs to the supplier, and the supplier plans how to meet those needs.

In practice, there has turned out to be a lot of incentive to keep collaboration very simple, requiring very few iterations between the supply chain partners and no meetings. Why? In spite of some excellent software having been written to support supply chain collaboration, the nature of the joint decision making required of true collaboration means that there is no good way to automate these iterations, to just let the computers talk to each other and collaborate. Generally, true collaboration requires a lot of people time, and that makes supply chain collaboration expensive. Many stories exist about how "collaboration worked well at the pilot level for 20 key products and everyone was enthusiastic, but when we tried to implement it 'at scale' for 700 products, we did not feel so good about it any more."

With contemporary communication and planning tools, supply chain partners will keep trying to figure out the best way to collaborate: how much to let the computers do, how much time staffers and managers should spend with the supply chain partner to accomplish what objectives. Supply chain collaboration, as well as internal collaboration within the enterprise, is becoming an increasingly important aspect of planning, but it does not represent a revolution in planning.

5

PLANNING UNDER DIFFERENT OPERATING PHILOSOPHIES AND SUPPLY–DEMAND STRATEGIES

BRITANNUS (shocked): Caesar, this is not proper

THEODOTUS (outraged): How?

CAESAR (recovering his self-possession): Pardon him, Theodotus; he is a barbarian and thinks that the customs of his tribe and island are the laws of nature.

George Bernard Shaw, *Caesar and Cleopatra,* Act II

In Chapter 4, we devoted considerable energy to the thought that product flow planning is a child of an enterprise's business strategy and the way that business strategy has been actualized with supply–demand strategies. That is, how you should best plan the flow of material depends on the big decisions that have been made about how product will be provided to meet customers' demand.

In this chapter, we are going to go a little deeper into these issues. The last forty years have seen an interminable debate in production and inventory control circles, and to a lesser extent logistics circles, about the best philosophy for operations management to adopt. Some popular educators and practitioners have come to believe fervently in a particular school of practice and advocate only that practice. Our approach in this chapter is to sort out these philosophies by a couple of criteria and to show where the planning techniques associated with them can be applied most usefully. While we very much believe that planning structures should be designed for individual enterprises and reflect the peculiarities of their unique competitive strategies, to do that in a sophisticated way we also have to understand the operating philosophies and their implications. We do not attempt to teach and "sort out" the philosophies in detail here; that would take a (long) book itself to do the subject justice.

Professionals in planning who come from different kinds of businesses often are unable to communicate effectively — they "talk past each other," because there are subtle, usually inexplicit differences in their assumptions and worldviews. Many experts in planning remind one of John Godfrey Saxe's poem "The Blind Men and the Elephant" (see Landvater's use of it [pp. 17–18] where he presents a parody for this context attributed to Ollie Wight[53]). Most are extremely familiar with one or two types of operations and can describe the world in terms that are appropriate for those operations but not others. We attempt here to take a very broad view and to present as much perspective as we can muster.

We will begin with an essay on categorizing supply chains and then progress into the actual operating philosophies.

VARIATION IN MANUFACTURING AND SUPPLY CHAIN DESIGN

There are, of course, countless ways to characterize supply chains and the manufacturing step(s) within them: push versus pull, job shop versus flow shop, discrete versus process, and so on. After many years of studying variation in the design of operations, this author has come to the conclusion that the single most useful way to understand the variation is based on the total customer order cycle time in a particular industry: How long do customers expect to wait from when they decide they want something until they can have it in their hands? We have found this particular cardinal measure of supply chains more useful than other general categorizations.

Rather than discuss this in terms of the number of days or weeks, we have chosen to use a slight variation, namely the ratio of how long that order cycle time is compared with realistic manufacturing and distribution time for the complete supply chain that could provide that product at a competitive cost (i.e., rather than discuss something in simple terms, we have chosen to present it as an abstract ratio — just to keep the reader thinking!). Figure 5.1 shows a

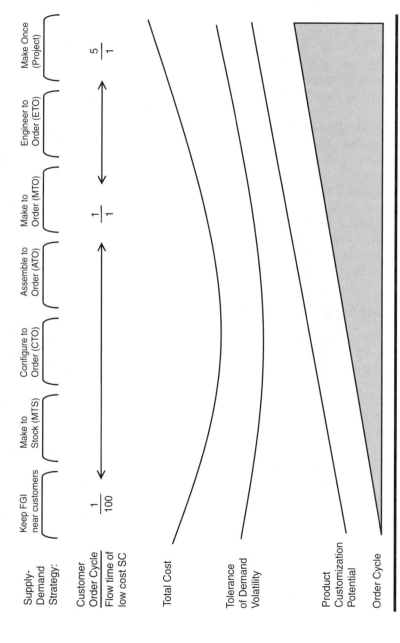

Figure 5.1 Customer fulfillment cycle/flow time of low-cost supply chain.

complete range of supply–demand strategies organized by that ratio and a few other characteristics of the strategies.

The numeric values of the ratio vary from 1/100 to 5/1, but they are illustrative and not to be taken too literally. Here is how to interpret it. Suppose you want to want to buy a jar of salsa. Consumers expect to get that jar in, say, half an hour, by going to a nearby grocery store and buying it. If you had to wait for it to be made from its ingredients and shipped to you, it might reasonably require two days or forty-eight hours. One-half hour to forty-eight hours is 1/100. On the other end of the spectrum, if I want a highway bridge built, it might take four years, or five times as long as the ten or eleven months it should take if the engineering and approvals were already done and the materials at hand to begin construction. It is thus an example of a 5/1 ratio, typical of true projects. Classic make to order is, by definition of the ratio, a 1.

We have also included in the diagram curves representing product customization, the tolerance of the supply chain for volatility in demand, and the total cost — all without scales, but just to show relative capabilities.

Let us consider these supply–demand strategies, beginning with the lowest ratio and shortest cycle time.

Keep Finished Goods Inventory Near Customers

Where immediate availability is required, there is no substitute for keeping finished goods inventory (FGI) near customers. The customer may be an automobile assembly plant, and you may be a supplier that keeps parts minutes away for immediate delivery to the line. Or suppose you are a consumer with a fondness for corn chips. For 99 percent of the U.S. public, a bag of corn chips is available for purchase perhaps no more than ten minutes away (for quick eating with your salsa). To provide that kind of availability, premium transportation is not an option — not Federal Express, not a courier — only distributed inventory will do. The cost of the distribution network to provide this kind of immediate availability is, of course, enormous. Indeed, the salty snacks supply chain is arguably more about physical distribution than about ingredients or manufacturing. But because of that distribution network, the customer can get product in his or her hands in perhaps one hundredth of the time it takes to get from corn meal, oil, and salt at the frying plant to the grocery or convenience store (we will not worry about the even longer cycle time to obtain the corn, oil, salt, and packaging materials). This supply chain has a significant tolerance for demand variability because there is quite a bit of inventory in the network (and in this particular example also considerable surplus production capacity maintained for holiday peak sales periods). There is no opportunity for product customization for the consumer.

Make to Stock (MTS)

Having differentiated the situation where inventory is stocked in the field, the pure MTS central stocking-only situation actually becomes a bit rare. For example, you may be an MRO (maintenance, repair, operations) equipment manufacturer that sells through industrial distributors, but your biggest distributor has decided that a portion of your product line will be direct ship from you (the distributor chooses to carry no inventory of these items) and requires that you be able to ship within forty-eight hours of its passing you a customer order. You have chosen to keep inventory of these finished good items rather than build them to order, and so you and the supply chain are MTS on these products.

For another example, let us suppose that you are a catalog/Internet clothing retailer. You keep your product ready for shipment in one central warehouse and rely on premium transportation or surface transport to get it to customers one to seven days from their order, based on their wishes. Note: the clothing manufacturers in your supply chain likely view their supply chains as make to order.

Costs in this supply chain are lower than with field inventory, but there is still little product-customization potential. There is more tolerance of unexpected demand variation geographically (because the inventory has not yet been deployed), but generally less tolerance of variation in total demand because there is less total inventory in the system. Customer order cycles are longer due to transport time.

Configure to Order (CTO)

You are a printer manufacturer and have most of your product built by contract manufacturers in the Far East, but you maintain a "postponement" center centrally in the U.S. to quickly add the right hardware options and install the right firmware in the printer and ship it off to customers. There is no FGI in this system (other than in transit to customers), but there are plenty of nearly finished goods required to make this strategy deliver high service. Or consider the example of an automobile manufacturer that plans production rates and commits to most materials weeks in advance, but finalizes each individual automobile configuration only a few days ahead of assembly based on actual orders from dealers.

With CTO, your customers' order cycles are a little longer, but you have cut FGI dramatically and probably achieved lower total supply chain costs. The concept can work even in products with little assembly. Say that you are a canned foods processor. You can leave generic product in "bright" unlabeled cans and only label and ship it as customer orders are received. You have reduced total costs (including scrap costs reduction through greatly reduced chance of shelf-life expiration) and retained flexibility for your customers, but you probably cannot deliver product in the seventy-two-hour order to delivery cycle common in the food industry. You can support peaks in demand as long as you have plenty of labeling and case-packing capacity.

Assemble to Order (ATO)

Dell Computers famously advanced supply chain design when it realized that because of the enormous obsolescence cost of holding inventory in the personal computer business, it was actually more cost effective to give up the economies of scale of mass production and assemble computers to the customer's order. Those customers were happy with the few extra days of order cycle time that design required because they could then buy a computer much closer to their specific needs. Pushing most of the responsibility for component inventory onto suppliers and doing away with distribution channels altogether completed the economic advantages of this supply chain.

Reeve[54] presents the fascinating case of Wendy's restaurants, where hamburgers are assembled to order in less than a minute. Of course, that is still much longer than just picking up an already assembled hamburger, but it allows considerable product variation without having to stock numerous finished goods (potentially every conceivable combination of condiments), instead relying on the simpler stocks of components. Most critically, it is within the acceptable order cycle time for fast-food customers, a small fraction of the complete hamburger manufacturing time that includes frying.

With either example, your ATO-based supply chain is at or near minimum cost, in part because you are getting some nice economies of scale on component part manufacturing or purchasing with significant lot sizes. You have stayed within customer-accepted order cycles while providing classic mass customization, but you have little tolerance for sudden demand spikes unless you maintain quite a bit of excess assembly capacity, which is usually not economically feasible.

Make to Order (MTO)

As a semiconductor production equipment manufacturer, you promise about six-month order cycles to your customers. Most of your cycle time is really your subassembly manufacturer's cycle times (and in many cases its component suppliers' cycle times as well). Before the tech bust of 2000–2002, you tried be more of an ATO manufacturer by keeping more subassemblies "in the pipeline" coming to you, to shorten delivery cycles and help overworked suppliers. But with only sporadic customer orders during the bust, there was not enough volume for a real pipeline. During the bust, and not coincidentally, your suppliers had excess capacity and gave you reasonable cycle times. Your supply chain is MTO because it includes manufacturing all major components to order, and it has been assigned a 1:1 ratio in our table because the cycle you promise your customers is approximately equal to the true time it takes to make all the higher level components, subassemblies, and finished goods.

It is tough to deliver product at the minimum conceivable cost in this mode, because both you and your component suppliers are setting up once for each machine you make. You offer great customization of product, and every machine produced is somewhat unique, but the order cycle times are commensurate.

Engineer to Order (ETO)

You are a manufacturer of air terminals, the air-conditioning outlets that modulate air flow in office buildings. While you make standard products, most of your largest sales are of custom products that have been engineered to order: special trim, special paint, special control circuitry. While a customer for standard product is quoted a one- to two-month order cycle time, for engineered products you quote your customers four months to make sure you have time to design the unit, review it with the customer, and build the (custom) bill of material before you begin manufacturing. Note that our customer order cycle is now longer than our "supply chain" flow execution time. You have a fair amount of tolerance for demand volatility, as you have time to add staff, add temporary workers for a few of the jobs, or even subcontract out major portions of engineering or production.

Make Once (Project)

An aficionado of houses decided to build a custom home and placed an order with himself to fulfill it. He spent one year finding the lot; two months interviewing architects; eight months designing the house with the selected architect; two months interviewing builders, getting bids, and selecting a building contractor; and ten months constructing the house. Elapsed supply chain time from ordering the building materials to completion of construction was ten months, out of a total thirty-two-month project, a factor of just over 3.

While numerous examples of projects with order cycle times much greater than supply chain time can be found, perhaps the most interesting is the time line of the Joint Strike Fighter aircraft program, commissioned by the U.S. government. After a few years of research by the government to determine feasible objectives for the new fighter, the initial RFP for designs was issued in 1995. Finalists were selected in 1997 and commissioned to build experimental fighters (the X-32 and X-35), with the projection that total build for the domestic armed forces would be about 1,500 fighters and total build for the world would be about 3,000. The experimental aircraft were built, tested, and the final lead manufacturer, Lockheed Martin, selected in 2001. Preproduction prototypes will be built in 2005, and the government expects to get the aircraft into service in the 2011–2012 time frame, about fifteen years after originally identifying order quantities. While manufacturing lead times on some of the more exotic parts contained in these aircraft can be more than a year, they pale in comparison to the total customer order cycle time. Our government is willing to tolerate a fifteen-year order cycle in order to advance the state of the art in tactical fighters.

Other Characteristics

Looking at some of the other characteristics plotted in Figure 5.1, we see that product-customization possibilities increase steadily from left to right, as one would expect, from none to "advancing the state of the art." Total cost of operation (including the cost of assets such as inventory and manufacturing capacity) dip from field inventory and MTS toward CTO/ATO and then rise steeply toward ETO and research projects. Why have we plotted total cost as decreasing toward the center, i.e., CTO/ATO cheaper than MTS? While it varies by industry, in businesses where technology exists to efficiently configure small numbers of units, it is likely that the total cost of operation is less by doing that and shipping directly to customers than to make large batches and stock finished goods. It is certainly more expensive to stock product in the field close to customers for quick access (the extreme left of the diagram). However, if no manufacturing technology exists for small-scale production that is competitive with larger scale manufacturing, then MTS is less costly (consider the cost of mixing just enough shampoo to fill a one-case order versus the cost of making enough at one time for twenty pallets and keeping some FGI).

The next curve up the diagram is the tolerance of the system for demand volatility, the ability to deal with highly variable demand without creating extra confusion and cost. Research projects and ETO, where we at least partly design the product for the customer, accommodate great flexibility in design and capacity — indeed, some of the production resources may only be hired once the product has been defined for the customer. Think of designing and building a ship, for example.

Classic job shop manufacturing systems, in which customer orders drive manufacturing orders, make no assumptions about consistent volume by product or product family, although facility and staff size are certainly planned to a forecast of total volume. Indeed, the classic way that job shops run into trouble is by pretending that they do not need either enormous extra manufacturing capacity (to accommodate peak loads in specific work centers) or highly variable order cycle time promising ("Yes, I know that last week we said we could make that for you in two weeks; we had some similar orders come in and now the best promise I can make you is seven weeks.").

Flow systems (often executed with just-in-time (JIT)–type pull of materials under a Lean philosophy) are notorious for requiring that demand be managed within the planned range. Finally, MTS systems can be minimally tolerant of volatility if the volatility is unpredictable and inventory modest or significantly more tolerant if inventory is large (left margin of figure) or the variation predictable. Highly predictable variation is, for example, the extreme sales peaks that a corn chip manufacturer experiences ahead of holiday weekends — demand that is filled primarily through prebuilding inventory.

Thus we are dealing in this spectrum with quite a range of product — from fighter aircraft to corn chips. The supply chains and the customer expectations have grown up together in these industries, a sort of "chicken and egg" type of phenomenon. Customers got used to what industries could provide at a reasonable cost; industries strove to provide what customers would pay for. The individual enterprise in an industry has a limited amount of flexibility in choosing where to operate along this spectrum and in the supply–demand strategies it will use. If you are in a consumer packaged goods business, your supply chain will stock product everywhere. If you deliver military aircraft to the U.S. government, you will manage decades-long programs to advance technology. But in many businesses there is some flexibility: As discussed in one example above, if you are an equipment manufacturer, you might be able to push "left" into higher customer service by moving from pure MTO to some elements of parts "flow" and ATO. Dell led the computer industry in pushing "right" by demonstrating that retail personal computer customers would wait a few days for delivery. You may also, for example, be able to push "right" in spare parts distribution by stocking parts in only one location if you and your customers can afford overnight air express and a twelve- to twenty-hour wait.

We should also point out that this measure will vary by product line within a business. A manufacturer might decide to keep FGI of its standard, high-volume stockkeeping units (SKUs) (MTS) to be able to fill an order for them tomorrow and not lose any sales to swift competitors, to build B and C items on an ATO basis to be available in a week, and to build really low-volume specialty items on an MTO basis requiring custom parts fabrication and promised availability in six weeks. A food retailer will issue purchase orders for product that will go through its central distribution center and thus commit to the manufacturer for the product perhaps a week in advance of sales to customers. But meanwhile, other items are being delivered to stores by the manufacturer on a direct-store-delivery basis and the store manager can (although they seldom do) tell the route salesman not to fully replenish shelf inventory because he expects few sales today.

Customer Order Decoupling Point

While we have chosen to display the differences in supply–demand strategies in terms of the ratio of customer order cycle time to fundamental supply chain time, it is also possible to characterize them with an almost exactly equivalent concept called the customer order decoupling point or "decision point analysis" (see Hines et al.[55]). As shown in Figure 5.2, this concept characterizes supply–demand strategy based on how far up the supply chain a customer order is kept distinct. That point can be as low in the supply chain as finished retail goods waiting for a customer on the store shelf, to as high as product that is completely engineered to order. For example, if a customer order goes back to component production, that is the equivalent of MTO. One of the nice things about this approach is that it frees us from using the conventional CTO/ATO/MTO/ETO terminology.

Now let us move on to how different operating philosophies apply in these realms of supply-demand strategies.

OPERATING PHILOSOPHIES AND THEIR "SWEET SPOTS"

Over the last four decades, there have been three highly publicized philosophies of operations control competing for practitioner mind-share and an ongoing evolution in the operations research/academic space. Let us reconsider them now as comparative operating/planning philosophies (we first covered them "historically" in Chapter 2). Figure 5.3 shows where these philosophies have had the greatest impact, plotted in the dimensions of order cycle supply–demand strategy as discussed above and of planning complexity. They are:

- Lean operations
- MRP II and enterprise resource planning (ERP)
- Theory of Constraints (TOC)
- Fully Scheduled (Operations Research–based [OR] techniques)
- Project management techniques

Note in Figure 5.3 that these sweet spots may overlap, and a given real-world system may represent more than one philosophy, e.g., a system might be both Lean and Fully Scheduled.

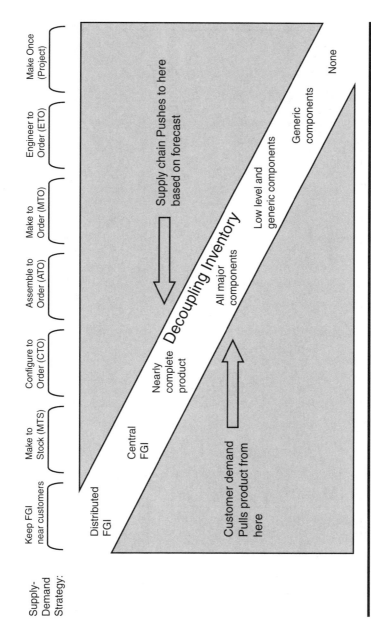

Figure 5.2 Customer order decoupling point.

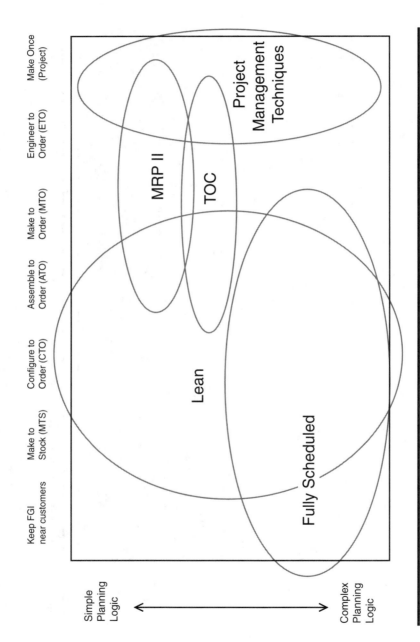

Figure 5.3 "Sweet spots" for planning philosophies.

Lean Operations: Planning for Flow

Lean manufacturing was first introduced to the world through the JIT concepts and the kanban techniques pioneered as part of the Toyota Production System. But as a philosophy of operations, Lean is much more than that and of much broader interest. Lean manufacturing and Lean operations in general have presented a convincing case for organizing production, and production control tools, by forcing product to flow briskly. Intuitively, and proven in practice, flowing product briskly through a supply chain makes economic sense.

Material requirements planning (MRP) does not assume or even encourage rapid flow. TOC helps prevent plants from getting bogged down, but does not really push flow. OR-oriented full scheduling can support flow or not, depending on whether a supply chain and production system are designed for it. But Lean forces flow, by making it a primary objective.

Parts of the Lean philosophy have little to do directly with our flow planning concepts, such as visual control (5S), poka-yoke error reduction, or continuous improvement, and they can certainly be used in non-Lean environments as well. But by reducing error and variability, these nonplanning elements of Lean are a big part of creating the environment where flow can occur — because they contribute to the process reliability that is essential for constant product flow.

In a classic Lean environment (the Toyota Production System for example), production levels are very carefully planned and modulated (and hence have a need for excellent planning capabilities at that level), and production is pulled through the plant with kanbans. Hence Lean is often equated with "pull" operations, and FGIs are forbidden. This author is a Lean revisionist in the sense that I feel that FGI is an absolute requirement in some supply chains and is not going to disappear no matter how long some purists hold their collective breath. Instead, the appropriate challenge is to design operations and planning techniques to keep *just the right amount of inventory* for effective service, operations, and total cost based on the supply–demand strategy you have adopted to deal with the order cycle/flow time ratio your industry demands.

Lean has had the greatest impact thus far where there is enough volume of product movement to plan operations around a regular flow, in the MTS, CTO, and ATO realms. But again, if production can be pushed "to the left" in Figure 5.1, a recognizable flow can be improved or MTO job shops can be converted to flow shops. Lean thinking can prevail there as well, and cost and service can improve. Most manufacturing strategists today recommend shifting supply–demand strategy to flow when that is feasible or finding subsets of the product line for which flow operations can be established (see Reeve[54] for example).

Flow-oriented planning is a fundamentally high-performance technique because it involves using neither much inventory nor much excess capacity to balance supply and demand, but rather finding ways to balance them directly.

Performing this delicate dance is at the core of Lean operations and of product flow planning in a Lean environment.

Example

Let us suppose that we are a major appliance manufacturer; we make washers, dryers, dishwashers, and refrigerators. We have some seasonal sales variation due to seasonal home completion and a few other factors, but it is minor. We have redesigned our supply chain for flow, so that our dealers keep little stock in their stores or their warehouses, but instead rely on us for replenishment within a few days. So we do keep some finished inventory in our regional distribution centers, but we have figured out how to keep it very modest. Part of what we did was to move as much of our product differentiation into accessory kits and either supply those kits to dealers when they order a dryer or install the kit at the distribution center after we receive the dealer order (thus applying the classic logistics postponement principle: delay of product differentiation). But we have also learned how to resupply our distribution centers from tiny flow-through inventories (two days of production) at our plants and to manage production to meet demand.

We use rate-based planning in our plants, combined with smaller production lines that are relatively specialized to a family of products, to keep a constant flow of each family and easy conversions between the items in the family. We never have national promotions of our product, only rolling regional promotions so that the load on the plant that makes each of our products stays reasonably constant. We have designed our operations to work efficiently between upper and lower bounds, and we have a planned rate of production each week for each family. This rate is planned with a tactical tool that looks many weeks into the future, but we only freeze that rate out as far as next week. Beyond that, we still have room to maneuver. We have monthly Sales & Operations Planning (S&OP) meetings to review the planned changes in these assembly rates, our sales promotions, and service levels. We assemble product to a combination of dealer orders and replenishment orders from the distribution centers, as shown on our assembly schedule for the day (we do not know tomorrow's assembly schedule until tomorrow). Components we manufacture in each plant are fabricated and assembled based on classic kanban visual replenishment orders. (And to consider the formal question of how production is authorized, final assembly is authorized by the final assembly schedule, and assembly operations authorize materials replenishment through "empty" kanbans working their way upstream in the material flow.) Purchased components are, depending on the relationship with the supplier, delivered to replenish inventory or on a JIT basis to coordinate with production.

The combination of small FGIs, small component inventories, and a flow supply chain allows us to provide very high service levels at quite low cost, including minimal risk of being caught with much obsolete inventory when we change models.

What kind of planning is required to make this work? We need good forecasting to drive our integrated tactical planning and S&OP processes and good tactical planning to set the production rate for each product family/production line combination and to manage our fifteen days of inventory very carefully. In order not to disrupt operations in the plant, we do go ahead and finish planned production each week even when we do not have a dealer order or distribution replenishment requirement, and this then needs some logic to push my excess to the best distribution center. But this inventory flexing is not a key planning need because it happens a minority of weeks and usually represents little product.

The key planning processes are shown in Figure 5.4. With this approach, I do not have to perform a great deal of planning, but I do have to do it very well. By deciding on rates of production within a predefined range, I have eliminated a lot of the change for which I would have to plan in other approaches. But with this operating philosophy, I have also pushed some of the more difficult problems out to others in the organization:

- Sales and/or marketing: How do they plan promotions so that I get fairly constant demand for my manufacturing and distribution operations? Can they convince big customers to spread out delivery of big orders that would be disruptive to my operations?
- How well does manufacturing management respond when I need to change capacity outside the modest range for which we have planned the flow? Same question for distribution management. They probably do not have resources on tap to let them do that easily, as that reserve capacity would cost money.
- Senior management: How do they deal with a lot of push-back when they want to add new products, new types of customers, or new sales models that would disrupt this highly engineered flowing stream of product?

Role of Inventory and Production Smoothing in Lean

There are also subtler decisions, such as whether we will track sales closely with our production rate or build to a constant production rate. This latter issue is particularly important because it represents a significant decision by the organization as to whether it wants to be directly customer demand driven or not

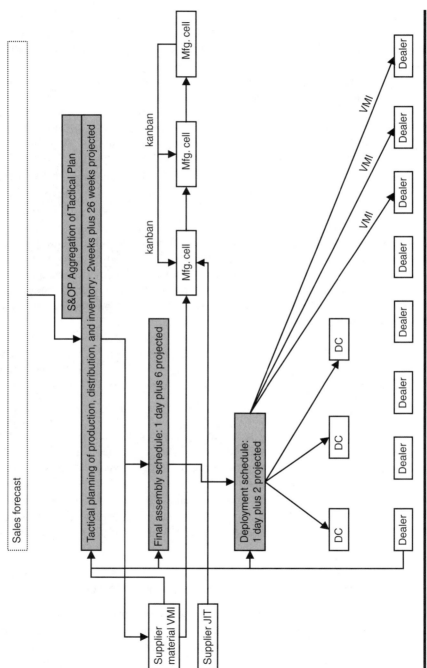

Figure 5.4 Planning processes in our Lean appliance business.

and what the role of inventory is. While many organizations espouse being directly customer demand driven, some authorities argue that "the goal is generally to stabilize production by level-loading the plant while smoothing out the demand."[56] FGI, of course, has to be manipulated in order to do that. There are reasons to do that for manufacturing efficiency and financial reasons: By building to a certain production level, a manufacturing organization can lock in profitability in the short run, pleasing financial management and the stock market. Because of the accounting rules that we operate under, product produced for an inventory build adds to profitability in the short run.

Example

A printer supplies manufacturer in Japan operates a beautifully Lean system, carefully planning production level changes, managing component suppliers to bring just the right amount of each component into the assembly plants when they will be needed, and shipping full containers of product as soon as it is produced to the distributor in each country where it is sold. In the U.S., where much of the product is sold through big-box office supply stores and electronics-oriented mass merchandisers, these powerful retailers expect and get almost 100 percent order fill to replenish their distribution centers, three- to five-day complete order cycles from the distributor, and plenty of quick supply to support promotions. The retailers are able to operate rather leanly as well. In the middle of this supply chain is a North American distributor that is required to make orders on the manufacturer four months in advance of U.S. delivery of the containers, with the power to adjust orders slightly if they are more than three months from delivery. To provide the kind of service to retailers discussed above, with this four-month replenishment lead time of its own, the distributor generally holds about two months of inventory. When inventory climbs, the distributor has no way to throttle its arrival, must fill up its warehouse, and typically ends up shuttling product to outside storage or paying container demurrage charges.

Is this a Lean supply chain? We would argue that it is not a very good one. In this supply chain example, most of the operations power is possessed by the manufacturer and the retailers, and they successfully force their operating models on the distributor and force the inventory to its warehouses and balance sheet. Depending on actual costs of manufacturing schedule changes, there is probably a different model of operation in this supply chain that provides equal service to the retailers but at lower total cost. The manufacturer and distributor have an ongoing dialogue and may yet arrive at a better way to modulate product flow.

To summarize, well-designed Lean systems (both intraplant and supply-chain-wide) are the gold standard for high-volume, reasonably predictable supply chains, i.e., supply chains that can be made to "flow" product because both customer demand and production quality are under control. As shown in Figure 5.3, they can successfully span a broad range of customer fulfillment cycles and successfully utilize planning tools from the rather simple to the very sophisticated. They must be carefully designed, implemented, and kept tuned up, or they fail in fairly obvious ways. That obviousness, like the old JIT rubric about "lowering the water level to expose the rocks," is part of the power of these systems to encourage good design and execution.

If a truly Lean system can be made to work, it will certainly beat MRP II by virtue of its low-cost flow and may also beat Fully Scheduled because of the low overhead associated with planning and production control. Lean remains dependent on high-reliability production and distribution processes and well-managed customer demand.

MRP II: Driven by Manufacturing Orders

As we discussed in Chapter 2, much of the industry-based thinking about operations control over the last four decades has been around MRP, MRP II, and ERP. The MRP "sweet spot," where this philosophy actually works well, is where manufacturing velocity is low; bills of material (BOMs) and routings are complex, deep, and long; and hence where more powerful philosophies of flow and more powerful scheduling techniques are difficult to use. MRP II is equipped to deal with as complex a BOM as you might have and as erratic production rates as you might need to have (including the capability to plan material acquisition for one-time projects, the most "erratic" that the world of production can experience).

MRP is, of course, a form of time-phased planning, different from the static economic order quantity (EOQ) approaches generally assumed to be the norm prior to its development. What is also special about it is that it is a form of production control *based on manufacturing orders* — not that it uses a BOM, which is used in some form by all of the manufacturing-oriented supply–demand strategies, nor that it plans hierarchically, which is also universal.

MRP in practice is tied to manufacturing work orders that can be time phased to reflect finished goods needs, sometimes on a one-for-one basis with customer orders. Often management is attracted to MRP because it wants to stay oriented toward manufacturing orders, which get launched into the shop and then have a life of their own. With the orders issued, let the shop make them as it can, and let the expeditors and planners worry about the details.

Example

Let us put ourselves in a business that uses manufacturing order-based planning. We manufacture measurement and control equipment for drilling. Our products range from measurement equipment up to complete control "cabins," actual control room structures that we outfit with instrumentation and equipment and then send off to drillers. All of our major products are made on an MTO basis. Most of our products are very low volume, and demand for them is sporadic. The idea of making them to stock, given that most are heavily customized, or trying to "flow" production of them, given that for a given product we may make one unit three times a year, seems silly. However, we do have work cells, each with one or two operators, which produce subassemblies or machine parts that will go into other products. There is no FGI; finished, tested product is simply shipped to the customer.

We use manufacturing orders to plan and control our production. We can not only see whether we have the material in stock to make an item as soon as we turn the customer order into a work order, but we can also peg material inventory that is several tiers down the BOM to a manufacturing order and the customer order. We can logically commit a part in inventory to a manufacturing order without physically segregating it, and we can account for cost by a manufacturing order based on both the parts and operator time that get charged to that order. So we have a good idea what it costs to build a unit and fill an order, we know whether we made money on the order, and we learn more with each order about how we should price the next similar order that we receive.

We use fairly standard MRP II techniques for planning, and they are generally adequate for us. We have a large plant relative to the volume of product we produce, with generally plenty of equipment for operators in each cell to use to fabricate or assemble product. We are quite an effective job shop: We get good utilization out of our staff by having them cross-trained to perform many functions, but we have poor utilization of our plant and equipment. We are careful to quote major items far enough into the future that we can finish other jobs promised closer in time. We have customers that are used to waiting for our industry-leading quality products and have pretty good margins built into our business as well.

In this environment, the basic tenets of MRP II make a great deal of sense. We have deep BOMs, and we are constrained primarily by specialized materials, most of them purchased, some with fairly long (but standard) lead times to us from their suppliers. Manufacturing capacity is not much of a constraint. We can forecast our demand many months into the future based on business conditions in our customers' industries. We perform a fairly standard production planning process at the level of highly aggregated product families to plan changes in workforce levels and to add equipment in particular work cells. We can master schedule finished goods, make sure that we have appropriate lead times for components based on how busy a given work cell is, and check for any potential capacity problems with rough-cut capacity planning.

It is easy to see why planning processes and system tools of the type described here, designed for this type of business, are inappropriate for high-volume CTO/ATO or MTS environments. When volume increases and margins decrease, manufacturers want high-capacity utilization. In the diverse job routings of a job shop environment, high-capacity utilization can only be achieved if customers are willing to accept outrageously long order cycle times. In most higher volume, lower margin operations, knowing the "cost" of individual customer orders or tying specific material inventory to an order is not very important, probably not worth the cost of collecting the data.

With more sophisticated planning approaches and tools, better performance can be achieved in the basically manufacturing-order environment described here. We can adopt TOC techniques like drum-buffer-rope scheduling around bottleneck resources. Complex planning approaches can consider the BOMs, capacity constraints, and manpower constraints more completely and generate schedules that find a way to get more product through the manufacturing maze. But the fact remains that planning production in an environment of deep BOMs and complex routings that rely on shared equipment is at best extremely difficult and at worst impossible from which to get a steady flow of output.

MRP II is competitive as a production planning and control technique in environments with complex assembled products, chaotic demand, and no real possibility for converting into a Lean or Fully Scheduled operation. While distribution requirements planning (DRP) represents an extension to the physical distribution milieu and ERP is, of course, a general purpose enterprise management system, MRP itself remains a plant-centric view of the planning problem, most useful in job shop and semi-job shop environments with deep BOMs. For enterprises that are not manufacturing based, it is not generally applicable. For enterprises where a principal problem is deciding which plant to make an order in, it has little to offer. When manufacturing processes are essentially unitary from one end of the plant to the other, and BOMs are shallow, MRP may be unnecessary overhead.

Theory of Constraints

If we throw jobs into the shop without really understanding their impact on the shop except in the simple rough-cut capacity planning way of MRP II, are we not going to create some horrendous delays? Yes indeed, as proven many times over. But given that we can probably predict where bottlenecks will occur in production, why do we not preidentify those areas, and then make sure that they are doing only the work they need to do, are well scheduled, and always kept busy? That apparently simple realization has made many a production environment work better.

TOC applies best in the same kinds of hard-to-structure environments that MRP is used in, but represents a higher level of sophistication and certainly an increase in planning complexity (and hopefully a decrease in operating complexity). Good plans take key resource constraints directly into account rather than trying to plan them as afterthoughts. While TOC does not attempt to identify all capacity constraints, scheduling around known critical resources is an excellent heuristic to achieve better flow in an otherwise unpredictable plant environment.

Perhaps even more important, TOC includes, as a fundamental part of its philosophy, elevating (relieving) constraints — not just coming up with the best way to produce convoluted schedules that respect constraints that should not be allowed to continue. Product flow planners may not have direct responsibility for the capital investments necessary to relieve regular bottlenecks, but they are sure a good place to begin identifying the need for those investments.

Several years ago, we worked on a new production scheduling system for a jams and jellies processor. Production had the classic two steps for grocery processing: mix and cook it, and then package it (mostly in jars in this case). Scheduling was tied in knots (and this example was not Knott's Berry Farm product!) by the limited but complex network of pipes to move cooked product to jar filling lines — or having to use the very labor-intense backup process of putting bulk product into wheeled transfer tubs. A little investment in more pipes to "take the piping diagram out of the scheduling process" would have been far more valuable than the client's enthusiasm for advanced planning! Certainly the TOC methodology would have quickly identified the need to not only "exploit" this piping constraint, but to "elevate" it as soon as possible.

TOC is a powerful addition to a fundamentally MRP-ish work order–oriented production environment. It has a limited amount to offer in a truly Lean plant, where routings are tightly restricted and bottlenecks are not really allowed to exist. Nor is it particularly helpful in a Fully Scheduled plant or supply chain where all major activities are finite capacity scheduled, not just the bottleneck ones. TOC can also be quite valuable in some project management environments, when the project time buffering strategy developed by Goldratt[57] is applicable.

Fully Scheduled Operations

This is a phrase coined for this book; it has not been used before. It is intended to reflect the vision held since the middle of the twentieth century by academic operations researchers: While operations are complex, they are not infinitely complex, and smart algorithms on fast computers should be able to figure out the best way to conduct them. The best way to conduct them; end of discussion. OR-based planning techniques (mathematical optimization and related algorithms) have been a lot slower to impact popular practice than might have been predicted fifty years ago, but they have had substantial impact, and their influence is slowly increasing.

Their greatest impact seems to have been towards the left of the Figure 5.1 diagram, where cycle times for the supply chain are shorter, uncertainty is much less, and precise planning offers greater rewards. For example, there are powerful and practical optimization techniques for deploying FGI that go well beyond simple DRP deployment logic. Both FGI and the transportation system in the U.S. are highly "reliable," and inventory deployment operations that rely on them can be planned in quite sophisticated ways with great success. Optimization has also been used quite successfully to do integrated tactical planning of multiplant production/distribution/inventory (and every full-spectrum advanced planning software provider has a linear programming-based tool to do that).

OR techniques have been less well used where BOMs are deep, total supply chain cycle times high, and production uncertainty high — towards the MTO and ETO end of the spectrum.

Mathematical optimization of real-world-sized planning problems is inherently fairly challenging, but that challenge has been successfully managed in many situations.

Example

Let us suppose that we are a maker of name-brand grocery products. The combination of customer expectations for seventy-two-hour order to delivery cycles, dense low-value product (which precludes much use of airfreight), and the lack of cost-competitive techniques for very small-scale production forces us into an MTS operation, with inventory distributed across five locations in the U.S. High-volume products are made in all of our three plants; low-volume products are typically made in only one of the plants. We try to ship truckloads of product directly from the producing plant to large customers, but a third of our volume must go through the mixing distribution centers.

Figure 5.5 shows the backbone diagram of our planning problem and general approach. The most critical planning decisions are what we will make each day next week (the part of the production schedule we will be freezing) on each major filling line, any changes we have to make in the production schedule this week, how much of each product we will move from each plant to each distribution center tomorrow, and how we will source some customer orders from

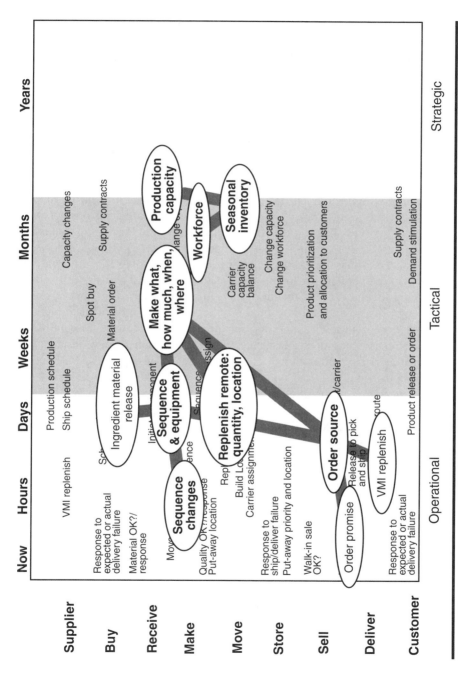

Figure 5.5   Backbone diagram for Fully Scheduled example.

boundary regions (areas that could reasonably be sourced from more than one distribution center). Virtually all these decisions have to be made at the item level, because major components (case boxes, glass containers) are nearly item specific. But good production schedules fill different package sizes of the same item simultaneously, so we also must schedule at the family level as well.

These most central decisions are shown in heavy ovals in the diagram. Also shown, with just a line connecting them, are slightly less critical decisions about ingredient supplier material releases, customer order promising (99 percent of orders must be automatically accepted in this business), and our own vendor-managed inventory responsibilities to a few retailers. Looking out several weeks and months into the future, we also need to make decisions about seasonal inventory builds and manufacturing capacity. These form another cluster of very important, slightly longer range, integrated tactical planning decisions. We will ignore operating and strategic decisions in this example. Packaging materials, by the way, are delivered on a JIT basis based on daily coordination between the materials coordinator and the packaging suppliers that have inventory a few hours away. We operate with about twenty days of FGI total and about five days of ingredient inventory. This inventory is significant in terms of storage space, not very significant in terms of capital requirements (our cost of materials and manufacture are both low relative to sales price), and somewhat susceptible to shelf life (freshness) and obsolescence (when we switch to new products or discontinue a strictly promotional package) issues. Consequently, we have to be quite good in our physical operations at managing inventory first-in–first-out and quite good in our product transitions at making sure retailers take all of the old item before we start shipping the replacement SKU.

Looking at the backbone diagram we have drawn, it is noteworthy that we have a lot of key decisions that we have to make, but they are quite "concentrated." They form two compact clusters in the diagram. Good planning tools are available to us from multiple software providers for the problems we have to solve, but there is potential beyond those software capabilities for even more decision integration and additional savings from planning.

How does this enterprise address the key planning decisions? A good forecast is important and, in fact, achievable in this business. We know a lot about sales for each of the next several weeks because we know trend for each product, expected cannibalization of old products by new, seasonal variation, promotion plans (a critical part of grocery marketing), and major customer demand plans (because we collaboratively forecast with them). For the last ten years there have been powerful tools to address production scheduling, distribution center replenishment, and customer order sourcing, and the state of technology and our traditional silo organization make it easy to manage the three separately. But the decisions are fundamentally intimately related, and we are tempted to merge the decision making and find tools powerful enough to support that integrated decision making. For example, if we can change evaluate order sourcing simultaneously with production scheduling and inventory deployment, we can avoid having to replenish a distribution center and thus avoid having to make more of a particular product for another three weeks, a total cost saving. But if we just look at order sourcing independently, it appears that shipping from an alternate distribution center would incur additional transportation costs and we should not do it.

We also need some type of S&OP process to oversee short-term decisions that should be raised to the management level and to finalize our seasonal production, distribution, and inventory decisions. Do we need a separate planning process (numbers generation process) to support S&OP, or can we support it using our scheduling tools by just running extended horizons with them? That approach would certainly minimize data management work and logical gaps between plans.

Fully Scheduled operations have demonstrated great value in environments where the product was not horribly complex, but where the marketplace was very dynamic, i.e., a lot of ups and downs in demand. Two of the industries with those characteristics are consumer packaged goods, where planners spend much of their time chasing product promotional activity, and certain parts of high tech, such as microprocessors and personal computers, where products never achieve a steady state but just go from initial shortages to obsolescence. In both these environments, Fully Scheduled techniques have made huge contributions (although with different tools in these two industries).

Engineering and Project Orientation

We will not spend much space here on production that essentially requires project management techniques to manage it properly. A product that requires only a modest amount of engineering on the front of the production process to customize it can be managed with the customer order = manufacturing order (usually via MRP II) approach discussed above. More complex products require true project orientation, where the issues of product flow become secondary to the complexity of keeping the project organized and all the participants moving in the right direction.

Most of the planning action for a project occurs in the work breakdown structure and work plan, which collectively are analogous to the routing and production schedule in a more typical production environment. The objective of the work breakdown structure is to identify all tasks within larger modules of work, so that no required work is forgotten. In the project schedule, usually expressed as a Gantt chart, we identify which tasks are precursors to others and which can be performed simultaneously, estimate the work required to perform each task, estimate the elapsed time required by that task, and identify the critical path through the tasks so that additional resources may be applied to that critical path and the total elapsed time of the project minimized.

Consider a shipbuilder. Its production process begins not with a customer order, but with a customer-written RFP, to which it responds with preliminary engineering and a proposal. If it receives the order, it must generate a complete project plan, reserve capacity in a suitable construction facility, do more engineering, create a largely custom BOM, order components at the right time, continue to do deferred engineering work, fabricate and assemble parts, launch the vessel (or first of a series of vessels), outfit it, and test it. To produce product, the shipbuilder must execute a complex program to create something unique. Indeed, that is the definition of a project: A project creates a unique good or service.

Our bottom line conclusion (very near the keel) is that when product becomes so custom and complex that it requires a project to produce it, it is clearly planning intense, but the nature of the planning is mostly different than that discussed elsewhere in this volume. Projects are managed as one-time activities, different than the regular flow of product on which we focus here. For a good summary of project management techniques, see *A Guide to the Project Management Body of Knowledge.*[58]

SPECIFIC PLANNING TECHNIQUES IN THE CONTEXT OF OPERATING PHILOSOPHIES

Let us go one level lower and review some specific planning techniques in the context of the broad philosophies discussed above. Most of these techniques were introduced in Chapter 2, but now we can better orient them for contemporary use. Figure 5.6 shows these techniques in the context of the operating philosophies we have just discussed.

Manufacturing Materials Reorder Point (ROP): Does Not Really Fit within Any Contemporary Operating Philosophies

This author had assumed, probably like many others, that using ROP techniques to control production materials was obsolete, dead, not worth considering in the twenty-first century. Wrong. A couple of years ago we saw a small plant within a plant that made display gauges for industrial use and repaired gauges returned from the field. Production volume was low, several gauges per day, each of them different (and hence a typical production lot size of one). There were really

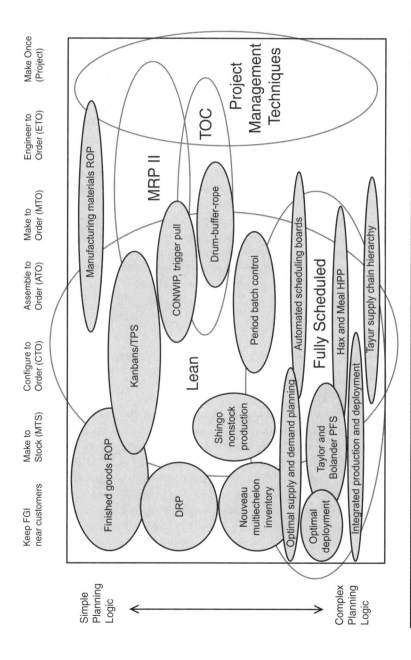

Figure 5.6 Specific planning techniques in the context of the operating philosophies.

no expensive components in the gauges. They consisted mostly of bezels (which came in several sizes from an outside supplier), glass covers, faces (which were printed from a computer file as needed), and indicators. Most of the components were stacked around the periphery of a few workbenches that were the "cell" for gauge production. Components were replenished with an EOQ from mostly outside suppliers when they dropped to their respective ROPs.

There was no flow, no optimization, and no time-phased ordering of materials (although there was an MRP system controlling the larger plant and ordering some of the gauges produced by this shop), just build and repair gauges as needed and reorder components when they hit their ROP. This was a time machine of sorts as it represented classic workshop-type production, not advocated for several decades and not high efficiency for either the parts inventory used or the floor space consumed. Labor efficiency was good, however, as the gauge builders worked elsewhere in the plant when not working on gauges.

For the very specialized, low-volume product that this example represents, ROP is probably the optimal, lowest cost technique for managing materials. For production scheduling, the work cell could effectively trade off the priority of production for larger systems, production for independent orders for gauges, and repair of returned gauges. ROP lives on in the right kinds of production environments.

Fixing MRP II: CONWIP and Trigger Pull Systems

We discussed the major components of MRP II in Chapter 2. Here we introduce two techniques invented to improve the performance of MRP. The first is a planning technique that is designed to correct one of the classic limitations of MRP II–planned production environments, their tendency to build very large work-in-process (WIP) inventories and not complete finished goods in a timely fashion. Hopp and Spearman[2] propose a Constant WIP or CONWIP technique for directly limiting the amount of WIP, by controlling the number of manufacturing orders released to the plant at any one time. To this author's knowledge, the technique has not been used in practice, but it is interesting and refreshing for its attempt to control a specific MRP problem.

George[4] advocates the addition of a Trigger Pull mechanism to MRP so that, for example, options that are added to a core product at a certain stage of production will not be released blindly by traditional MRP logic, but rather will be triggered based on actual knowledge of the status of production on the shop floor, say with a nightly triggering process. This addition of Trigger Pull to MRP is intended, like CONWIP, to substantially reduce WIP inventories and make the still MRP-driven production system Leaner.

Drum-Buffer-Rope (DBR): Theory of Constraints and Enhancement to MRP II

While TOC has broad applicability for operations management (and even life management), it began as an attack on the unwieldiness and order delays of complex, multirouting manufacturing shop environments. The TOC principle to "exploit" a capacity-constrained resource can be operationalized with DBR. The "drum" in DBR is the schedule for the bottleneck resource, the "buffer" is a time buffer of jobs arriving at the bottleneck (they are planned to arrive before the bottleneck is expected to be ready to process them, which then, of course, turns into inventory), and the "rope" is the connecting device from the bottleneck upstream to regulate the release of materials. Normally, work orders are released into the plant so that an appropriate sized buffer of time (which turns into inventory) is maintained ahead of the drum (schedule) in order to get the absolute maximum production out of the capacity-constrained resource (see Schragenheim and Detmer[17]).

Kanbans/Toyota Production System: Lean

The specific technique through which many of us first got exposure to post–World War II Japanese manufacturing thinking was the kanban, the famous ticket or other type of token by which more production is authorized at an upstream production cell in a JIT manufacturing environment. Easy to criticize as a myopic control technique versus computer-based systems, the kanban lives on in numerous manufacturing environments and Toyota plants (see Dennis[59]) as a simple — but sometimes actually sophisticated — way of visually controlling the flow of product through a manufacturing facility.

JIT production requires a substantially different approach to scheduling than other philosophies. For example, it self-schedules upstream steps, where conventional department-based manufacturing requires some type of schedule or work list for each work center in order for the operator to know what to work on next. It directly eliminates much of the need for manufacturing execution systems, which track work progress and inventory at each work center. Mature versions of JIT, such as the Lean Production described by Dennis[59] at Toyota Canada, rely on multiple levels of production planning to set production rates for product groups and rely on kanbans only to fine-tune the flow by ±10 percent. In this light, JIT is not as radical an approach to directing flow in the plant as one might have thought from its 1980s advocates.

Do not underestimate the power of visual techniques, such as kanbans, which are quick to read, easy to understand, and difficult to make mistakes with. Many of the most highly publicized computer-based shop floor control techniques involve using tools like handheld computer terminals, which are, conversely, slow to read, sometimes difficult to understand, and easy to make mistakes either reading or inputting data (which is also quite time consuming). In warehouse management systems, for example, there is great interest in converting from handhelds and keyboards to voice response systems to be able to get the best combination of speed, the computer's visibility of the whole operation, and both hands free to do work.

Shingo's Nonstock Production: Lean

Always ready to ask "Why can't this be done better?" Shigeo Shingo's later writings implicitly criticize kanbans as wasteful and propose more advanced techniques for controlling flow of material through a manufacturing facility.[7] Most notably from a product flow planning point of view, Shingo's Nonstock approach relies on the synchronization of processes through which product moves so that there is essentially no dead WIP inventory in the plant, only a little live inventory on conveyer, and no need for kanbans. To make a system of this sort work requires the underpinnings typical of other Japanese advanced manufacturing approaches, such as near zero quality defects in production, process-oriented rather than machine-oriented layout, and respect for human dignity. The Matsushita Mikuni washing machine plant is a better example of Shingo's thinking than is the Toyota Production System.

Period Batch Control: Lean

Most manufacturing systems of the early twentieth century relied on inventories of materials and WIP to feed each stage of production, thus decoupling manufacturing processes from their predecessors and successors. However, a technique called period batch control was developed in England during the 1930s by R.J. Gigli and was used for producing a number of products, including Spitfire fighter aircraft (see Burbridge[61,62]). As shown in Figure 5.7, period batch control requires that work be divided into explicit stages of production, preferably, according to Burbridge, via Group Technology. Using uniform time periods, often a one-week period, all the work for all jobs at each particular stage must be completed in that period. Each job then moves on to the next stage of production in the next period. By imposing this strict discipline, the technique is able to "march" all products through the plant in a uniform number of periods.

Period batch control is not a well-known technique, at least not in the U.S. Although originated long ago and certainly not of Japanese origin, the technique

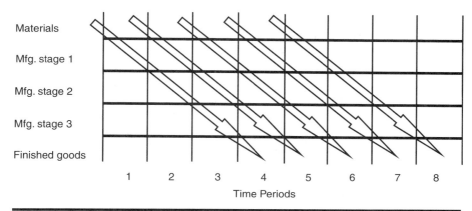

Materials

Mfg. stage 1

Mfg. stage 2

Mfg. stage 3

Finished goods

1   2   3   4   5   6   7   8

Time Periods

Figure 5.7   Period batch control.

is now taught in some Lean production courses. It is a uniquely powerful and simplifying way of forcing a uniform flow of product through an otherwise complex manufacturing facility and a remarkable way of achieving Lean production — as long as:

■ The plant can be successfully organized into cells that can take responsibility for finishing their production steps during each production cycle, and those cells can be grouped into stages (see Riezebos[1]).

■ Production can efficiently occur in short cycles, with components mostly manufactured on a lot-for-lot basis.

We believe that the power of this approach can be maximized by combining it with a sophisticated finite-capacity master scheduling tool and capable-to-promise (CTP) order promising for customers. Unlike a typical MRP factory environment, where we really do not know what the load will be on any given work center each week, with a plant organized for period batch control we can know precisely: It will be whatever work is performed by that work center on the products scheduled to be completed X weeks from now. Consequently, it is straightforward, as part of master production scheduling logic, to create master schedules that will be capacity feasible not just in final assembly but in each period/stage of production leading up to final assembly. With CTP based on that master scheduling tool, product promised to customers and put into the master schedule each period will be within the capacity of each manufacturing cell, and the right product to fulfill those promises to customers can come marching out of the plant each period, as expected.

Automated Scheduling Boards/Solvers: Fully Scheduled

This class of scheduling techniques is better known as finite capacity scheduling, but we avoid that terminology as being misleadingly general. As we discussed in Chapter 2, by the late 1970s planning software creators realized that the computer could be an excellent tool for both displaying a detailed hour-by-hour production schedule as a dynamic Gantt chart and also for implementing algorithms to generate and improve proposed schedules. There have been scores of finite-capacity detailed scheduling tools made available in the software marketplace as well. These tools can be very powerful helpers in creating manufacturing schedules, but they are challenging to implement because they require a detailed model of the manufacturing environment. The detailed model also requires heavy manual maintenance to keep up with changes in the plant and product line. When the tool does not earn its keep by proposing very good schedules, it tends to be discontinued rather quickly because of those maintenance requirements.

Hax and Meal HPP: Fully Scheduled

This is an academic technique, but we wanted to remind the reader of it because it is well documented (see Hax and Candea[25]) and typical of many schemes that have been proposed and sometimes fully implemented over the last few decades to fully schedule a production environment. As computers become more powerful, the computational requirements of these kinds of tools become less and less of a limitation. The current advanced planning software suites from all of the leading supply chain planning software providers provide multiple ways to perform essentially complete hierarchical planning of production and much of the supply chain. We review the challenges of implementing these kinds of tool sets in Chapter 8.

Tayur: Fully Scheduled

Again, an academic example of complete supply chain planning and scheduling, as introduced in Chapter 2 (Figure 2.3). To our knowledge, no one has implemented a system with all of these components. There is no end to the complexity and degree of planning detail that can be computerized in a semi-integrated planning environment composed of many modules. As we will discuss in Chapter 8, the issue comes down to the degree of investment in development, implementation, and maintenance (feeding the planning monster) an organization believes is truly cost justifiable.

This particular planning framework involves a large number of distinct plans, and thus is architected rather differently than our "minimum number of plans" principle would suggest.

Finished Goods ROP: Not Really Part of Any of the Operating Philosophies

Relatively simple ROP logic remains a favorite of distribution center managers and independent smaller businesses. Software packages have been available for the last forty years for inventory control in an independent location and continue to be available in many forms: as stand-alone tools, as part of specialized software suites for "distributors" and other types of businesses, and as part of both large-scale- and mid-market-focused ERP suites. As we discussed in Chapter 2, the ROP model of operations was always a better fit for managing inventory at independent sites than it is for most manufacturing environments.

Distribution Requirements Planning: MRP II Family, Although Quite Different Applicability

Billed as an extension of MRP II–dependent demand thinking when first introduced but really quite different, DRP continues as a mainstay of multiechelon finished goods planning and execution.[14] It is available in most ERP systems and is robust. Because it does not typically recognize capacity or attempt to minimize costs, it is often replaced by the "supply" modules in advanced planning systems (see below) that use linear programming or advanced heuristics to try to be smarter about inventory deployment.

Nouveau Multiechelon Inventory Planning: Independent or Fully Scheduled

Renewed academic work on multiechelon inventory management in the last twenty years has led to a number of tools from several software providers (still mostly independent software companies at this point) that are smarter about planning multiple echelons of inventory than simply applying ROP logic one level at a time. It has long been recognized that when multiple layers of inventory are managed together, total inventory investment can be reduced relative to independent safety stock setting for each level. Multiechelon logic is fundamentally much more complex than single, but there are now commercial success stories confirming its value. Part of the value of tackling inventory with sophisticated tools is in re-emphasizing the importance of doing the fundamentals that impact inventory requirements, as well as possible better forecasts, better inventory accuracy, finer categorization of the product line (more specific than A-B-C), frequent updating of inventory policies as SKU sales patterns change, etc.

Taylor and Bolander PFS: Fully Scheduled

In their book *Process Flow Scheduling,* Taylor and Bolander[63] do a nice job of both empirically describing the planning techniques that have been developed for process industry production scheduling and of developing a theory of how this class of planning logic should work in various process manufacturing environments. The dominant concept underlying these scheduling schemes is that the scheduling logic is based on the structure of the production process. These process-oriented techniques typically authorize production with a schedule, not with work orders, and that production schedule is a valid, finite capacity schedule. This class of scheduling techniques can be implemented with a complete range of computerization, from simple manual calculations and spreadsheets to sophisticated heuristics or optimization algorithms.

Optimal Supply and Demand Planning: Fully Scheduled

All integrated advanced planning tool sets now have capabilities to optimally plan product supply over the next several weeks and months, based on location-by-location field demand for product or on direct forecasts. The specific technology employed varies with the tool set, but the objective is to successfully match supply with demand over the tactical planning horizon, so that all projected demand is cost-effectively fulfilled. The production/distribution/inventory models discussed earlier are predecessors of these tools.

Optimal Deployment: Fully Scheduled

If inventories are considered, say, daily by a planning tool that looks simultaneously at all locations to evaluate both supply and demand of inventory and looks ahead in time for several days or weeks at expected additional supplies and forecasted/ordered demand, and even considers any capacity constraints on loading, unloading, and transportation, then very intelligent decisions can be made about how much inventory to deploy tomorrow. This kind of logic will consistently outperform simple DRP in terms of how much customer service can be provided with a given amount of FGI. It can also include subtleties like the ability to reflect differences in which customers are more strategic to us and hence should receive more product under shortage conditions. These kinds of capabilities are available in some, but not most, supply chain advanced planning software suites.

Integrated Production and Deployment: Fully Scheduled

Given the computational resources available today, it is well within planning technology capabilities to both schedule production and manage distributed inventories of FGI simultaneously. This kind of approach can simultaneously consider current forecasts and customer orders, current inventories by individual location of each SKU, and capabilities of each major production system in multiple plants. It can then, for example, recommend making the next batch of product B at only plant X next week (thus saving a setup next week at plant Y) and distributing it to three of the distribution centers from there, while sourcing certain large customer orders directly from the producing plant. It expects to make a batch of the product at plant Y the week after next and distribute it to some of the same distribution centers. Thus it attempts to simultaneously minimize costs for manufacturing, distribution, and inventory in a multilocation enterprise while maintaining a high customer service level.

These systems have been discussed for fifteen years, but few, if any, implemented to date. They suffer not only from "bleeding edge" size and complexity in a single planning module, but they also cross all traditional planning boundaries: between central and plant planners, between manufacturing and distribution, and between customer service and operations. In certain consumer goods businesses, however, considerable economic incentive exists to solve this problem, and planners will continue to chip away at how to implement a fully unified finished goods planning solution.

THERE IS NO ONE BEST WAY TO PLAN (REPRISE)

Every philosophy and technique discussed above has usefulness and is in fact the best technique for some particular problem and context. The planning problems we are trying to solve are usually difficult problems, and identifying the best technique is not easy. Selecting the best planning approach has several dimensions: operating cost, asset requirements, management requirements, staff requirements, training, system requirements, etc. We must be constant skeptics to confirm that what we want to do is valid, that we are using the best models and techniques, and that we have not been sold something that sounds plausible but actually violates common sense or is a very poor technique in one of those dimensions.

Advocates of a particular operations philosophy and planning structure have generally argued that their approach was universally applicable and superior to all others. Plossl, for example, says that "Principle 1. The system framework needed for effective planning and control is common to all manufacturing industries" referring to the basic MRP II structure.[13] We believe that the needs of different enterprises vary so much that it is incorrect to specify a single system framework that is always best, even for just the manufacturing-based subset of enterprises. Enterprises are highly differentiated, even within the same industry, and should probably *differentiate their planning processes and technology even further* to seek uniquely successful competitive positions.

The range of planning problems presented by different enterprises and supply chains in different industries is more like a whole zoo full of animals of various shapes and sizes than it is like just one elephant. Fortunately, to improve planning in an enterprise (and its supply network) you do not have to deal with the whole zoo; you just have to improve the performance of one "beast," your business. The next chapter presents a good way to do that.

6

METHODOLOGY — CREATING BETTER PRODUCT FLOW PLANNING: FROM A "GLEAM IN YOUR EYE" TO IMPROVED OPERATING RESULTS

"Would you tell me, please, which way I ought to go from here?"
"That depends a good deal on where you want to get to," said the Cat.
"I don't much care where—" said Alice.
"Then it doesn't matter which way you go," said the Cat.
"—so long as I get somewhere," Alice added as an explanation.

Lewis Carroll, *Alice's Adventures in Wonderland,* Chapter 6

The four previous chapters have provided the foundation for improving planning. We have discussed the history of the field (Chapter 2), defined some fundamental concepts (Chapter 3), reviewed some fundamental planning structures (Chapter 4), and considered planning under different operating regimes (Chapter 5). But how do we actually change to better planning processes and systems? That is the question we will answer here as we present methodology.

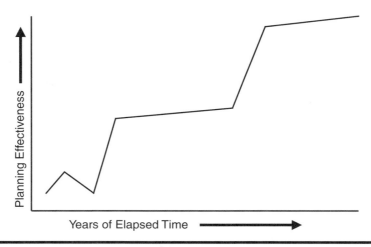

Figure 6.1   Big leaps and continuous improvements in planning approach.

First, a caveat. Most of the methodology presented here is not unique, and it certainly contains no magic. It is mostly common sense and a lot of experience applied to the domain of planning. But there are a number of principles presented that are very important and about which practitioners frequently become confused and try to go the wrong way. We will try to explain why we recommend the various components of the process, why the perspective on planning that we take is important, and how to use some of the specialized tools introduced in Chapter 4.

In this discussion, we will assume that the reader is about to undertake a program to improve planning for an enterprise. As illustrated in Figure 6.1, the "planets will align" occasionally in such a way that an organization is ready to take a major leap upward in the effectiveness of its product flow planning. However, much of the methodology we discuss here can be applied usefully regardless of where one is in the cycle of improvement — much can be used during the periods of steady continuous improvement that should occur between these leaps.

By the way, we use the word "program" rather than "project" because typically enterprises will benefit from comprehensive efforts to improve planning that are multiyear programs encompassing many projects.

OVERVIEW OF METHODOLOGY

Figure 6.2 presents an overview of the methodology we will study. It is based on five nominally sequential phases, although you may be in a position currently where you must begin somewhere other than Phase A. The phases are:

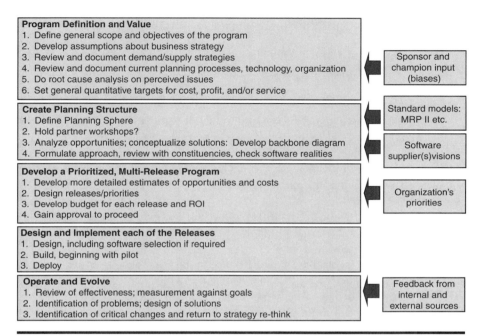

Program Definition and Value
1. Define general scope and objectives of the program
2. Develop assumptions about business strategy
3. Review and document demand/supply strategies
4. Review and document current planning processes, technology, organization
5. Do root cause analysis on perceived issues
6. Set general quantitative targets for cost, profit, and/or service

Sponsor and champion input (biases)

Create Planning Structure
1. Define Planning Sphere
2. Hold partner workshops?
3. Analyze opportunities; conceptualize solutions: Develop backbone diagram
4. Formulate approach, review with constituencies, check software realities

Standard models: MRP II etc.

Software supplier(s)visions

Develop a Prioritized, Multi-Release Program
1. Develop more detailed estimates of opportunities and costs
2. Design releases/priorities
3. Develop budget for each release and ROI
4. Gain approval to proceed

Organization's priorities

Design and Implement each of the Releases
1. Design, including software selection if required
2. Build, beginning with pilot
3. Deploy

Operate and Evolve
1. Review of effectiveness; measurement against goals
2. Identification of problems; design of solutions
3. Identification of critical changes and return to strategy re-think

Feedback from internal and external sources

Figure 6.2 Methodology: improving product flow planning.

A. **Program Definition and Value**. We begin by defining what we are trying to accomplish, the scope over which we are trying to operate, and the value we expect to deliver. Often, this work leads to some type of budget authority to expend resources for more of the program steps.

B. **Create Planning Structure**. This phase asks us to figure out how we think we ought to plan. We rely heavily on the planning structures and related concepts we learned in Chapter 4. We want to finish this work with a shared vision of where we are trying to get, in the enterprise and in the larger supply network.

C. **Develop a Prioritized, Multirelease Program**. If you are part of an enterprise of any size and a supply network of any complexity, there are many facets to good planning. They cannot be successfully tackled at once. It is essential to break the path to the vision into reasonable releases, each of which will demonstrate value to the people sponsoring the work and paying the bills.

D. **Design and Implement Each Release**. This is where most of the work is. What processes are we really going to use in a given area? Do we have the software we need to execute those processes, or will we need to acquire more? Let us build the models, load the databases, set the planning parameters, pilot the approach, run parallel, and then roll it out for live use.

E. **Operate and Evolve**. Okay, we are live with our new process, but we are still not planning very well. Let us figure out why and fix it. Now let us fix the next problem, and the next. Let us get some advanced training from our software provider. Let us spend the next few years making incremental but very important adjustments as we figure out how to get better and as the business changes.

Does this sound exhausting? It is a lot of work, but it is easier work than the alternative, which is trying for years to operate successfully in a morass of poor processes, the wrong systems, and daily firefighting. And while there are many steps, they do not necessarily require big budgets or large staffs.

Why do we need a formal program to figure out how to improve planning? Given that planning does not involve huge numbers of staff, why can we not just rely on the planners themselves to figure out better processes and to speak out when they need better systems? To a degree, we can rely on them: If there are regular crises around a particular issue, experienced planners will speak up loudly and demand a solution. But in the more typical situation, where things seem to work acceptably a majority of the time, planners will not generate a lot of complaint volume. Typically, planners get lost in the trees and cannot see the forest. As shown in Figure 6.3, most planners must devote their best attention to dealing with very short-term service-oriented issues — they have multiple layers of these between their immediate attention and the longer term issues. Typically, they are not able to think about cost optimization or improvements to the planning structure on a daily basis. Nor are the typical planners given responsibility to think about how to change the planning processes themselves.

Six Sigma

The methodology we present here emphasizes the special requirements of redesigning planning. However, the dominant approach in recent years for industrial process improvement has been the Six Sigma methodology. Six Sigma has been successfully used in numerous environments to attack problems that include flow planning (see George[4] for example). If your organization is committed to Six Sigma, we recommend that you use it for improving planning as well, but incorporate some of the specialized, planning-oriented techniques we present here.

We are now ready to jump in and think through our approach, phase by phase.

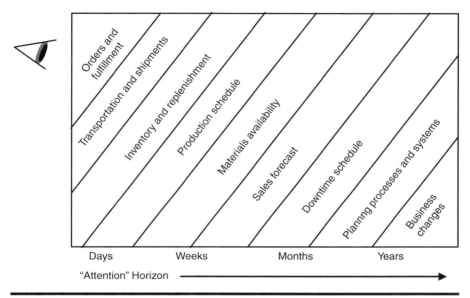

Figure 6.3   The planner's perspective.

THE METHODOLOGY, STEP BY STEP

A. Program Definition and Value

Like most methodologies, we must begin by figuring out what we are trying to do and approximately how we will do it. It is not difficult to define the necessary steps.

1. Define General Scope and Objectives of the Program

We need to write a page of prose or create a few slides to communicate what we are trying to accomplish, what our objectives are (increased sales, improved service, lower costs, all of the above), and who we are going to "go to war with" (who will be on the team). What business units will be involved and what suppliers or customers will participate? We will almost certainly create some type of core program team, so we need to find the appropriate participants from management and staff. Who is going to manage the team, who is going to be on the team, and who in senior management is going to champion the effort (whether the person knows it yet or not that he or she is going to be the champion)? Here, and later when we discuss rollout, we will have some important choices to make about securing the right full-time program manager and guarantees from key participants of enough time to contribute meaningfully. This challenge is particularly difficult because many organizations have been "task forced" to the limits of their patience, but it is necessary because no organization of any size has one individual who understands everything about planning its operations.

We are not believers in making big productions out of setting scope and objectives and of defining vision. There is no better way to lose momentum at the beginning of a program than spending days trying to get agreement on and produce elaborate directional statements. But simple statements of direction have to be written down and referred to periodically during the program. Without that written charter, there is great risk that organizational pressures will morph the program into something it was never intended to be and result in neither the original nor the unconsciously revised goals being achieved.

Being explicit about goals can also quickly clarify how deep support is for a program. Recently, we saw a situation where a planning manager wanted to kick off a major program to improve product flow performance. This major automotive parts manufacturer had made considerable progress over the last few years in improving inventory and cost performance, but the manager could see where major opportunities still existed to jump to a higher, near industry-leading level. He championed an initiative to set ambitious targets, such as a further 35 percent reduction in finished goods inventory, and proposed some significant changes in how product flow would be managed in order to accomplish that. His management was supportive, but only of a program with modest improvement goals and process changes. Rather than undertake a program with too weak a charter, the planning manager decided to defer the whole initiative for six to nine months and then try again.

2. Develop Assumptions About Business Strategy

In this volume, we generally present the relationship of business strategy, supply–demand strategy, and product flow planning as they are diagrammed by decisions in Figure 3.1. But it is also valid to think about these planning issue sets hierarchically, as shown in Figure 4.5. This way of thinking emphasizes that, logically, business strategy should drive product flow strategy, which should drive how we plan the actual product-level decisions. Simple, right?

Wrong. One of the first issues that will probably be faced is that there are few usable business strategies already documented and few supply–demand strategies laid out. No one ever figured out explicitly whether we wanted to be oriented toward operational excellence, customer intimacy, or product innovation (see the discussion of these in Chapter 4). Often no one has specified whether our growth is going to come through better customer service, product line additions, price reductions, or some other source. That does not mean that these decisions about the business do not exist. They probably are understood by the organization to some degree of vagueness and perhaps by certain individuals in some detail. If we can find those individuals, a quick conversation with them can be enlightening. It is, for example, perfectly legitimate for a planning improvement program champion to go have a conversation with the corporate strategist.

In most cases, what we think we know about where the organization is headed can be quickly documented in a few slides, certainly relative to issues that directly impact product flow planning. Of course, if business strategy that defines what we need to know is already documented, we can simply highlight the portions of it relevant to us and go on to step 3. We are not trying to create a business strategy here, just to document the assumptions about strategy that impact our immediate work. We will present these assumptions to other managers as we work in the first three phases of the program, and they will be welcome to correct us or take specific concerns to appropriate executive vice presidents and chief operating officers.

A few years ago, we began a logistics strategy project with a client (a very large industrial distributor) that knew it had not "finalized" its future business model, and there was in fact a lot of contention in the organization about what it should be when it grew up. We began the project with a series of quick management workshops (one per week) that progressed from articulating business strategy to reviewing the primary logistics options we thought were worth considering. By using these workshops, we developed enough working consensus on strategy that we could move forward and complete the analytical project. Of course, we did not finalize business strategy with this technique, and when the time came to authorize the massive investments required to implement the results of the study, the strategic issues were again raised, but our workshops built enough foundation that we were able to move forward in an otherwise contentious environment. If simply documenting and "reporting" strategic assumptions is not going to be adequate, consider a management workshop approach as used in this example. But workshops on strategy must be tightly disciplined as they can deteriorate into endless philosophical debates if not carefully controlled.

3. Review and Document Supply–Demand Strategies and Policies

There will probably be more concrete information available at this level about how you operate as a business:

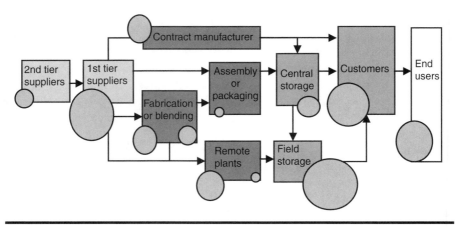

Figure 6.4   Where is the inventory in the supply chain? Where is there almost no inventory?

- Do you sell from finished goods inventory, configure to order, assemble to order, make to order, or engineer to order? For which portions of the product line?
- Where do you keep what pools of inventory? Determining "where the inventory is" in the supply network is often a great way to understand what is really going on and where the greatest opportunities are for improvement. As shown by the inventory balloons in Figure 6.4, there are a lot of places inventory can be, or perhaps not be, if a given participant in the network has figured out how to push it to its suppliers or customers.
- If you manufacture, are you organized by departments, cells, or a combination?
- Do you know why you buy some materials to replenish stock and others specifically to support a master production schedule? Are you about to switch some key materials to just-in-time (JIT) delivery or switch some away from JIT because you have found a cheaper supplier (one that will not play that game).
- Have you adopted strict Lean policies for operations; do you always attack problems with the Theory of Constraints methodology?
- And so on.

You will almost certainly find it valuable to document aspects of current operating strategies that are not explicitly understood by the organization. But there is also a distinct possibility that when you review existing operations strategies and policies, you will come to the conclusion that they are not the best ones for current business conditions (or consistent with your apparent corporate strategy). If you arrive at that conclusion, you have a choice to make. If changes in supply–demand strategy are relatively small and likely to be noncontroversial, you can try to simply make policy decisions and implement them as part of your planning program. For example, if you come to the conclusion that inventory policy for goods stocked at your five distribution centers is simplistic and poor, and you know you can do better, and the vice president of logistics is on board and the vice presidents of finance and sales do not care about these details, you are well positioned to "just do it" in terms of fixing inventory control (to borrow a slogan from Nike). If, on the other hand, you come to the conclusion that you are not going to be competitive in your industry without shifting from make to stock to, say, make to order with a one-week order cycle time, you have a much bigger challenge on you hands than just changes in planning. Every major supply chain process — how you relate to customers, how manufacturing plants are organized, how distribution processes work — is going to have to be changed.

If you reach the conclusion that truly strategic operations policies have to change, you are going to need to shift the program up a level in Figure 4.5, from working on product flow planning to operations strategy. You could easily spend the next two years getting a few strategic issues settled and implemented. But if you truly believe that change is necessary at that level, it is better to approach it there, and work explicitly with appropriate management in the enterprise on those issues, than to try to pretend that you are just working on product flow planning problems. Better short- to intermediate-range product flow planning is not going to fix a truly broken operating strategy, and the time and money you spend on flow planning will be mostly wasted. This book does not focus on the issues of designing operations strategy, even though we discussed some alternatives in Chapter 5.

4. Review and Document Current Planning Processes, Technology, and Organization

There likely will be some documentation already in existence here, but you will want to revise or complete it. Draw some process maps of how things work today. Write summaries of what each player does in the process. Do not worry about lengthy documentation, but you will find that a little time spent studying the present will both educate the working team and provide a few pages or slides that can (and will) be frequently pulled out during the discussions of the next several steps.

5. Do Root Cause Analysis on Perceived Issues

As part of the review of the current planning approach, you will identify apparent problems such as customer service issues, or money left on the table by inefficient operations, materials prices that are too high, or too much inventory. In addition to whatever can be learned from the formal key performance indicators (KPIs) your enterprise tracks, you will hear many anecdotes and probably some horror stories. What are the real causes of these problems, these inefficient uses of resources? Often it is good to diagram perceived problems in a root cause diagram, shown in an example as Figure 6.5.

6. Set General Quantitative Targets for Improving Cost, Profit, and/or Service Performance

Having studied how we operate today, it is time to try to estimate how much better we could do and what that would be worth in improved customer service, improved sales, improved profit, reduced costs, and reduced long-term investment requirements (for example, in new plant capacity) and reduced short-term investment requirements (usually inventory). Let us go ahead and build some kind of business case, large or small. We may need to estimate total program costs at this point, and do a formal return on investment (ROI) analysis to justify our effort and expense to management, or we may be able to weasel through another small phase of work before having to build that large, formal business case.

Based on our knowledge of what good planning can do, we can certainly estimate some very rough cost and savings numbers now in Phase A, but we will be able to do an even better job in Phase C. We should now, if we have not already, begin collecting the appropriate KPI data for the "before" state, so that we have something against which to compare our "after" the new planning approach is implemented. More than a few excellent new planning approaches have gone unrewarded because we could not quantify the situation beforehand.

One supply chain planning software provider developed a rather elaborate methodology around root cause analysis and benefits estimation. In that case, the analytical process was sometimes abused by estimating benefits aggressively and then using them as a basis for "value pricing" the software license to the client. But the basic concepts of this analysis are fundamental and should usually be performed: consideration of current problems, money currently wasted by inadequate planning processes, the root causes of these problems, how better planning can address these problems, and realistic budgets for upgrading planning.

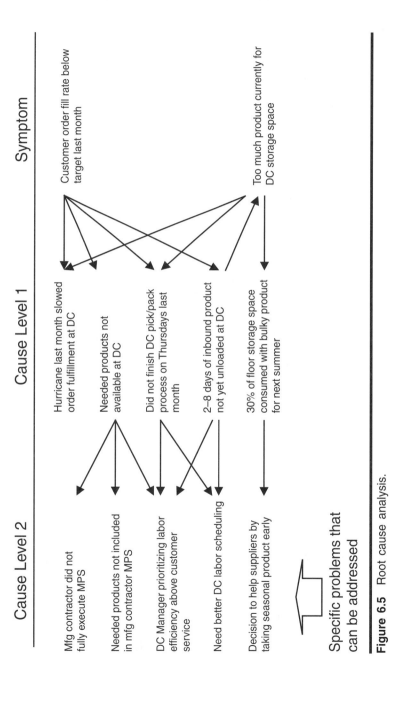

Figure 6.5 Root cause analysis.

B. Create Planning Structure

This phase is perhaps the most creative of the steps involved in improving operations planning. The challenge here is to design a planning approach that will truly give us a competitive advantage in our industry (including being practical and implementable), versus one that is ho-hum, perhaps no better than our competitors already use. How do we go about that process?

1. Define Planning Sphere

It is time to use one of the concepts we defined in Chapter 4, the planning sphere. In what part of the supply network can we take the lead on planning processes and systems?

■ Our operation division or multiple operating divisions? Do we have logistics on board, or are we going to have to plan around them? Do we have manufacturing on board?
■ Key suppliers or most suppliers?
■ Key customers or most customers in one of our sales channels?

Note that defining the borders of the planning sphere precisely is not critical, although it needs to be done. Planning on the borders will generally end up being planned in a delegated or collaborative way, so the borders of this system can be a little vague. Our improved planning approach will be driven by what is central to the sphere, not by what is peripheral. That is good, because as the business and the organization change, the borders of the planning sphere will change, and an approach that was highly dependent on its periphery would have to change radically on a frequent basis.

Let us draw some candidate diagrams that look like Figure 4.11, think about where the current inefficiencies are in those diagrams (where is there money being left on the table?), decide how big our aspirations are, and make go-forward plans.

2. Hold Partner Workshop(s)

If we think we can include suppliers or customers in our planning sphere, let us hold a series of workshops with them to figure out how we can plan better together. Workshops should be a day or two in length and ideally include a few customers or suppliers that we feel we would work with in the same way and may work well with each other. Generally, suppliers and customers do not mix in one workshop, nor do direct competitors. We will talk through the inefficiencies of what we do today, talk through the ways in which we value our independence from each other, and devise some high-level processes that will reduce the problems. You may be amazed at how frank and honest these kinds of conversations can be when conducted away from the heat of the day-to-day business and procurement battle, away from the "Why did you just raise prices?" kinds of issues. Obviously, everyone involved has to adopt the attitude that all the supply chain participants need to make a profit, and the goal of the workshop is to figure out how to raise the supply chain's collective profitability.

It is also helpful to hold workshops with managers and staff from your own enterprise who are not part of the core program team. Everyone who is involved with planning or the use of plans has a unique perspective on the planning processes, and you genuinely want to capture their input for purposes of conceiving new approaches, as well as begin the process of making them feel that they are part of the solution and enthusiastic about adopting it. Yes, involving more people requires more time, but as discussed elsewhere, people will only support and execute plans they believe in. If a plant planner does not believe in a new planning process, you can be sure that his or her managers (plant manager, production supervisors, production control supervisor, etc.) will not believe in it either, resulting in nonimplementation or poor operating results. While not too many people directly create product flow plans in the enterprise, a lot of people have to have confidence in the process and be willing to execute enthusiastically based on it.

3. Develop Backbone Diagram

At this point, we know where the quantifiable opportunities are for better operations because of better planning. We understand the politics of our own enterprise, and we have a sense of what is possible and attractive for suppliers and customers. It is time to draw some diagrams of the type we saw in Figure 4.12. It is time to start to diagram what we think the major planning processes can be in our part of the supply network, our galaxy in the supply universe.

What is critical to the business? Where is the greatest leverage of better planning on cost and performance? (Almost the same question.) What logically needs to be planned together in order to optimize the business and to avoid creating overlap and overcommunication requirements among separated plans?

As discussed in Chapter 4, the backbone represents a picture of how we want to plan. Now is when we decide what flow planning decisions are made together, essentially simultaneously, to do it right, to take most of the currently wasted money off the table. These complex(es) of decisions will form a backbone for planning, perhaps multiple backbones, and dictate the processes, the staff executing the human part of those processes, and the planning technology and data that are required.

It also starts to become evident from the backbone diagram how planning should be organized. Do we really need a central planning group or can we plan from multiple separate perspectives? What part can plant planners do largely on their own? What are we going to do for suppliers; what are they going to do for us? Can some customers give us essentially final replenishment plans, and so on? Which parts of planning need to report to the executive vice president of supply chain, or the vice president of manufacturing, or the plant manager, or the distribution center manager, or the customer? The organizational implications must be considered simultaneously with data, processes, and algorithms/systems, because the best designs must work well in all these dimensions.

In either this step or the next, it is time to get some help on understanding what is possible with contemporary planning technology, unless we have internal staff with unusual breadth and depth of knowledge. If we have had professional assistance since earlier steps, we may be able to obtain all the needed knowledge from that source.

It is difficult, however, to find professional, outside help with sufficient breadth and depth of knowledge. Most professionals have their domains of expertise and preference and limited knowledge outside them. An MRP II specialist may have learned JIT but still know little about what can be done with the most sophisticated factory planning heuristics. An academic "operations researcher" will understand optimization but may be prejudiced against MRP II. A certified Six Sigma practitioner may be excited about designing new Lean processes but know nothing about MRP, heuristics, or optimization.

Software providers are another important source of expertise at this stage, and it is entirely appropriate to initiate conversations with them now on the conceptual approach(es). However, for this purpose they suffer not only from typically limited personal knowledge, but from an enormous economic incentive to propose only what they can uniquely deliver. Primary reliance on a software provider to design the planning structures reduces the probability of successful planning improvement at a reasonable cost. Nominally independent professionals with strong implementation ties to one software provider may be almost as biased as the software providers themselves.

Ultimately, it is the enterprise's inescapable responsibility to design a planning structure for itself that represents the right vision of the future, perhaps with some unbiased outside counsel.

4. Formulate Approach(es), Review with Constituencies

Let us go ahead and flesh out our planning design. We can finalize a backbone diagram, create a general description of where we are going in prose or slides, finalize a brief set of process maps, and write brief software requirements/ specifications. If we did not do so in step 3, we can now solicit from software providers their sales presentations, design input, and preliminary cost estimates, that is, if we think new software will be needed. As we will discuss in Chapter 8, we may need no new software as it may already be licensed, or we may need only an additional module or two from a current software provider.

We are also now in a position to present what we want to do in enough detail that general management and staff can get excited about it. Good planning structures are cool, attractive things, because they allow organizations to function well, like sleek, well-coordinated animals. If they are presented well to the enterprise, they are exciting and will naturally draw support from most parts of the organization (there may be, of course, some parts of the organization that lose influence in the new process and really cannot be enthusiastic). Planners who are not part of the core team, of course, have to be included in this process and their input used to modify the structure in ways that they support. We should certainly review our plan with key executives and incorporate their input (which is not to say that we do not have to defend key parts of the design which we understand and they do not). If we decide to make changes, we can do that quite cost effectively at this stage.

C. Develop a Prioritized, Multirelease Program

The transition from Phase B to C is quite subtle. In fact, you might want to combine them in practice, although we have kept them separate to emphasize the importance of both the planning structure design (in Phase B) and the program design (in Phase C). Having figured out our vision of what we want to build, we now have to figure out how to construct it and pay for it.

1. Develop More Detailed Estimates of Opportunities and Costs

We made an initial attempt to assess benefits in Phase A, but now we have to get serious about it. We can ask software providers to give us estimates of software costs, if we do not already have them. We can estimate software-interfacing costs and estimate custom development costs for pieces we do not think we should license. We can estimate training costs, other process implementation costs, and travel expenses. We can perform a detailed benefits analysis of where the new planning structure will impact service, sales, costs, and asset requirements. It is important that we do this analysis to the extent possible for each aspect of the planning structure that we need to invest in, because we are going to have to break the work out into implementation releases and cost-justify each release.

2. Design Releases/Priorities

As a general rule, comprehensive new planning structures should not be implemented in any kind of a "big bang." Figure 6.6 shows a different view of our complete methodology. The first three phases are performed "once" in the program, because they are unified. But the fourth phase, design and implementation of each "release," is performed multiple times. In recommending multiple releases, we suggest a methodology similar to that advocated for many years by i2 Technologies, which it called "business releases" because of the emphasis on delivering measurable value, i.e., business case justification, with each release. We believe that i2 figured this out basically correctly, that this is generally the best way for businesses to make progress in planning approaches when there are some significant investments that have to be made.

The release methodology lets management approve a budget quantity for each release that represents an acceptable risk, see that part of the program successfully implemented, and approve funds for an additional release. It also avoids the disruption caused by a big bang that throws the whole planning process up in the air simultaneously and asks that you correctly assemble all the new pieces instantly. There are trade-offs, of course, such as having to spend money to construct software interfaces that will only be used temporarily, while part of a new system talks to part of an old system. But potential budget changes work to the favor of a multirelease approach more often than not. Considering that budgets may get tightened in the future, it is generally preferable to have a smaller release nearing completion that leads to an improved interim planning

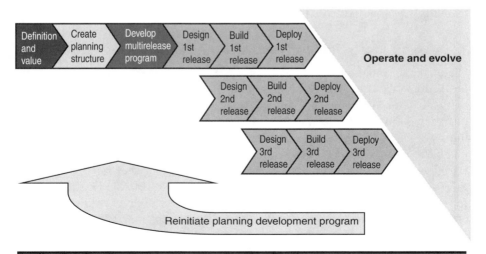

Figure 6.6   Release-oriented view of methodology.

state, where you can "rest awhile" pending more budget availability, than to be in the middle of a huge integrated project and be told you must halt it, perhaps with no planning gains whatsoever.

The criteria that are typically used to decide how to group and prioritize the releases are:

- **Logical precedence**. If some steps have to be performed before others, they need to be in the same release or a release prior to the one that relies on them. If moving to real-time inventory information is a pre-requisite to implementing a new available-to-promise (ATP)/capable-to-promise (CTP) approach, then real-time inventory has to happen first. Note that in this example we have already stumbled over the issue of grouping work so that each release shows a financial return. If there are no significant quantifiable benefits associated with real-time inventory (as compared with, say, the "accurate as of midnight last night" inventory data we have been using for the last several years), then perhaps we ought to put the inventory information improvement and the new ATP/CTP process into the same release. That leads us to our next criterion.

- **Each release has an attractive ROI**. Management may approve re-leases one at a time if they want to keep you on a short leash. That is their prerogative, and you have developed an approach that delivers value to them with each release and will still ultimately get to the vision.

- **Bigger benefits first**. Of course, both the working team and top man-agement want to make the business more efficient as soon as possible. We may have stock options to exercise, we may have college tuition to pay now, and we may not live till the end of the program! Seriously though, good gains early on will help build credibility in the program and typically make it easier to get approval on later releases.

- **Easier releases first**. Some of our improvements may be quick and easy. For example, we may first implement a small process change like convincing a supplier to regularly update a data form that is already on our Internet portal for suppliers. Of course we want to do things like that before we have to develop new systems or build, say, an ambitious optimal planning system/process. On the other hand, often the larger benefits are truly associated with relatively exotic new communications or planning technology, and we cannot have them without paying the price.

- **The stuff you are not so sure about comes last**. Chances are that you will have learned enough by the time you get there that your uncertainty is gone or, more likely, you have redesigned the release to take advan-tage of new understandings, new technology, or changes in the business.

3. Develop Budget for Each Release and ROI

The details of budgeting and financial justification tend to vary with the enterprise and will not be detailed here. The vast majority of the budget for planning structure change should be in the human activities: training, data collection, model structuring, piloting, developing systems interfaces, parallel execution with old processes, and so on. Software licenses and new hardware for computing and communications should be a small fraction of the total. We have seen guidelines published which indicate that other activities should be about one to two times the software license cost. This guideline is generally wrong. It is correct only if you are:

- Paying too much for packaged software
- Custom developing truly leading-edge, specialized software that is very expensive
- Putting zero (or minimal) cost on significant amounts of internal staff time, so that the budget does not reflect the true cost
- Badly shortchanging all the other activities associated with changing planning approaches

The most cost-effective planning changes involve better use of software to which you already have access. Two to four times license fees for other costs is a better guideline, even when you are paying full ticket for relatively expensive packaged software.

4. Gain Approval to Proceed

Good planning should be a high-leverage activity. You should not have to be selling releases to your management that are near the approval "hurdle rate" for capital expenditure by your enterprise. If you are, you should question whether you are paying too much for what you are getting or whether you are trying to implement approaches that you really question the value of. Perhaps a simpler, lower cost approach would be more appropriate. More importantly, with a good explanation of your proposed planning structure and development program, you can make it obvious why doing what you want to do will simply result in the business being better run. In most enterprises, selling truly good investments in planning is easy.

D. Design and Implement Each Release

Now that we have defined what we want to accomplish in a release and likely committed to quantitative goals, it is time for the hard work to begin.

1. Design, Including Software Selection If Required

Processes are often the best place to begin design. They will drive our software and data requirements and influence organization. We have probably generated high-level process maps in our earlier work; now it is time to extend them to the mid-level and to a very detailed level for some selected processes (but not for all; planners are smart people and will generally figure out the best way to do each step as they work). If additional software is required, you must have it identified by now. This step may be easy if, for example, your organization has already made a concrete commitment to one vendor and the vendor's offering is reasonable for your purposes or you have already chosen software for several releases in the design of a prior program release.

Much has been written about the process of selecting application software, and we will not add much to that here. Certainly, the selection process has to be driven by a brief definition of functional requirements. In addition, other concerns such as ease of interfacing with your existing systems, fit with the information technology architecture, vendor financial stability, completeness of offering relative to all potential needs, ability to support implementation, and license price are valid issues with planning tools, as they are with any business application software selection. It is probably not worth the time to generate extremely long lists of functional requirements (more than a couple of pages) because your choice should be driven not by how many "yes we do that" checkmarks a given provider gets, but by how well its software will support the key four or five functions you must perform. We will discuss this further in Chapter 8.

Note that we are supporting here a very traditional "user defines the needs" kind of selection process, rather than an "Okay supplier, you tell us what we need to do and then propose on that." Remember that we spent some time talking to potential suppliers in Phase B, we understand the concepts they are promoting, and we have decided for ourselves what we most value in planning tools.

There are variations to consider in software selection. You may be able to have access to the software in an application service provider (ASP) mode, in which either the supplier or a third party offers use of the software. Because planning tools are ideally accessed from many sites and by both full-time and casual users, they are excellent web-based applications. They are thus particularly amenable to delivery through the ASP approach, although few organizations have in fact adopted this model thus far.

2. Build, Beginning with a Nonlive Pilot

There is probably a lot of work to build the new planning structure. There are data to assemble and test, probably some systems to interface in order to get regular automated access to that data, and planning models to design and configure. Much of this work should be performed in some type of nonlive pilot, known generically as a conference room pilot. At CSC Consulting, where this concept was refined and used heavily, we called them Solution Demonstration Laboratories[SM]. The primary purpose of a laboratory pilot is to test the processes you have designed and test the ability of new software to help execute those processes. Without exception, you will find that processes need to be modified, both because they simply will not work in their originally conceptualized form and because they are not compatible with the software.

The second purpose of the "laboratory" is to learn what any new packaged software you want to use actually does. Planning software is complex and subtle, and the chances are zero that you will be able to understand adequately what it does from the software provider's descriptions, demonstrations (even heavily scripted demonstrations based on your data), and documentation. You have to get your fingers dirty with the software at some point — to put data into it yourself, to build models with it yourself — and that point is now. It is also important to perform this pilot prior to a payment of a large license fee or final commitment to pay that license fee. While the purpose of the pilot is not to break the software, it may prove, for any of several reasons, to be unsuitable for your use and you may need to be able to escape. It is perfectly legitimate to pay a vendor's costs of participating in the pilot and even nominal license fees. But you probably do not want to work with a provider that insists on a large license fee prior to your trying to use the software. Doing that represents blind faith on a large scale. A planning improvement program can recover from having to switch to another vendor if the investment in the initial vendor has been kept modest.

For collaborative planning, it is very appropriate to get staff from suppliers and customers involved in the laboratory. They will provide key insights on the workability of new processes and systems. Assuming that the new planning processes are reasonably well conceived, these supplier and customer representatives will become close colleagues and as committed to making the new program work as your own enterprise is.

Typically, the laboratory will begin with training on new software, perhaps training on existing systems for staff unfamiliar with them and completion of any remaining process design. It then moves on to it, and loading of data necessary to execute the pilot and actual daily simulated execution of planning processes. The core team needs to be assigned to the laboratory on a full-time basis. This usually will lead to a staff crunch to get all the live "real" work done in their absence from their regular jobs, but that is a price that has to be paid. The real work often gets done with the supplemental help of temporary staff or experienced staff or managers who you can "draft" in between other job assignments.

There are a couple of exceptions to the need for the conference room pilot. If there is considerable hands-on experience using new software among the project team in environments very similar to the current situation, it may be an acceptable risk to go forward to deployment without a conference room pilot: You have staff who feel they understand the software almost perfectly, and you and your management trust them to project carefully from their previous experience into your new situation. The other exception is where there is a perfect opportunity to do a live pilot of the software at little risk, perhaps in a small business unit or with just a portion of the product line or a fraction of operating locations. Our experience is that good situations for low-risk, early live pilots are rare. Not only do they raise tougher issues about when license fees will be paid, but they generally involve more people, create more expectations, and are harder to suddenly stop for, say, three weeks while you make changes in the software. You may want to consider a live pilot after the conference room pilot and before formal rollout. If you have significant concerns with the software, and tolerant management that is comfortable with the team dinking around with new software for many months, moving from a conference room pilot to a live pilot will give you a deep test of the new software and process and help set you up for a confident large-scale rollout.

3. Deploy

There were likely some difficult interfaces with other systems that got deferred during the pilot process; they must be created now. Depending on the nature of the new release, it may be possible to perform parallel operations for several weeks, or even a few months, while live planning is still being performed with old systems. Just like staffing a conference room pilot, performing parallel planning creates quite a strain on staff time, but is well worth it. The objective here is to simulate live operations closely, while fixing the problems that are exposed. Typically more process issues are exposed here, as well as data problems that had not surfaced previously. Integrated planning typically forces the reconciliation of data from disparate systems, which have often not been used together before. This reconciliation can be as profound as discovering that "available inventory" means substantially different things in different systems to slight differences in coding for unusual business conditions. If you did not discover these problems in the laboratory environment, you must fix them now before going live and stumbling badly. This is also the period in which to provide basic training to additional users of the new processes and software.

Again, a live pilot may be a good alternative to parallel use of the new processes and tools. While it will probably require more elapsed time than parallel use of the software and tools would, it will provide a deeper test and provides lead staffing (the staff who were already responsible for planning with the old processes) the best training possible on new processes.

If processes, systems, and data have been worked out in the laboratory environment and honed in parallel operation, the cutover to live use is usually not overly traumatic. Unlike an ERP or other execution system with thousands of transactions per hour, planning processes mostly do not occur in real time, and adjustment to them can occur over a period of weeks. And typically there are tens of full-time users involved, rather than the hundreds or thousands in many ERP implementations. This is not to say, however, that your initial planning with new processes will be "good planning." There will be a flurry of changes and fixes necessary to overcome the initial problems with the plans, unless you have done an unusually good job with the previous steps.

In general, you will want to begin using a new planning approach on a subset of your operations and then roll it out to the appropriate full domain. That initial subset may be one product group in one plant, one product group for all distribution centers, all products at one plant, one supplier, two customers, or whatever is appropriate.

Software tools for planning are inherently, unavoidably complex and require deep and expensive training of users. Even training someone to use a planning spreadsheet created by someone else involves teaching the new user the assumptions and logic built into that spreadsheet — let alone the complexities of a full-blown advanced planning tool. The majority of training, and perhaps the majority of model building depending on the type of planning, will occur as part of the rollout. You will need to make decisions about how much conceptual training to perform up front, how much users should participate in initial model building, and how much training should occur when software is implemented enough that live models of planners' own products are available to play with in the software. In a distributed environment, you will need to make decisions about whether to perform initial training in a centralized classroom environment or whether to do all training "*in situ*" where planners or plan users work. Later rounds of training, often including helping them to evolve their planning models, must be done where they work.

One of the most elaborate and effective training programs we have been involved with was for advanced master production scheduling software to be used on site at all of a consumer packaged goods (CPG) enterprise's plants. It consisted of initial user training through bringing planners into a central training facility (about three to four plants at a time), teaching them the basics, and working with them on planning model design and construction. Meanwhile, two dedicated information technology staff set up downloads to those plants for the data supplied by other systems. After initial training, the users were sent back to their work plants to finish building their models and to begin experimenting with them on their own (so that they could truly internalize the challenge). The next step was a follow-up visit to each plant within two weeks by the original trainers to help fix the user-built models and really get the planners generating plans using the software.

Often it is also appropriate to perform advanced training of users a few months after they initially go live, in order to check their use of the process/ system, proactively solve problems they are still having, and teach them features or modes of use that would have just been confusing in the initial training. This type of advanced training was performed in the case of the multiplant CPG example above.

Needless to say, major releases for multiple operating locations typically require several months to deploy. In some cases, one release will still not be fully deployed while the next release is being refined in the laboratory.

Deployment of new planning processes and systems can sometimes benefit from formal change management support, that is, professionals who are trained to understand user concerns, develop approaches to alleviate those concerns, develop educational materials, and in general help with the more human side of the implementation process. In our experience, the use of project budget for that type of activity is usually controversial.

It is also our experience that a significant fraction of resistance to change is not simply foot-dragging by people who are set in their ways and resistant to new processes or systems. It is often legitimate objections by staff — who understand all of the complexities in making plans really work — to new processes and systems that are half-baked, poorly designed, hard to use, and may represent a step backwards in planning capability, breadth of view, or planning cycle time (e.g., the big new system is also slow and cumbersome). There is simply no substitute for designing new processes and systems that are "fully baked," have had the tough issues already figured out with the most expert "doers," are genuinely easy to use, are powerful, provide planners with a good view of the comprehensive problem, and are fast. That kind of design and development is hard work and may take much longer than you would like. But if you can achieve it, you will find that implementation goes much more easily, that planners are surprisingly excited about the new process and system, and that change management per se is really not much of a challenge.

Some of the nicest words we have ever heard were from a sixty-year-old career production scheduler/manager who had little experience with computers.

Attending an advanced training session about four months after rolling out a new scheduling tool, he commented one morning: "Hearing that we were getting a new optimization tool, I figured that it was gonna be a pain in the butt. But, you know, this thing just works! I'm amazed how easy using it turned out to be."

E. Operate and Evolve

Operation of a novel planning approach is the ultimate test of the work done in the prior phases and where most of the person-hours will ultimately be spent.

1. Review of Effectiveness and Measurement Against Goals

Improved planning approaches get measured in two ways. First, there should be careful assembly of quantitative data, showing how operations perform in regard to the KPIs that planning should affect. In Phases A and C, we developed general program improvement targets and then more specific targets for each release. If we have been collecting operating effectiveness data since at least the beginning of our program (and at best assembling KPI data from before our program began), we should be able to see the effect of better planning on changes in those KPIs over several months. It usually takes at least six months for better processes and systems to become fully effective. The unfortunate reality is that many enterprises do not measure the effectiveness of new planning approaches, just as they do not measure other new initiatives, and never know quantitatively how they have done. And of course, it is generally impossible to get a perfectly clear measurement of the impact of just planning, because many other business changes (level of sales, types of promotions, new products, product proliferation) will be impacting the same KPIs as planning at the same time.

Second, there will be a subjective reaction to the new approach on the part of its users and on the part of the people who are on the "receiving end" of planning decisions. Do they like using the new process and systems? Do they feel they are producing better plans? Do people executing operations based on the plans feel they are good plans? You and your management will hear compliments if people like it; you will hear silence or guarded criticism if they do not, and you will see overt or stealth refusal to use it if they really dislike it. The reality is that this subjective evaluation will probably be the ultimate measure of success and longevity. People will continue to use a planning approach that they like, regardless of whether they can measure results, as long as there are no negative results or the planning process is not too costly (we have seen a planning system dropped largely because of the enormous mainframe computation charges it was incurring at the corporate data center).

2. Identification of Problems and Design of Solutions

If you undertake a planning improvement program of any size or complexity, chances are small that the design will be perfected by the time you deploy it. There are always subtleties that must be improved, parameters to tweak, new steps to fill in missing parts of the processes, and planning errors for which you need to try to prevent recurrence. As we have mentioned elsewhere, the planning problem is constantly changing because the business is constantly changing: customers, products, production resources, supply chain relationships, and so on. So planning must evolve for both those reasons, and a good manager is constantly working to identify and make those changes. Indeed, one could argue that perhaps a majority of improvements in planning should happen as a process of continuous improvement rather than in major redesign programs (i.e., that Figure 6.1 should be drawn a bit differently).

3. Identification of Critical Changes and Return to Strategic Design

Nevertheless, there will be business changes and perhaps conceptual revelations that require major changes in planning. Perhaps it is the acquisition of a new but related division, perhaps the discovery of new planning technology or intelligence about what a competitor is doing that wakes us up and says, "We are not planning as well as we could." The time will come again for a rethink of what we are doing, the time to go back to Phase A and begin the cycle over again.

IDENTIFYING WHEN TO RETHINK PLANNING PROCESSES AND SYSTEMS

As we have discussed, improving planning is a never-ending process, both because it is difficult to claim we perfected it and because it must constantly adapt to an evolving business. There are really two levels of work that need to go on: to rethink our planning structure and to evolve it. In this section, we will be a little more explicit about when to consider an overhaul.

Is This the Time?

To consider a new approach, we need to re-evaluate the appropriateness of the planning structure we or our predecessors have devised and implemented:

- Do we still believe it is the best for the business; have we learned enough since our earlier implementation that we now realize there is yet a substantially better way to do it?
- Have our business needs changed: a new division, new products, new customer types, new philosophy of management?
- Have our supply chain partners evolved to the point where key ones are now ready to collaborate with us in more intimate, trusting ways?
- Is new planning technology available that will let us solve a problem we have not really solved well before?
- Are new data available that can substantially improve what we do, for example, from new supply chain execution systems, a new logistics provider, or a new contract manufacturer?

We need to be ready to explicitly rethink our structure every two to three years and ready to initiate it at any time in response to events like a business purchase or divestiture, major change at a key customer, or release of relevant new software from our software providers.

What Steps Should We Take Regularly?

Will re-examining how we plan actually lead to major changes every two to three years? Of course not! Often changes in the business or planning technology will be minor, or needed changes will be significant, but management will recognize that there is no time or budget available to make process and system changes now, and work on them will need to be deferred until next year. But at least considering the possibility every few years means that we are open and ready to change and that we take the first steps:

- Identifying which changes *can* be made right now, for little investment of time and money, and making those changes. By doing this, we actively do the low-cost evolving that we can do; otherwise we risk becoming complacent and miss changes that are well within our power (and budget) to just implement.
- Developing a business case (or cost–benefit analysis, or whatever we choose to call it), whether formal or informal, that evaluates whether bigger changes may be justifiable.
- Putting money into next year's budget for significant process and system changes.

CAVEAT: WHEN YOU ARE NOT IN THE DRIVER'S SEAT

The perspective assumed by our methodology is that you are in a position to initiate a comprehensive rethinking of the enterprise's planning approach. Indeed, one of the primary tenets of this book is that product flow planning deserves just such a rethink periodically to make sure that it is synchronized with the current business and the direction in which that business is evolving and that a comprehensive review allows you create good structures that situation-specific fixes would overlook.

Nevertheless, planning-oriented managers are often not in a position to control the forces that are changing processes in an enterprise. Initiatives come from many sources; for example, a commitment by the enterprise to pursue a Six Sigma program may mean that your planning redesign work is now part of a larger initiative with many goals beyond better planning. A purchase of a company (now a significant new division of your company) that supplies certain components to your business but also sells directly to your customers will create a host of change initiatives, some of which are oriented toward product flow planning.

These kinds of initiatives should provoke new thinking about planning and changes in how you plan. You may well be in the middle of rolling out the second release in a comprehensive program when suddenly the enterprise's "world" changes. Since the "best way to plan" is very much a function of the business you are in, planning may need to change direction as well.

But if you have used some of the tools we have discussed here, you are in a stronger position than you might think. If you have a planning sphere diagram, you should be able to figure out the implications of inter- and intraenterprise changes rather easily. If you have constructed a backbone diagram of your planning structure and you know why you designed the approach that you did, you should be able to think about how it should perhaps change and be able to draw new variants or a whole new approach. If you have some well-drawn high- or mid-level process maps, you should be able to propose the right process changes.

The big investments in planning are in data collection, management, and perhaps planning software. Most business changes will not require wholesale abandonment of the work already done. If real-time inventory data were of sufficient value to invest in before, they are still probably of considerable value. If most of your planning tools are packaged software, they probably have enough flexibility to accommodate much of the "new" world through model and parameter changes. Of course, the planning structure may no longer be able to work as perfectly as you had hoped it someday would, in spite of the adaptation and evolution you sponsor. Be patient; your time to lead the charge, to try to get planning processes and systems truly "right" for the business, will come again.

PEOPLE, ORGANIZATION, AND CHANGE

Planning organization is not a topic that is discussed very often. The process orientation we usually have today, which by definition is cross-functional, tends to de-emphasize it. The small number of people typically involved full time in planning, compared with the armies who execute business operations and use transaction systems, means that managing the number of staff involved is not a big challenge. And good planners are smart people who can quickly understand the dynamics of the enterprise and its supply net fairly easily and will largely manage themselves. Can we not just find a good senior planner, make him or her the planning manager, and move on? It is a little tougher than that. There are usually challenging issues around how well goals are aligned in the enterprise, what functional organizations planners should report to, and where they sit physically.

Goal Alignment

Organizations that take the time to review goals often discover that there are major unresolved issues, areas of controversy, or at least optimization gaps. What level of customer service are we providing (or trying to provide)? Are we seriously trying to be a low-cost provider relative to our direct competitors? Obviously, in any real organization a certain amount of controversy and uncertainty has to be tolerable at this level.

But in most businesses, a little of the controversy stems from these relatively esoteric issues, which do not tend to come up that much in daily operations. Instead, problems are caused by the somewhat different goals that different functional organizations have. We are often fragmented by our incentive systems: sales needs to hit targets to get incentive pay, manufacturing needs to cut costs, logistics needs to reduce inventories. Twenty years ago, many of us thought that the suboptimization issues created by departmental budgeting and incentive structures could be easily broken down. But in most organizations, they have proven quite resistant to change, apparently because the functional silos are fundamental to how organizations are managed. Managers want to use incentives that subordinates can control individually, and that means narrow incentives that tend to put functional groups in conflict with each other.

A few years ago, we asked a senior manufacturing manager if he could list his top five priorities in descending order. The response was:

1. Plant operator safety
2. Product quality
3. Production cost
4. Production cost
5. Production cost

That production manager faced the typical situation of being measured by his management primarily on cost. His response was certainly understandable and not unusual, but not very comforting for professionals who think in terms of supply chains, customer orientation, and total cost of operations rather just manufacturing cost. Manufacturing plants are, after all, at the center of most supply chains. If they are run with a strictly internal orientation, they create substantial additional costs both above and below them.

Fifteen years ago, we worked with a CPG organization in which the difference in perspective between the brand management "business" organization and the operations organization had become so great that they had "solved" the problem by building a wall between the two. Brand management (with some field sales input) would update the sales forecast monthly and toss it over the wall to operations. Operations would make and deploy inventory to that forecast — and its service effectiveness was measured against the forecast, not against actual customer orders! Operations had, from a performance metrics perspective, completely divorced itself from the customer, as well as eliminated the need to talk to marketing and sales management. It had also put a lot of pressure on marketing to forecast well. This approach was, by the way, not very effective, and the company has since been sold.

The perspective we take here is not that we, as planning redesigners, must align goals to be shared across the organization, although that remains a very worthy objective, but that we must recognize the degree to which the enterprise is ready to function as one organization. We have worked with businesses in which sales, logistics, and manufacturing goals were essentially aligned — they were on the same track already. If the organization shares a vision of where it is trying to go, and if the various functional groups understand the differences in their respective quantitative incentives and are still willing to work for the good of the enterprise as a whole, planning processes can be set up to be very comprehensive and very "globally optimal." Planning processes can reflect this collegial culture and be organized most effectively for the dynamics of the business. A Sales & Operations Planning (S&OP) process can be made to work much more easily in this environment as well.

If that is not the case, if the organization is locked in narrower silos, then planning processes must recognize that culture and broker differences among separate planning groups that have different goals.

John Bermudez[64] offers the example of profitable orders. Planning technology is now capable of determining the extent to which a given customer order, at a given sales price, is profitable to the business. If sales works hard to sell a big order and has to make substantial concessions on price to succeed, is there anyone in the organization prepared to tell the vice president of sales that the order will lose the organization money and cannot be accepted? Clearly, the organization that wants to optimize profitability in this way has to have not only systems and processes in place to make this work, but management structures and norms that support it as well.

What Organization Planners Report To

Part of the design of successful planning approaches is deciding not only what plans are required, what their scope should be, and how they should interact, but who should (re)generate them, who should review them, and who is ultimately responsible for what types of decisions. Do you need an enterprise planning group with responsibility across, say, customer service, manufacturing, and distribution?

Our experience has been that overcentralization of planning is not the solution. The goal is to place planning responsibilities at various places in the organization where they have the right balance of in-depth knowledge of that part of the business and an understanding of how their part needs to best interact with the enterprise and the supply network as a whole. Good planning is typically done by a confederation of very good planners who may be quite remote from each other in the formal organization, but work together well. Of course, detailed manufacturing planning needs to be in production; of course, logistics needs to perform transportation and warehouse planning; of course, the "business unit" organization needs to plan sales quantities and hence drive procurement, manufacturing, and distribution needs.

You may, in fact, need a central planning organization if you want to use planning processes and systems to manage flow from a global perspective. The most comprehensive planning approaches will support simultaneous optimization of what is sold, what is bought, what is manufactured, and what is distributed. And no traditional function within an enterprise has that broad of a perspective or responsibility. One option worth considering is having an "integrated planning group" report to a traditional function, e.g., manufacturing. We have seen surprisingly broad perspectives adopted by functional managers held accountable for "making the whole supply chain work." And they are much more likely to actually implement the plans produced by such a group if they consider them one of their own, rather than an independent, unrealistic, planning group reporting to a new vice president of planning. Of course, regardless of where planners report, if they attempt to do comprehensive planning, they will be successful only if there is a reasonable amount of understanding from top management and solid support for planning that crosses functional organizational boundaries.

Enough Horsepower in Planning

When an organization decides to upgrade its planning approach substantially, perhaps including new advanced software to support the process, a question should be raised: Do we have a powerful enough planning staff to effectively execute the new processes and take advantage of the new software? For example, in the second case discussed in Chapter 7, a new planning group is a significant part of the solution.

We have yet to work on a planning redesign effort where planning staff was reduced in number. We may live to see that or not, but the reality is that good planning does take planner time, and adding software tools has, without exception in our experience, delivered benefits through better plans and decisions, not through cost reduction of the planning staff.

New processes and software also raise the question of whether the existing planning staff members have the right capabilities for the future. Our experience is that in many situations they do, but in some situations there is clear value from adding an additional planner or two with more mathematical modeling experience (and sometimes this is the planning manager). There is also the rare situation where a planner really does not want to be part of a new planning process, in which case he or she probably should not remain in planning.

Optimizing Where Planners Sit Physically

Many organizations today operate in a "virtual" environment with manufacturing and logistics spread around the world. That is a fact of modern business, and we have a wealth of communication technologies to help make that work, including planning systems themselves (see "Architecture of Planning Data and Systems" in Chapter 8). But face-to-face human communication is still the most powerful and most likely to lead to trust and enthusiastic execution of plans. Hence, where planners sit is a critical issue.

For example, we have seen a situation where the master production schedulers were located at headquarters just outside where the customer service manager sat (and near all the customer service reps). This technique worked extremely well in terms of keeping the production process customer oriented, even though the master schedulers reported to logistics and were not near customer service organizationally. We have also seen a "central" planning group that had global responsibility for tactical planning of all production, physical distribution, finished goods inventory, and primary materials inventory sit at the enterprise's largest plant, not fifty meters from actual floor operations. This seemed to help the planners keep a very real-world perspective and "gut feel" for operational problems.

Careful thinking about where planners live physically is a must. Some kinds of valuable planning staff may not be willing to live in some plant locations, or plants may be located remotely (e.g., interior China) and not really appropriate for broader supply chain management activities. But most organizations should think about creative planner location as discussed just above.

While we present above the vision of good planning being performed by a confederation of separate planning teams, physical consolidation of planning has considerable value. We worked recently with a large high-tech firm that is perhaps fifteen years into the (realistically thirty-year long) process of consolidating very entrepreneurial operating units, beginning with shared logistics operations. Three global business units sharing two major distribution centers in the U.S. were having operations planned by five separate planning groups: some at the business unit global headquarters (all of which were in different places), some at other office locations that had responsibility for managing distribution, and none within one hundred miles of either distribution center. Needless to say, this approach to planning wasted enormous amounts of energy on communications, at the cost of having less time to plan. Most planners kept headsets plugged into their phones and spent a large fraction of their time in conference calls with each other.

Planning by Planners; Planning Done by Line Managers

In many environments, such as planning the operations of a complex plant or planning product flow through an entire enterprise, it is obvious that the operations challenges are sufficiently complex that dedicated planning staff is necessary. But operating line managers may not accept the plans that come from planning staff. The obvious solution is to institute a regular process of reviewing plans with managers and incorporating their feedback. The S&OP process, as discussed in Chapter 2, is an excellent example of this cycle. But not every planning process deserves the amount of time that is required to "turn the S&OP crank," and simpler approaches can also work. We have seen plant production management meetings held daily at 7:45 a.m. that included a three- to five-minute review of significant changes in plans, and sometimes led to a five- to ten-minute discussion of implications and modifications to the plan. This process successfully served to get the whole production management team on board.

There is an interesting trade-off inherent in planning. On the one hand, plans are only useful if they are implemented, if the decisions they imply are made and acted on. The easiest way to ensure that is to have the primary manager responsible for implementing those plans be his or her own planner — the plan is automatically "internalized" and likely to be perfectly executed, including appropriate adjustments along the way based on new information. The manager may not have time (or perhaps the skills) to be a good planner, but certainly one objective of planning support software should be to make planning so easy that it takes relatively little time. However, there is a more fundamental issue with having each manager do his or her own planning: We are back to the problem with competing plans discussed in Chapter 3, to plans that do not serve their coordinating role very well because they are not jointly owned by all the managers responsible for executing decisions made from them. Figure 6.7 diagrams this challenge and shows some alternatives.

Planner-driven planning + S&OP-like management review and modification

Pro:
- Opportunity for managers to understand and contribute to upgrading plans
- Benefits of shared, neutral plans, professional planning

Con:
- Very, very time-consuming planning process
- May still not get complete buy-in and dedicated execution by individual managers

Dedicated planning group(s)

Pro:
- Professional planning skills
- Neutral party in a sea of competing parochial interests

Con:
- Unless planners are very good, no one will implement the plan
- Creates extra players in process who must be paid for, communicated with, and in general cost time and expense

Manager plans his or her own operations

Pro:
- Automatically Internalized and enthusiastically executed
- Avoids costs of dedicated planners and undue complexity

Con:
- May not have the time or skills to plan well
- Easy to generate dueling plans among managers

Figure 6.7 Responsibility for planning.

Culture

Michael Schrage[65] tells the true story of a Fortune 250 company that built a superb information system that included letting executives see performance data essentially real time, in fact at the same time as the first-line managers saw it. Executives were quick to communicate to operating managers "demanding explanation and clarifications." Line managers began to game the system by delaying data entry and, in a few cases, even falsifying data.

This is a nice example of what happens when an organization does not have a truly healthy, professional business culture. Good executives do not micromanage their middle managers; they have more important things to do with their time. But, realistically, we have little ability to change management culture as part of a planning approach redesign program.

The bottom line is that we, as planning approach designers, must be aware of the culture of the enterprise. We must design planning approaches that will be effective in the corporate culture we are part of. While we can push it some distance in what we believe is the right direction, ultimately we are responsible for creating something that will work in the world that exists. Planning, like politics, is "the art of the possible."

OUTSOURCING OF PLANNING

Outsourcing of business processes has been with us for many decades, doing things like, for example, the now traditional outsourcing of payroll functions. But it first achieved widespread supply chain success in the 1980s with the use of third-party logistics providers (3PLs) to perform specific sets of logistics functions for the enterprise. By the 1990s, there were also numerous examples of large-scale contracts for the outsourcing of complete information technology functions, often with hundreds or thousands of employees being transferred to the outsourcing firm. As the 1990s progressed, more companies outsourced manufacturing, human resource functions, claims processing, customer service centers, and so on, all under the banner of these not being "core competencies" of the enterprise (or just cheaper labor in China or India).

With business process outsourcing (BPO) even more heavily promoted in the late 1990s, product flow planners have been wondering if flow planning was a good candidate for outsourcing, i.e., for having some outside agency do it for the enterprise, rather than the enterprise do it for itself. Few enterprises would claim that product flow planning is a core competency of theirs, either because it is something they really do well or because it is a competitive differentiator for them (although we argue in this volume that product flow planning is important enough and difficult enough to do well that it in fact can be a competitive differentiator).

So why not outsource it? Anecdotal evidence seems to indicate that most enterprises are willing to outsource processes that are labor intense, difficult to manage, and not central to the business. Indeed, outsourced planning has been available. Long's Drugs, for example, outsourced store pharmaceutical inventory replenishment decisions to NonStop Solutions (now Evant) during the 1990s. Outsourced systems logic managed inventory in retail stores, a very important and difficult challenge given the amount of inventory tied up in stores and the vast number of stockkeeping unit location combinations that retail represents. 3PLs often perform much of the transportation planning, certainly load building and assignment of carriers to loads, as part of their logistics responsibilities. And, of course, most contract manufacturers have responsibility for detailed scheduling of their production, so that kind of planning is naturally outsourced as part of the contract manufacturing relationship.

Most planning tools are now architected with web browser user interfaces and in some cases are now available as web services (see Chapter 8) as well. These system advances mean that accessing planning information from outside an organization and inserting plans into enterprise systems are now technically relatively easy, if organizations wants to communicate that information. But do they?

It seems that far more enterprises are prepared to outsource transportation management and warehousing, or manufacturing detailed scheduling, than are prepared to outsource the core product flow planning functions. Beginning with forecasting sales, and continuing through deciding how much inventory to carry, how much product to produce, how much product to order from contract manufacturers, and how much material to buy, most enterprises seem to hold on to product flow planning decisions rather determinedly. An enterprise may believe that its core competencies are in engineering or marketing, but virtually all businesses that we have worked with retain responsibility for major product flow decisions. For example, a common situation today for a distribution center operated by a 3PL is for the client enterprise to retain complete authority over replenishment of inventory and delegate to the 3PL the responsibility for the warehouse staff and filling and shipping customer orders.

Enterprises tend to want to keep in-house responsibility for planning processes that they consider core: accepting orders, allocating inventory (or capacity) to customers, planning seasonal inventory investment, planning and scheduling production in their own plants. There are few enough staff involved in planning that pay differentials between enterprise employees and BPO personnel should not matter much. It is probably more important to retain continuity in the planning group and to be sure of the loyalties of the staff performing the work by keeping them completely inside the enterprise. And of course, those insource versus outsource decisions have significant impact on how the total planning process will work, which functions will be performed using systems from the BPO provider, and how those systems will interact with planning (and operating) systems run by the client enterprise.

Consider an example. For a new product introduction in an outsourced manufacturing environment (say in the high-tech industry), would it be reasonable for the contract manufacturer to take on responsibility for deciding on the initial production run? In most cases the original equipment manufacturer, which is responsible for engineering, marketing, and sales, will also want to take on responsibility for production quantities, at least until there is a steady demand stream to react to. Even if it outsources the initial quantity decision to some type of planning specialist, it needs to maintain at least a skeleton planning organization to tie the processes and decisions together.

As execution-oriented processes continue to be outsourced (to be BPO-ed), we believe that low-level planning processes will continue to shift with them, consistent with the idea of keeping responsibility for planning near responsibility for execution. We will also see more situations where a planning technology so specific is required to optimize a difficult planning problem, like the NonStop services to which Long's subscribed, that the decision is made to employ an outside specialist and his or her powerful technology. But on balance, we expect to see organizations that have product flow to manage continue to want to make core decisions themselves.

What to keep in house and what to outsource along with execution processes (like manufacturing or warehousing) is an important aspect of how planning structures get defined for an enterprise. They are far too important to be left just to managers who structure outsourcing deals. Planning managers need to stay involved with these decisions throughout the BPO management process and to be very conscious of opportunities for changing the responsibility for certain types of planning when they go through the comprehensive rethink of planning discussed earlier in this chapter.

CONCLUSIONS ON METHODOLOGY

Good planning does not require a huge investment and thus should not require unusually elaborate business cases to support it. While the thinking about how to best plan product flow needs to be global, investments need to be modular, incremental, and justified because we know enough about how we want to plan that we know we need a particular process and systems capability to support it.

While the value of good planning is obvious, justification of investment is sometimes difficult because it is hard to connect planning to performance accountability. Usually there is no one-to-one relationship between a specific type of plan and a specific set of business problems. For example, inventory deployment planning is not inherently "more important" to customer service than the master production schedule. You have to do it all pretty well to deliver good customer service at a reasonable cost. The root cause analysis mentioned in Phase A above is not usually easy on a large scale. On the other hand, if an organization wishes to trace causality of specific problems, the customer order that was not delivered on time, the shift of overtime in a department that you really wish you had not needed, or a significant inventory overhang in a specific stockkeeping unit, that kind of tracing is pretty easy to do and often instructive as to where the planning process, the execution process, data accuracy, or the management policies underlying it all have broken down and need to be corrected.

As we stated at the beginning of this chapter, there is nothing magic about the methodology described here. It is a common sense vehicle for implementing a lot of the principles we have discussed previously and other principles pioneered elsewhere, such as the multiple-release approach for implementation of new processes and systems.

7

CASES IN PLANNING STRUCTURE TRANSFORMATION: SUCCESSES AND PARTIAL SUCCESSES

> *Joining the revolution is a fool's game.*
> *The real path to business success is evolution.*
>
> Jeff Adams[66]

This chapter presents four brief case histories in implementing new planning approaches. They cover a considerable range of industries, business challenges, and project methodologies. Some of the cases report on programs that were great successes; others were not. The standard of practice ranges from adequate to excellent, and we certainly discuss here the lessons learned as part of these cases. They are presented in chronological order, from near-ancient to contemporary. The cases report on:

- A custom production planning and master scheduling system for a tire manufacturer
- A tightly integrated planning package implemented at a soft drink bottler

- A comprehensive planning approach for a paper producer
- A short-range logistics planning/operating system

PRODUCTION PLANNING AND MASTER SCHEDULING OF TIRE MANUFACTURING

Manufacturers of automobile tires have long been aware of the complex problem they face in planning the manufacture and physical distribution of their product and how much value there is in planning approaches that deal with multiple factors simultaneously. They must balance their original equipment manufacturer manufacturing for the automobile companies (which is basically a no-profit business that requires 100 percent service, lest an auto assembly plant be shut down) with their aftermarket production where they can make some profit. They must maintain inventory of product in the field for quick replenishment of dealers' stocks, since a dealer without their product on hand in the right size, right now, will simply sell another brand of tire to the customer. They must build product very efficiently in a multistep manufacturing process where work-in-process inventory physically deteriorates, where production of similar products needs to be grouped together to avoid costly and quality-threatening changeovers, and where there are typically tight capacity constraints at both the tire-building stage and at curing. Curing is performed with a limited number of molds for each finished goods stockkeeping unit (SKU), and hence it is often desirable to simultaneously cure multiple SKUs that share the same "green tire" (the assembled but uncured tire — they are not actually green). Production quality is critical, both for competitive and for automotive safety reasons, and quite difficult to control. Aftermarket tires sales are both highly seasonal and promoted heavily, creating substantial peaks and valleys in demand that are only partially predictable. Overall, the tire supply chain is quite a challenging problem to plan.

Many decades ago, tire manufacturers recognized that trying to decouple this problem with conventional order point or material requirements planning (MRP) logic left a lot of money on the table. Hence there have been numerous attempts to implement fully scheduled solutions in the tire industry. Lasdon and Terjung[21] published an early paper on an integrated solution to much of this problem at Kelly-Springfield, and later work at Kelly (see King and Love[22]) won the prestigious Edelman award for best application of operations research that year.

In this case, we will discuss five years of work in the 1980s at another tire manufacturer. While this is an old case, and atypical of modern planning improvement projects in that it involves custom software development, it nicely illustrates a number of principles.

Project Motivation

In the early 1980s, this smaller North American manufacturer was acutely aware that it was not doing a good job of meeting the complex set of criteria outlined above. Its finished goods field inventories were bloated while customer order fill was only in the low 90 percent range. Its production schedules were far from optimal, with frequent breaks into planned sequences to try to meet immediate customer needs. The tire manufacturer had been doing manual production planning only. As part of a large body of work with an outside consulting firm and software developer, it decided to fund a new tool to help it plan monthly production.

Solution Methodology and Planning Approach

Working with the custom developers, a somewhat unique production planning tool was designed. It would figure out how much of each product to make each month for the next twelve to seventeen months (seventeen months at the point each year where planners needed to look out through all of the next budget year for planning purposes) considering current inventories, forecasted sales, grouping production by "green" tire, realistic minimum production quantities, tire-building capacity, and staying within the capacity of the molds available for each SKU. It would be a small, stand-alone, interactive system, running on a remote time-shared mainframe computer — and using manually maintained data (except for current inventory and sales forecasts that were electronically transmitted to the remote system).

The solver that would suggest production plans was composed of a network linear program optimizer, plus a heuristic that interacted with the linear program and caused it to reoptimize several times to achieve each finished solution. Since different kinds of tires were both assembled and cured in different departments, the problem could be decoupled and solved one department at a time. Note that the problems being solved here were a bit different than classic production planning: While they dealt with monthly buckets of production, they were modeled at the SKU level in order to comprehend curing capacity constraints, which dramatically affected how much of each SKU could be produced each month. Some long lead time materials were being ordered from this production plan.

The little custom system was a raging success. After using it for a year, headquarters production/inventory planners cut finished good inventory 31 percent while slightly increasing customer order fill rates. Performing the required manual data maintenance was a nuisance for planners, but actual planning was quick and easy. Solver runs would take ten to forty-five seconds depending on the size of the department, most of them thirty to one hundred SKUs, and manual editing (and quick resolves around the edits) was easy.

Given the success of this small planning tool and the obvious limitations of dealing with monthly buckets of demand, the manufacturer and its consultants were eager to take on the more ambitious problem of weekly master scheduling. They had been relying on a manually generated master schedule that was then entered into their MRP II software. They designed a new system that performed both monthly production planning and master scheduling of production with week-sized time buckets. This system would run on the company's small mainframe computer and use complex heuristics for all logic rather than the network linear program.

The master schedule would go well beyond classic MRP master scheduling in that it would build near-optimal sequences of green tires on the tire-building machines to minimize changeover problems, while simultaneously observing constraints on molds and curing press capacities. Furthermore, it would support a very specific allocation of responsibilities between headquarters planners and plant schedulers. Revised master schedules would be initiated each week at headquarters and immediately (usually the same day) reviewed by plant planners (on the same planning system screens) to approve or quickly propose changes back to the central planners. Thus, collaborative scheduling between headquarters and the plants was a fundamental part of the design, with central planners initiating the schedules, but plant schedulers having final approval.

Results and Lessons Learned

The second, much more complex planning system had a considerably more challenging implementation process. Initial testing indicated four or five areas where the system design was not quite what the business needed. For example, it had been designed for too few weeks in the "frozen" period of the master scheduling cycle, and the plants and planners wanted more protection via a longer time fence. The system had cost the better part of a million dollars to build, and the manufacturer was eager to get it up and running (and end the invoices from the external consultants/developers). The developers, who had invested considerable off-the-books time in the initial development, were not enthusiastic about supporting additional evolution of the software at their expense. Thus, there was huge budget pressure to perform quick, sometimes inadequate fixes to the software to get it operational and the project completed. The most significant problems were fixed, the small ones were not, and no one was very happy. The system was used, grudgingly, for a few years, and finally dropped.

There were some important lessons learned over the course of this program:

- Higher level, more aggregate planning problems are much more amenable to computer support: Production planning required less data maintenance than master scheduling, the models were much simpler, and users found the solver outputs easier to understand. While this case did not attempt to get down to the level of scheduling individual pieces of equipment (although it did get to the level of sequencing on each tire-building machine), many other applications of detailed scheduling software have shown just how challenging it is to maintain automated scheduling tools at the most detailed level.

- A mathematical optimization, linear program solution could work well for nonmathematical users if it was well designed, so that the users only had to worry about the business problem, not "infeasibilities" and other artifacts of mathematical optimization. Users loved a system that came back with good answers in less than a minute and into which they could plug their own ideas and have the system resolve around them in several seconds.

- An extremely complex heuristic is a difficult animal to deal with, both for users and systems developers/maintainers. It is often difficult to truly understand (and hence fully accept) its proposed solutions, and tweaking it to provide improved results is an arduous process because of the hard-to-predict interactions among the different parts of the logic. With sufficient development time, however, complex heuristics can be quite effective, as they can quickly generate good solutions to tough problems.

- Custom planning projects with tight budget limitations from the beginning are perhaps not worth attempting. In this case, no one felt good about spending the money to really finish developing the tool. In more recent situations where organizations have spent big sums on license fees for packaged software, they often fail to appreciate the need to spend even larger sums on user training, "tuning" how the software models their environment, and perhaps enhancements to the software. This is a common source of project failure today, and the best solution is a realization that the road to better planning is a long one, and you had better start down it with enough "fuel" in your tank to command the right resources for long enough to achieve success. It may take several more miles than you expect.

- While its planning logic left something to be desired, the system functioned very effectively as a specialized communications vehicle between the plants and headquarters, supporting a kind of collaborative planning process.

ADVANCED TECHNIQUES IN A RAPID-CYCLE PRODUCTION/DISTRIBUTION OPERATION

Project Motivation

A regional soft drink bottler with three bottling plants and seven depots had had a change of operations management and realized that it had a serious service problem in supporting its (retailer) customers and end consumers (soft drink guzzlers). Business volume and SKUs had grown to the point where the bottler was heavily utilizing its plants and distribution centers, but providing only about 96 percent case fill of the orders it received. This was far below acceptable norms in the food and beverage industry. The company was losing sales and upsetting customers and needed to do something about it quickly. It was performing essentially no integrated planning of the plants and depots and realized that it could probably solve much of its problem through better planning. It decided that there would be two components to better planning:

1. Establishing a small central planning group responsible for both master scheduling the plants and determining daily deployment of product to the distribution centers
2. Implementing some new software tools to support the central planning group

Planning short- to intermediate-term operations of a soft drink bottler is complex because operations are integrated and intense. Higher volume products are produced in multiple plants; low-volume products in only one. Best manufacturing efficiencies are achieved by adhering to container size and flavor (light to dark) sequences that are typical of the food industry. This particular bottler had an unusually large number of items to produce, a few hundred, many of them licensed from other soft drink brands. And finally, an operationally excellent bottler provides high fill rates to customers with only six to seven days of total finished goods inventory — counting all plant, depot, and in-transit finished goods inventories! It can operate with these small inventories only because bottling production processes are quite reliable; it can generally (but not always) count on making the product it plans to make each day.

Solution Methodology and Planning Approach

The global soft drink company with which this bottler was affiliated had already identified a planning software package that used powerful optimization logic (both linear programming and heuristics), was tightly integrated, and was fairly suitable for bottling. It had also negotiated very attractive license terms for bottlers that wanted to employ the software (a few hundred thousand dollars in license fees per bottler). The software contained four relevant modules:

1. Integrated tactical planning of production and distribution to set production rates, change product production responsibilities among plants seasonally, and plan seasonal builds before holiday sales peaks.
2. Master production scheduling to figure out which products to make on each bottling line each day for the next several weeks. Unfortunately, this module was not designed to deal with continuous sequences of production stretching several days at a time, so it was not the perfect tool for bottling.
3. An optimization-based "distribution requirements planning"–like tool that would both project daily requirements for product from each depot and also optimally allocate and deploy available inventory on a daily basis to the depots based on understanding transportation costs from each plant, how badly each depot needed each product, how much of each product was available in inventory, and how much was being produced in each plant in each of the next few days.
4. A truckload-building module, designed to take the distribution center replenishment shipments planned for tomorrow and turn them into specific truckloads.

The bottler agreed to use the software selected by its "parent" and contracted with the software provider to implement it. Because the software was already tightly integrated and parametrically controlled (no coding required; we will discuss this issue more in Chapter 8), implementing the software would not require a large systems integration or development effort. However, because it required building a comprehensive new data model of operations, it required substantial up-front classroom training of its users and model construction.

The bottler assigned one experienced planner to lead the new central planning group and hired a couple of very young planners with plenty of "potential" to complete the staffing. They were installed in a conference room (the conference room at headquarters was the first casualty of the project) with three new big-screen personal computers appropriate for planning use. Plant-based planners would continue to do the detailed minute-by-minute scheduling of production.

Results and Lessons Learned

The planners were trained, built the data models with software provider support, and proceeded with parallel use of the software (with real decisions made continually) over about a sixty-day period. They then went live with the new system, and five months after project initiation had succeeded in raising case fill to over 99 percent while reducing finished goods inventories by 12 percent, material inventories by 36 percent, and manufacturing/distribution cost by 12 percent. Computer-assisted master scheduling was effective even with the software missing some of the desirable continuous production logic, and the new inventory deployment software and process worked great. A depot manager reported that: "Operations just feel different now. We start to get low on a product, and the next morning it is being unloaded from a truck here — like magic. I am spending more of my time on other operating issues, not worrying about having the right product." The bottler continued to use the planning software for several years, until it was replaced by a later-generation tool.

After establishing the planning group and getting the new planning processes into operation, management realized it still had coordination problems among plant management, the sales/marketing folks who were driving the promotion programs, and the operations folks who were supporting those promotions. The next step was to adopt a Sales & Operations Planning (S&OP) process, and so several months after the planning software was initially implemented, it also became the primary support tool for an S&OP process.

There were different lessons learned here than in our earlier case:

- Top and middle management were highly motivated to make something happen quickly in this situation, and they successfully did so. They put a planning staff in place very quickly. They changed the replenishment process and immediately changed plant and depot managers' norms for how operations would be controlled. They invested in very capable planners who were able to meet the high expectations placed on them.
- Having good software "waiting in the wings" because of activity by corporate-level staff was a blessing. Doing an independent software search in this situation would have added months to the process and might not have resulted in a good choice.

- Creating a new centralized planning process for what was in fact a tightly integrated business (but which had not previously been recognized as such) was perhaps the key management decision. Field management knew they were in enough trouble that they accepted some loss of individual control.

- The mostly optimization-based software was "black boxes" for the planners and for their management; they understood conceptually what the tools were doing, but did not understand the details. They were willing, however, to accept and implement the proposed solutions (with human oversight and edits, of course) that came out of the black boxes — because the planners were thoughtfully trained and the black boxes were good black boxes for this business.

A MODERN SOLUTION TO A CLASSIC PROBLEM IN PAPER

Project Motivation

A few years ago, a major paper producer realized that customers were receiving an unacceptable level of customer service because of its inability to deliver to promised delivery dates. Finished goods inventories were climbing as well. Better planning was identified as a key part of the solution. A vice president became the champion of a program to fix the problems, but the director of information technology for the particular operating division was also a strong supporter based on the improvements she had seen from better planning at another firm.

The old approach had suffered from a poor sales forecasting process, which was used to drive a classic paper industry "block scheduling" approach. Block scheduling is a technique common for paper production in which the paper company planners define a block of future production and planned sequence of papers that will be made in that block, and then customer service sells customers slices of that planned production. The technique is a kind of traditional "collaboration" between producer and customer, because it shares the pain between the customers' need for product when they need it and the producer's need to make product in a desirable sequence in order to kep production costs low and stay competitive in this commodity business. But in this case it was working poorly because salespeople were forcing the planners to abuse existing blocks. They were jamming too much production into them as customers discovered they needed more product; the most important customer was "the one on the phone right now." These violations of block discipline were delaying the cycles and making most orders for most customers late. These regular delays then resulted in some customers gaming the system by ordering early and then deferring delivery if the product actually became available on time — a good way to achieve chaos in a supply chain. Blocks were planned in a monthly cycle, with a block opened up for orders when it covered the production time from six to ten weeks into the future.

This particular business involved several paper mills, with considerable overlap among the mills in the products that could be produced, and about 600 customers. But individual customers would, in many cases, only take a product from one mill because of the slight differences (or perceived differences) in product characteristics between mills. About 40 percent of sales were to other converting divisions of the same manufacturer. Mills operated somewhat autonomously; they might, on their own initiative, add production for favored customers into their existing, already full production blocks or continue running a grade (if it was running particularly well) for orders in later blocks to improve production efficiencies.

Historical sales data to drive the forecasting process were fairly accurate, but this business suffered from two classic problems in the mechanics of sales forecasting:

1. It had not maintained discipline in its customer records, so every spelling error and every "Ave" versus "Avenue" in an address was a new customer or location.
2. It had no formal procedure for linking new SKUs to the sales history of the old SKUs they replaced.

In addition to the block schedule/operating plan, the company maintained a sales plan that was updated quarterly and disconnected from the operations plan and a budgeting/financial planning process that was equally disconnected from either.

Solution Methodology and Planning Approach

Managers agreed that something needed to be done and that modern planning software could help, so a software-oriented project was initiated, beginning with a packaged software provider and professional services firm performing a small assessment project to confirm the value of new software and propose a comprehensive solution. When the estimated cost of a solution came in at approximately $60 million, the paper manufacturer decided to reconsider its approach.

With support from a different professional services firm, it reinitiated the project, focusing on designing a comprehensive planning process and, only secondarily, selecting software to help execute that process. A team was assembled that included several full-time staff members from the manufacturer and several external consulting staff. Both the mills and the converting divisions were represented on the team. There was no one immediately available within the manufacturer who was prepared to manage the project, so project management for both internal resources and external resources was performed by a (external) senior consultant with the requisite skills. The external consultant had a standard general purpose methodology for software package selection and implementation, and it was used loosely, with considerable modification and simplification.

A week was spent documenting current processes, followed by almost three months of "to be" design on a new set of planning processes. A business case was constructed, with much of the hard dollar benefits expected to be achieved via inventory reduction — in inventory purchased and held by the converting divisions of the manufacturer — while most of the expense would be borne by the mills. Thus benefits were primarily on the "customer" side, but real dollars for the company because so much customer demand was part of the same corporate P&L. Inventory reduction within the mill system was also substantial, and an increase in on-time delivery would lend an advantage in a commodity-based business. New processes were defined in which customers, particularly these internal customers, could quickly reforecast their needs, reorder product weekly as needed (rather than the traditional monthly ordering), and cancel orders when appropriate.

A planning approach was designed based primarily on a fairly standard, broad-spectrum planning software suite, plus specialized "trim optimization" from another software firm. The block scheduling approach would be retained, but now customers would be given a precise promise date based on dynamically optimizing trim (the detailed design for how to cut individual order lines from a master roll of paper) when each order was taken. A new forecasting software module would be implemented from the planning software family, and the data maintenance problems fixed with new processes.

Implementation of new processes and software was broken into multiple modules of work, but the modules were largely performed in parallel with each other rather than being organized into sequential phases. Pilots of various processes/systems were performed simultaneously, and the decision to graduate from parallel use of the new planning system to live use was made independently for each planning module.

One of the pilots was a new "S&OP" process between one mill and one customer division. Because it crossed the supplier/customer boundary, it was as much a form of collaborative planning as it was classic S&OP. It was piloted as a pure management process, based on a monthly meeting and weekly con-

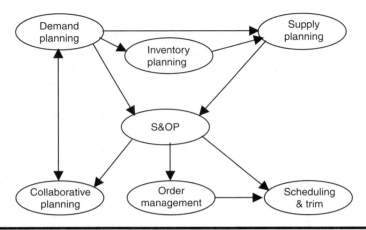

Figure 7.1   New planning processes for a paper company.

ference calls, with no software support. It was initially difficult to get the groups to work together, but quickly became easier as they produced positive results.

Figure 7.1 is a diagram of the new planning processes. Ultimately, the S&OP process was supported by new demand planning (meaning forecasting in this case) processes and software and a new supply planning process based on the primary software provider's integrated tactical planning (one- to six-month horizon) software. S&OP came to rely on reports from the tactical planning software, plus new spreadsheets to assemble data just the way they wanted it. They also began a formal collaboration process using the software provider's "collaboration" module, not between supplier and customer but between the mill system sales force, the converting company planners, and the central forecasting group (this is actually a quite common use of collaboration software). They would do one collaborative iteration as part of each reforecasting cycle, as multiple iterations were too time consuming.

The mainstream software provider's tactical planning software supported the process of planning changes in production capacity and rates, on an ap-proximately monthly cycle. This provider also had a scheduling tool that explicitly supported block scheduling, and it was adopted to help generate and maintain better block schedules. The original plan had been to use software from a paper industry specialist to perform dynamic trim optimization as customer orders were received and quickly promise customers shipment dates (as part of a capable-to-promise process) based on cost-effective trim during each part of the block. After an extended attempt to implement this software, and not achieving usable results, the dynamic trim optimization approach was abandoned in favor of just promising orders by a date late in the block, enforcing block discipline, and then negotiating early delivery if necessary as production actually occurred.

Results and Lessons Learned

This was a large-scale effort, both in terms of its cost and its benefits. About $20 million was spent externally over a twenty-two-month project, 90 percent of that on external professional resources and the balance mostly spent on software. Data cleanup took a great deal of work, particularly to support forecasting with corrected customer histories and good mapping of product successor relationships. On-time delivery of customer orders was dramatically improved. Mill inventory over 120 days old was reduced by 25 percent in the first six months. Eighteen months after completion of the project, the business was on schedule to deliver payback of the costs through inventory reduction at the twenty-eight-month mark.

A large-scale project of this type typically demonstrates both positive and negative lessons:

- The multiple pilots of various new processes and software modules, many run in parallel with each other, worked quite well. The team knew how the planning "pieces" should fit together, based on experience with this software elsewhere and careful process design here. Because of the prior knowledge, no "conference room pilots" were required. Intermediate releases of functionality allowed more immediate benefits to the business and a graduated learning curve for the planning staff.

- The "process first, software second" methodology produced excellent results. In a complex business environment such as this, with multiple divisions and multiple mills, figuring how they wanted to plan was the essential first step; the tools to implement those concepts could then be selected based on an agreed process. This kind of approach depends, of course, on project team knowledge of available planning tool sets, so that a planning approach is designed that can be practically implemented.

- A policy decision made early in the project not to attempt to customize the planning software worked out well. In some cases, this meant adapting processes to the software's capabilities; in some cases, it meant coding reports in an external report writer or spreadsheet because the reports that came with the planning software were not the ones needed by the business.

- The team failed to perform "due diligence" on the trim-optimization software early in the project, which could have been done with an immediate conference room pilot of the software as soon as it was selected. The software provider's statement of "we can do that" turned out to be a belief in their ability to add certain functionality rather than a current capability. A scripted demonstration, as used here (and on many other software selection efforts, see Chapter 8), was not adequate. The team only learned its true capabilities later. The team also skipped early piloting of the mainstream planning software, but this was acceptable because multiple team members had experience with that software elsewhere and already knew its capabilities rather precisely.

■ There was adequate information technology involvement from the principal business division, but insufficient involvement from the corporate information technology group that had responsibility for deep support of the legacy information systems. Hence, systems integration with those legacy systems took longer than it should have and in some cases was cut short of final optimal design.

PLANNING NEAR-TERM LOGISTICS OPERATIONS

This final case is interesting because it is in a domain where a lot of innovative thinking has happened recently in planning: planning the very near term and responding to operational issues almost immediately. It concerns a particular manufacturing site of a very large consumer packaged goods (CPG) manufacturer. As is typical in many industries, this manufacturer has a tendency to increase production steadily at its plants, consuming warehouse space originally intended for finished goods with production equipment and materials. It then leases new space at other sites nearby and shuttles finished product to those other locations for storage. The product may be shipped to customers from those other locations or shuttled back to the plant for customer shipments. Either way, there are a lot of decisions to be made about where to send product, from where to ship to customers, and what additional shuttling needs to be scheduled.

A few years ago, a small but enterprising planning software company and management at another plant that belonged to the same CPG manufacturer had agreed to construct a custom software package to optimize management of these shuttles and loading locations for customer orders. The system was wildly successful and quickly adopted by other plants that belonged to the manufacturer as well. The software evolved considerably as it received expert attention and refinement by the software firm.

The planning software tool is driven primarily by the warehouse management system (WMS) that is used by the manufacturer, which knows about: (1) all current inventory and its location and (2) orders that need to be picked and shipped in the next day or two. Secondarily, it is driven by the manufacturer's: (1) order entry system, which knows about orders further out in time, and (2) an ERP production scheduling module, so that the next several days of production can be considered as well.

Project Motivation

Interestingly, as this producing plant had been forced into using more outside storage over the previous several years, corporate-level planners had come up with a scheme for allocating customer orders by customer type to one of the several potential ship-from locations. This approach to allocation order sourcing had its limitations, as there was considerable overlap in which products each class of customers ordered and hence a temptation to stock and ship most products at most of the outside storage locations. The solution discussed in this case was a locally sponsored effort to dynamically, day-to-day, optimize those shipping locations and inventory allocation so that high efficiency could be achieved in spite of the rather muddled facility strategy.

This particular plant was under increasing pressure to reduce local logistics costs (by reducing the amount of handling associated with shuttling product and reducing transfers of product from one location to another to complete orders for customers) and to improve customer service. Logistics management here had heard about the successful application of software to the shuttling/customer shipping problem at other plants and came to the conclusion that it would be useful for them as well, even though they were smaller than most of the plants already using it.

The outside software vendor would largely manage the implementation process. There were no significant license fees for the plant to justify, really just the cost of a very modest amount of implementation support from the software provider, an analysis of appropriate inventory policies to be used, and any additional enhancements to the software that were needed for this particular plant.

Solution Methodology and Planning Approach

The implementation of the software was extremely straightforward. Because the systems with which it would interface were standardized across the manufacturer's locations and the planning software already had interfaces built to these systems, the planning software could be brought up very simply: by acquiring a new personal computer; installing it on the local network for access to the WMS, order management system, and ERP scheduling modules; and giving the planning software access to the relational databases used by those tools.

Unlike typical planning tools, where there is a substantial model of operations that must be built, this tool relied mostly on the model of operations implicit in the WMS database. The implementation plan was to start up basic features first and then, with follow-up visits from the software provider, turn on more advanced features (such as doing planning based on tomorrow's production schedule).

The primary user of the tool and his backup were trained on the tool in their offices using live data and told to "have at it" in the daily planning cycle, initially in parallel mode and then in live mode. While the logic employed by the tools solver is heuristic, the results it produces are sufficiently intuitive that users do not need much training on how to understand the output, nor do they question its logic.

Results and Lessons Learned

The tool immediately began to identify significant operational savings in shuttling and customer order shipping. After a few days of parallel use, the users began to implement a fraction of the systems recommendations, saving perhaps $1,000 per day in reduced handling and transportation. Full implementation of system recommendations and more comprehensive changes in operations were delayed, however, and, as of this writing, were still not fully implemented. As additional work was identified to really complete the implementation process, the project's sponsor became unhappy about the need to find more budget. Local management, while eager to get the easy part of the savings, was reluctant to "rock the boat" by pushing for more fundamental changes, for example increasing warehousing staff slightly at the union workforce plant so that more product could be shipped to customers directly from the plant.

There are some interesting, perhaps controversial, lessons to be learned from this project:

■   This case is a counter example to one of the major themes of this book, that planners should develop an integrated vision of their planning needs, craft a better process for their planning, and then find software that can help them implement that process. This CPG plant pursued an almost pure software approach and "skimmed the cream" of benefits that it could with almost no operational changes. There were very special circumstances that made it possible for this approach to be effective: The parent company had already licensed the software and the software was already fully integrated with the company's standard systems. Training requirements were minimal and the software easy to use, so overall investment by local management could be kept to a minimum.

■ Perhaps because of this minimal commitment, there was also a reluctance to make even modest changes in operations to exploit much of the economic gain the software identified each day. So perhaps it is not as much of a counter example as it might first appear to be. Even the modest use of the software changed the job dramatically of the primary shuttle/customer load planner.

■ It is also a counter example to the principle that "planning is not a Band-Aid® for poor operations." In this case it was just that, as the multilocation shuttling was inherently expensive regardless of the quality of daily planning. In fairness to the plant, however, it had already obtained funding to consolidate outside storage and shipping in a single location. Hence, the importance of this short-range dynamic planning was expected to be greatly reduced in the future when the new consolidated facility was available, though it was expected to still be a valuable tool and process for optimizing sourcing and inventory between the plant and the one future outside location.

■ Good planning can be as effective at the micro level as at the macro level. While the dollar amounts involved are not as large, there is a whole class of operating problems that unassisted humans often do not do a very good job of solving at the daily level. We are most familiar with these kinds of short-cycle problems in production operations (and the scheduling of those operations), but this case illustrates a profitable attack on them in short-range local logistics as well.

COMMON THEMES DRAWN FROM THESE CASES

1. All these cases involve planning software, which plays a critical role in executing the planning approach for the business. We cannot escape computers and software when it comes to planning product flow. On the other hand, does one generally initiate better planning by going out and looking for software to license? Not if one intends to gain the full benefits of better planning. We should begin by defining the planning vision and processes that make sense for our business and then build software, license software, or implement already licensed software.

2. As with most significant accomplishments in life or business, improving product flow planning requires wise direction, focus, energy, and persistence. In business, persistence sometimes translates into "enough budget to finish the project properly." Other times, it just means managers who are determined to see something through to successful completion. Planning improvement projects always have some problems that have to be

overcome. Any poor decisions up front create bigger problems that have to be overcome.

3. Budgets for external software and support ranged from $100,000 to $20 million across these cases, a vast range reflecting differences in business scale, various arrangements for acquiring software tools, how much work was done by external versus internal resources, and the scope of planning issues addressed.

4. Partial successes are common. Good planning is, as we discussed in Chapter 1, a very high-leverage activity — meaning that successful projects should have big payoffs from better planning. Here we have seen cases where a project failed to achieve all its goals, but was still considered a quantitative and qualitative success because of the improvements that in fact were achieved.

5. Where the scope of the case was in the area of general product flow planning, these companies were very interested in having strong S&OP management processes and in using the quantitative tools to support an S&OP process that sat on top of detailed planning.

6. The planning approach diagram used in the paper industry case (Figure 7.1) is more process oriented than the backbone diagram presented in Chapter 4, which attempts to get at the fundamental logical issues of how planning decision should be made. Nevertheless, it serves as a unifying map or vision of how planning should work and a guide to what is expected from software modules and associated processes.

8

DATA AND SYSTEMS FOR PLANNING: THE COMPUTER'S CONTRIBUTION

There is...no longer any such thing as an IT project.
Every project we're involved in is about business change.

Bob Lewis[67]

In Chapter 1, we discussed the fact that it is the information and communication technologies of today that make modern planning conceivable, that make it possible for us to get our arms around big parts of the supply chain and plan them rationally. In this book, we have chosen to emphasize planning processes as the core issue for improved planning, in part to redress an economic imbalance: To promote software, there are powerful marketing machines financed by software providers and fed by the information technology analyst community; to encourage good practice and effective processes, there are only the professional societies and educators. We also, of course, strongly believe that understanding how an enterprise should plan ideally must come before decisions about software — to avoid attempts to plan product flow in inappropriate ways — but with expertise and awareness of what kinds of planning approaches are technically possible.

Information systems for planning are a critical part of how to improve planning. Every one of the case studies in Chapter 7 involved new software.

Good planning in medium and larger enterprises depends critically on using good planning tools. In this chapter, we will address software selection and implementation issues head on. We will attempt to arm the reader with insight and guidelines to help with the systems side of planning improvement. We will take you through the major steps of software implementation and then into some of the more esoteric issues.

SOFTWARE SELECTION AND IMPLEMENTATION

In the methodology of Chapter 6, during the Design and Implement Release step, the project team may well be required to select packaged software, implement packaged software, design and develop custom software, or do all three. Packaged software for planning is quite mature at this point (although there is always some immature software available for license), and most planning process upgrades rely on using packaged software. There are still, however, exceptional situations where there is no attractive packaged software available for a particular problem, and custom software development is appropriate.

Most of us who have worked around packaged software for a few decades can recall the classic approach to selecting software. First, a "business requirements" study of some type is performed to determine what the software needs to do, and then a detailed requirements list is generated, usually with hundreds of specific requirements that should be met. The requirements list is sent to a long list of software providers, their responses are tallied ("Yes, we do that. Yes, we do that. Yes, we sort of do that."), and then a short list of vendors is identified for more detailed study.

While we do not particularly advocate that approach, a business requirements study is not a bad place to start, particularly if it includes some quick documentation of current processes and some serious work on identifying an integrated vision of how we want to plan in the future. Business requirements lists, however, can be a problem because they can focus too much attention on voluminous superficial requirements ("Here are the seventeen specific reports we would like to see.") and not enough on the core functions the software is designed to perform and the planning approach its designer had in mind. Long business requirements documents can produce a classic "can't see the forest for the trees" situation, resulting in poor decisions. Software has to be selected for its essence: What does it do? How well does it do it? How efficiently and quickly does it do it? Can users work easily with it? Is the software provider a company you want to have a long-term relationship with? Of course, we would like the software to include a modern daily "dashboard" so that management can see whether the business is on track, but that kind of relatively peripheral feature should not have much impact on what software we choose.

If a vision of integrated planning has already been formulated, part of the process of selecting packaged software is to compare that internal vision to the vision designed into each software package. Almost without exception, software reflects the operating/planning vision of its original designers, which may be broad or narrow. This author, for example, designed planning software early in his career that he later realized was a "rifle shot" — extremely powerful if the vision fit the business problem, but probably not the best tool if the built-in vision did not closely fit. This issue is not unique to planning. Certain enterprise resource planning (ERP) systems have been criticized with the observation that "to successfully use the system, an enterprise really had to adopt the system's vision of how to run a business."

As software matures, it often becomes better able to accommodate a broader vision of a business. The most extreme example of accommodating many visions is where software is really more of a tool kit than a true application system and the implementers have to "program," one way or another, a specific set of business processes (and implicitly the vision those processes represent) as part of the implementation. In this situation, of course, the implementers must have developed some kind of explicit process and planning logic map, a planning approach design, from which to work.

During the software purchase cycle (or sales cycle from the point of view of the software provider), the vision "range" of the software may be discussed explicitly or it may be hidden. If the software is not, in fact, a very good fit for the business or for the vision of planning that has been defined for the business, the software sales team may try to hide the actual vision built into the software or pretend that it is something that it is not. If the sales team has good presales "consulting" support from the software provider, the sales team at least understands these issues and deals explicitly with them internally. If the sales team consists only of pure "salespeople," who classically are most sensitive to buyer personality and management dynamics in the target enterprise and really not oriented toward the specific capabilities of the software anyway, the salespeople may not really understand what the software is capable of. Experienced readers may recall the old joke: "What is the difference between a used car salesman and a software salesman? The used car salesman knows when he is lying." Fortunately, as supply chain planning software has matured, most software providers have come to provide quite knowledgeable sales teams.

A good way for software procurement teams to identify what software is really intended to do is to ask about in what industry it was first applied. Who was the alpha client for whom it was initially developed and what did that client use it for? Who were the beta users?

Unless the project team has prior knowledge and experience with the software (see the paper industry case in Chapter 7), you also need to perform some type of conference room pilot of the software to get a feel for what it actually does. This experimentation with the software should occur before major license fees are paid, to see how well it can execute the planning processes you have defined. A scripted demonstration of the software is not sufficient, as there is too much opportunity for sidestepping issues of function or performance, as well as simple misunderstandings between software providers and potential customers.

More often than not today, a project team may have very few software options it can realistically consider. For example, one software vendor's supply chain planning suite may have been selected already for planning in another division or for certain types of planning in this division, and there may be pressure to continue to work with that provider. If, for example, management has decided that "all supply chain packaged software will be provided by our current ERP vendor," then it may be quite an uphill battle to select software from another source. If the ERP vendor's offering is clearly not suitable, a planning team may be able to take on this battle and win it. But if the software provider already selected by your organization is reasonably capable relative to your needs, but not perfect, you may have to use it but become more creative. You may have to design a software architecture that supports your specific planning approach through a combination of packaged modules (which were not of your choosing), custom-programmed reports, personal computer spreadsheets, and perhaps one or two essential highly custom modules that are executed as "outcalls" from the packaged mainstream software provider.

Considerable ingenuity is appropriate in designing these kinds of software architectures to support your real needs, but there is an important caveat here: Anything you construct is going to have to be maintained and evolved as the business and your planning needs change and evolve. Jerry-rigged, Rube Goldberg types of information flow will cause problems for years. Custom changes to packaged vendor software cause another class of problems, as the changes have to be reintegrated with each new release of the vendor's software that your business decides to implement. These issues are, of course, trade-offs inherent in the decision to employ packaged software. The cleanest way to handle it for the long term may be a decision to simply not customize vendor software (see the paper industry case in Chapter 7), but to either develop and maintain a custom-designed module for truly unique planning needs or to leave the truly unique part of the planning process manual (or personal computer spreadsheet-based) rather than supported with software.

A client of a few years ago had the perennial problem of more demand than product that it could produce. It had developed elaborate logic for allocating product among different customers and classes of customers and had custom coded this logic as an outcall from an order management system. Unfortunately, the logic was implemented in an extremely convoluted way that left customer service representatives, product flow planners, and management frequently mystified. While what this business really needed, of course, was better production capability to meet demand, it also needed a redesign and redevelopment of its custom allocation system.

MODEL BUILDING

Product flow planning software typically proposes plans based on a mathematical "model" of operations. That is, it asks that you build a description in the planning database of facility locations, production systems, products, business policies, decision rules, throughput and storage capacities (so that it can propose plans that are feasible), and costs (so that it can propose plans that minimize costs). Running the "solver" or executing a "model run" generally consists of running dynamic data such as customer orders or forecasts of orders, and current inventory, through that model and letting the solver come up with a plan that hopefully can meet all customer needs while staying within capacity constraints and minimizing costs (no overtime, no premium transportation). Solvers that perform very short-range tasks, such as an immediate response to an available-to-promise type of inquiry, typically look at only part of the overall model of operations and are thus "local" rather than "global" in their scope.

In integrated software suites, multiple planning tools and solvers share the same data model of operations, thus helping users get more value out of their investment in maintaining that data. If a planning tool has been designed to be truly integrated with an ERP system's more business transaction–oriented model of operations, it should be able to use some of that model data directly (and perhaps transaction data as well), further reducing data maintenance effort.

"Modeling" or "model building" is typically a significant intellectual effort that must occur in the early stages of planning software implementation. Considerable thought must go into how to describe operations for planning and solver purposes. For example, should identical machines that operate in parallel be modeled as one machine (which would be adequate and more efficient for high-level planning) or as individual machines (which would be necessary if we are going to sequence production on each machine to minimize impact from changeovers)? The last case described in Chapter 7 is an interesting exception, because it involves a detailed planning tool that was designed to integrate directly with the warehouse management system (WMS) used at most of the consumer packaged goods manufacturer's sites, allowing it to rely mostly on the model of operations already built into the WMS.

Packaged planning software can be categorized to some degree by how models are built. Some software is designed to be "data driven," that is, pretty much the complete range of what it can do is controlled by data inserted into it (hard data like locations and products) or control parameters (like "use this policy to control production of these items, use that policy to control those items"). Other planning software is intended more to be controlled by logic that has to be programmed as part of the implementation process, often using some type of pseudo-code that looks rather like a programming language. Sometimes this programming can be performed graphically on a screen, but it is still programming.

The conventional wisdom is that the former data-driven tools look more like finished applications and are less work to install but less flexible, while the latter tools are more like tool kits and are more flexible and more work to install. However, every mature software package is a mix of these capabilities, well designed or poorly designed for user understanding and control, and must be evaluated on a case-by-case basis. Either type of tool may include the capability to make "outcalls" to completely custom computer code that performs completely unique functions. These types of features (data-driven versus programmable versus outcalls) cannot be evaluated in a scripted demonstration and are one of the reasons why a conference room pilot or prior experience with the software is so important.

DATA ACQUISITION AND CONSISTENCY

Planning systems and their users are very large consumers of data about operations:

- Transactional data, such as current customer orders and current inventory
- Corporate structural data, for example the item master file(s)
- Parametric and policy data, like how to prioritize stockkeeping units (SKUs) or customers for scarce production capacity

The first two of these classes generally are maintained in corporate systems and are provided to planning systems via interfaces or directly if planning is performed by the same systems that manage these fundamental data. Policy data typically are not stored in other systems and often are recorded first in an advanced planning system.

With more organizations having preintegrated ERP systems in place, the problems of making transactional and corporate structural data available to planning are typically less today than they were a few decades ago, but they are still often considerable. The data integration approach(es) chosen to support new planning capabilities is an information technology decision that will depend largely on policies established by the information technology organization. Does it employ EAI (enterprise application integration) software; does it write custom integration software; does it try to rely almost entirely on preintegration and adapters built by the application software providers? How often does it refresh these data for the planning tools' use? The planning manager is, of course, very interested in the effectiveness of data integration, but he or she typically will not have final say over the technical approach taken to provide that integration.

In any case, the systems that support short- and intermediate-range product flow planning must work in conjunction with the enterprise's other operations-oriented systems. Data flow from the transaction systems into planning, and to a lesser extent from planning back to transaction systems, are structured and highly repetitive. It is not ad hoc, to be changed by a planner lightly, or only to be executed once in the way that, for example, data collection is performed once every several years when distribution refreshes its strategic model of the warehouse network.

Planning's use of transactional data may require that an effort be undertaken to clean up some of that data. For example, product classification fields may already exist in the product master table, but may be populated inconsistently due to the fact that no previous systems or users really depended on that data. While most of the data cleanup work is typically manual effort (Ugh!), there is specialized data cleanup software ("data quality" software to check data and perhaps correct them) available that can perform some support functions. Of course, the key step in maintaining clean data is to have validation checks built into transaction systems so that important fields are always correctly populated. Well-trained and disciplined users make a big difference as well.

Often when data are extracted from multiple systems and pulled together to drive planning systems, there is, in effect, a first-ever test of data consistency between these otherwise separate systems. Let us consider a complex but real-world example.

A new tactical planning system was being implemented and needed to use current customer order information from the order management system, current inventory of finished goods, and manufacturing near-term expected output. The order management system and the finished goods inventory system were built on the same database and their information was consistent. But the near-term scheduling system for manufacturing used some different product codes because its implementers (years before) did not want to deal with all the issues of fully aligning the manufacturing system with the order/inventory system. The implementers of the tactical planning tool faced an expensive quandary: Should they try to create an interface that would make assumptions about which finished goods products would be coming out of production, or partially reimplement the production scheduling system, or adopt some other approach? There was no easy answer.

There was an additional integration challenge. The tactical planning system was designed to operate above the level of individual customer orders, and the initial intent was to use the zip code in the "ship-to" field of the order management system to understand where the order was going and hence to aggregate demand by geographic area for tactical planning purposes. But it was discovered that the zip code field was empty or full of junk on about 40 percent of customer orders, because the ship-to for orders was really controlled by a location code passed between the order management system and the customer master file. The tactical planning implementation team was faced with a quandary: Should they write code to do customer master file lookups for the tactical planning system as well, or should they force the order management process to begin populating the zip code field 100 percent of the time?

In general, implementing good product flow planning systems brings up issues of this type, although usually, thankfully, not quite as thorny as in the example above. In most cases, a new planning process and system will bring together data that have never been brought together in the same way before. Planning systems that have broader scope, which look at data from across the enterprise or across the supply chain, cause this to happen even more frequently. Typically, there are expensive solutions to these issues.

These issues are not exotic or novel to experienced systems professionals; they have seen similar issues crop up many times before in their systems integration work. The best solution to any data consistency or quality problem is generally based on a combination of the needs of the moment for planning and the strategy with which the information technology organization is trying to evolve its overall integration architecture. Consequently, the senior systems staff involved in the project need to make these decisions, supported, of course, by highly involved planning users.

Generally, the implementation of a new planning system forces better integration of other existing systems and better execution of the processes that drive data through them. This disciplinary effect can be good in itself, producing other ancillary benefits (such as fewer systems and process errors) elsewhere in operations. It does, however, typically require very significant investment of time in connection with the planning system implementation project.

DATA AND PLAN RETENTION

An issue that is often overlooked in the design of planning processes and systems is how the planning data will be managed. While keeping input data and plans in relational databases is a given in this era, exactly how that will work usually has to be designed or least configured as part of system implementation.

First of all, every planning environment needs to be able to manage multiple cases or "scenarios." For example, if you want to assume that demand for a particular set of products will be 15 percent higher next summer than the nominal forecast, and then build a set of plans for production, inventory, and deployment around that assumption, you need to be able to keep that complete scenario distinct from your current set of "live" plans. Most modern planning software suites make it easy to do that.

But there are subtler issues as well. If your planning process is designed to regenerate a new tactical plan the second week of each month, you probably need to retain a static version of all data associated with that plan throughout the month, and perhaps for much longer. As new ideas emerge, you will want to be able to go back and rerun that model based on the data as they stood: forecasted sales, "current" inventory, inventory policy, product master list, and so on. As your thinking evolves, you need to be able to test new ideas against a static set of data, in order to be able to compare apples to apples and know that all differences in results are due to the inputs you changed, not to changing live data continuously. Keeping this kind of data will result in some fairly large databases, but it is a requirement for professional planning and well within the capabilities of modern database software and a reasonable budget for data storage on disk (i.e., not backed up to tape, where you cannot readily use it).

Meanwhile, of course, your live plans may well be changing hourly, even minute by minute if some of your planning processes are essentially real time, such as customer order allocations, receipts of finished product into inventory, or whatever. Being facile with both real-time and historical "snapshots" is a requirement for a good planning environment.

TUNING: ARE YOU FEELING RELENTLESS?

Even after we essentially complete the implementation process described in Chapter 6, we will need to continue to tune and improve what we do. The "continuous improvement" philosophy applies to planning processes at least as much as it applies in Japanese operations philosophy. In part, the need to do this is driven by continuing changes in the business, of course. But for the first year or two of software use, the planners will need to experiment with tuning the software to produce better results from the solvers. There are parameters to be experimented with and/or programmed control code to be changed. Often, doing this well makes the difference between a planning system that is viewed as truly valuable and a planning system that generates somewhat "strange" proposed plans that are barely worth the effort to maintain the input data.

This tuning may be done by a master user who is quite expert on the software and also knows the enterprise's business, by the software provider, or by consultants who have assisted throughout the implementation process and are expert on both the business challenges and the planning software. Tuning is hard work intellectually and requires endurance (months, maybe years to get it right, and then some ongoing tuning as business conditions change). Running out of budget or patience before the planning software is truly tuned can result in disappointing results from the software, even after 90 percent of the implementation work has been well done. Of course, sometimes after several months of tuning, the conclusion may be reached that the logic in the software is just not adequate for the business problem, and different logic (and more investment) is required. Getting into this situation is rare when users really understand their planning needs up front (e.g., through the backbone diagram), when the software provider is knowledgeable and capable, and when the initial implementation has been thoughtful. But it may occur, especially when one or more of those principles is violated.

INFORMATION OR OPTIMIZATION?

There has been some debate in recent years about whether information or optimization is more important, driven in part by the recent large increases in the speed and volume of data that can be made available, both with internal systems and from partners in the supply network. For example, there has been considerable interest over the last five years in supply chain visibility and event management, an information-driven process that interacts directly with short-range planning. Optimization capabilities, on the other hand, have evolved more slowly over several decades. A quick reaction to this issue might be: "What a stupid question. Is engineering more important than finance? No, you have to do them both well if you want to be a successful business."

But the real issue is more subtle and complex. Part of the argument is that with new data, one can conceive of entirely new operations approaches, new supply chain relationships, while optimization is limited by the upper bound of perfect planning on a problem scope you have previously defined: As you approach perfect planning, you cannot really do much better on that problem as defined.

The perspective we take on the issue is twofold. First, new information technologies definitely do permit new supply chain designs with new performance possibilities compared with old designs (for example, transmit customer orders for items that are actually manufactured by one of your suppliers directly to that supplier and have the supplier ship directly to the customer). As we discussed in Chapter 1, the design of manufacturing and distribution systems is a vast subject with great potential. In this sense, data can transform what you do and how you do it and thus are at the center of large-scale business changes over the last several years.

The second way of looking at this issue is that with near-real-time data availability and new supply chain operations, the planning problems change as well. As we discussed in Chapter 4, the best planning structure for an enterprise is dynamic and needs to be rethought occasionally and continuously evolved. How to plan it, to "optimize" its operation, is a new challenge as the business changes and a very important one. It takes a lot of effort to get and stay anywhere near "perfect" planning as the business changes. Material flow planning and optimal plans are not about revolutionizing your business; they are about quickly figuring out how to operate efficiently every time you (or your marketplace) decide to revolutionize your business.

At any given time, an enterprise has to decide whether the highest priority is to change the way its business is conducted, to put in better information systems to understand and control the business, or to invest in new product flow planning processes and tools to optimize the business in its new form.

ARCHITECTURE OF PLANNING DATA AND SYSTEMS

Systems Architecture in the Era of e-Business

Planning systems are significantly different than their larger brothers, the transaction-driven business execution systems that we rely on to operate enterprises and supply chains:

- They need to pull data together from many sources in order to help generate good, comprehensive plans. For most planning purposes, data do not have to be up to the minute (in spite of the value of near-real-time planning), and, in fact, appropriate data retention is very important.
- There is typically a much larger component of calculation in the system, because it takes a lot of computer "thinking" to work out the logical implications of the broadly assembled operations data.
- They require extended interaction with thoughtful users, including very effective data display (hopefully graphical display), but yet they are not quite the same as the classic offline "decision support system" because

they may be in a very short-cycle (hourly) planning loop with the real world.

Good planning tools, like transaction systems, serve not only a "data processing" function, but also a communications function. The custom production planning and master scheduling system for a tire manufacturer presented as the first case in Chapter 7 is a nice illustration of the communications role. But any modern planning system with shared databases and browser access to planning functions should provide substantial communication to support:

- Data for planning
- A "collaborative" planning process
- Sharing of the plans with their users

Effective planning system architecture should support the communications function as well as user–computer interface, the computation of plans, and interfacing with transaction systems.

The larger trends in systems technology have determined the structure of planning systems, just as they have execution systems. Early calculations, such as the economic order quantity, required no computer. Early computer-based systems (see Lasdon and Terjung[21]), whether optimization oriented or material requirements planning (MRP), of course ran on batch-oriented mainframe computers. These machines were neither powerful (by today's standards) nor user friendly. With the advent of the Unix workstation and powerful personal computers in the 1980s, certain types of planning shifted to stand-alone machines. Functions like detailed production scheduling seemed well suited to that because of the relative isolation of the planners from the enterprise and supply chain as a whole. These machines also provided wonderful graphics capability for user displays, which considerably enhanced planner effectiveness. By the mid-1990s, these planning architectures had grown into full-fledged client-server implementations with multiuser relational databases, powerful user graphics, and fairly expensive installation and support requirements.

The widespread adoption of the very "thin client" architecture for most business application software, often only an Internet browser on the user's computer, has had a big impact on planning systems architecture. Planning systems are too small to drive architecture in the typical corporate environment; they are very much the tail on the technical architectural dog and get wagged by large systems' architectures. Planning systems have followed transaction systems into the browser world, with consequent ease of deployment and support of the software (since there is little or nothing to maintain on each user's machine), with excellent opportunity for plan communication through the system, but with a greater challenge in presenting data effectively to planners through the Internet browser, e.g., it is not easy to offer users interactive graphics through a web browser. Figure 8.1 shows this evolution of hardware and systems software in the left-hand column.

Approach to Systems Integration

Just as we must make choices about the degree of logical integration in our planning processes (Chapter 4), we must make choices about the degree of systems integration of our planning systems. Planning systems have traditionally been somewhat isolated from the transaction systems being used to operate the business. Over the last twenty years, it has become much easier for planning technology to receive and send information to other systems, and numerous technologies have been used for doing just that. Custom interfaces have been programmed thousands of times, EAI software has been used to speed up the building of interfaces, and adapters have been built by planning software vendors to provide a prepackaged way to interface their software to the most commonly used ERP systems, such as those from SAP and Oracle. More recently, the "web services" standards have been touted as an interfacing vehicle, and some of the software providers have begun to enable their software to be able to connect using these standards. The right-hand column of Figure 8.1 shows some of these evolving choices in planning application software and data integration.

While the term "systems integration" is applied to all these approaches, it is in fact a euphemism because they do not achieve the unified whole that the word *integration* traditionally means; rather, they achieve an adequate level of data interfacing. They are inherently a bit unstable since as software providers make major changes in their offerings, new interfaces must be implemented as well, but they do permit the enterprise to select "best of breed" software for each function.

As ERP providers have added more product flow planning capabilities, it has become realistic to think about having all software tools related to operations supplied by the same vendor and to then rely on the level of integration provided by that vendor. SAP, for example, developed its APO (Advanced Planning & Optimization) tool set separately from its core R3 transactional software, but has made communication between the two reasonably straightforward.

Another approach has been adopted by a small number of enterprises that have an operations orientation and relatively large information technology resources. That approach is to adopt a data-centered architecture, built around databases that they completely control (see Figure 8.2), rather than relying

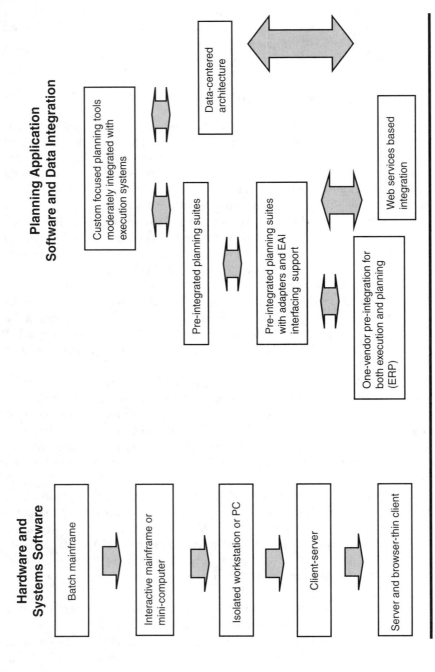

Figure 8.1 Planning system integration choices.

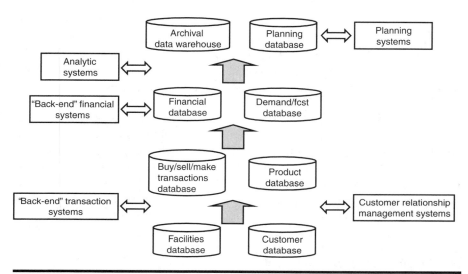

Figure 8.2   Data-centered architecture.

heavily on data structure designs provided by any software vendor. With this strategy, the databases are viewed as relatively permanent, and the application systems that update them and use data from them are expected to come and go. Technology developed by database software providers over the last ten years to permit integrated viewing of multiple databases as one logically "federated" database makes this data-centered architecture increasingly attractive.

The best approach for systems interfacing continues to be a subject of debate in information technology circles and competition among integration software vendors. One school of thought, the process-oriented school, argues that the correct approach is to use formal process management software to capture business processes "abstracted" from the application software (see Smith and Fingar[68]). Integrate these processes, and then the mere data integration can logically and robustly follow. By dealing explicitly with processes, it may be easier to change the processes as business needs change than the traditional situation where no one can accurately describe the current processes.

Supply Network Collaborative Planning Architectures on the Internet

If, as Oracle's Larry Ellison once famously said, "the Internet is the computer," then does it not make sense to plan product flow there as well? As we discussed in Chapter 1, planning product flow along a supply chain path in the supply network is obviously an interorganizational activity. Not forgetting our point that planning will remain rooted in individual enterprises and that interenterprise collaboration will remain limited because supply chain partners cannot completely trust each other (Chapter 4), there are a lot of activities that must go on between enterprises.

Traditional technologies for collaboration include the telephone, the telex, and more recently the facsimile machine. In the 1980s, electronic data interchange (EDI) was heavily promoted as the appropriate technology for interbusiness process execution. While most EDI transactions are, in fact, business transaction oriented, like an order or an advanced shipping notice, EDI is also used to transmit planning data like production schedules sent to suppliers. EDI is famous for both the cost of configuring internal systems to speak the language of EDI messages and the cost of using third-party value-added networks (VANs) to, in fact, move the messages. Consequently, it has seen limited adoption, mostly between larger trading partners.

The Internet has reduced the cost of EDI (including transmitting EDI messages over the Internet rather than via VANs, which has led to significant recent additional adoption of EDI). It has made available the completely unstructured communications vehicle of e-mail, and the partially structured approach of having users in other enterprises log into your website, and the very flexible vehicle of Extensible Markup Language (XML), on which the web services standards were built. Because of its flexibility, XML is used as the foundation for specific schemas for messages to be sent directly between execution systems, such as those defined by RosettaNet for the high-tech industry. As this is written, there is continuous progress in the technology of supporting the transfer of information, but as yet no breakthrough in making it easy to communicate directly between different enterprises' planning systems. The web services approach to systems interfacing is being developed, but there is by no means agreement across software suppliers on all the standards that would be necessary for fully interoperable systems.

At the logical level of planning, however, more collaborative progress has been made. The VICS committee has published a formal standard for collaborative planning, forecasting, and replenishment (CPFR), originally intended for collaboration between retailers and the manufacturers supplying them, but broadly applicable in most industries. In addition, Syncra Systems developed a system from scratch to specifically support CPFR processes between enterprises. Most of the SCM/APS software vendors have added software modules to their suites to encourage collaboration. Collaboration in product flow planning has generally taken the form of collaborative forecasting, and then the communication of projected specific needs for product and confirmation that those needs can or cannot be met.

While CPFR was envisioned and is used primarily between pairs of enterprises, collaboration can be executed through a hub that supports many enterprises. Many of the interactions would still be pair-wise, but some, such as communication of shared statistics to all users of the hub, need not be. One of the better-funded industry-sponsored markets, Covisint, created by the North American automakers, pursued the technology platform to provide planning as a hub between and among supply chain partners. Syncra was able to adapt its CPFR software for hub planning use quickly, and it was adopted by multiple Internet markets.

Figure 8.3 shows three fundamentally different ways that planning systems may be connected to support the integrated supply chain:

1. Suppliers and customers of a dominant channel master (e.g., Wal-Mart) can function as satellites of that enterprise and use its communications standards.
2. Enterprises can communicate freely using standards such as web services.
3. Enterprises in an industry can each connect to a hub for planning purposes.

Each chain-planning architecture has issues associated with it. Most enterprises would prefer not to have to adapt to the multiple channel masters with which they do business. Web services standards are progressing slowly, and it is not clear how well standards are going to support planning processes in the foreseeable future. With the initial enthusiasm for the role of Internet markets having now passed, it seems even less likely that enterprises will want a "process hub" (Renner[69]) to take on a significant planning role for the supply network of an industry.

Stay tuned, and we shall see what emerges as the dominant architecture for supply network planning.

INTERVIEW RESULTS: CHALLENGES IN IMPLEMENTING ADVANCED PLANNING TOOLS

We had an opportunity to conduct a set of interviews with organizations that had extensive experience using sophisticated planning tools for product flow planning. These were "early adopters" of advanced planning software. Many were using their second and even third generation of tools at the time of our interviews. Several had begun their odysseys with custom tools and

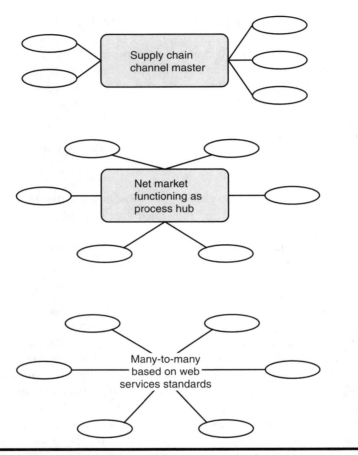

Figure 8.3   Collaborative planning architectures on the Internet.

moved on to packaged software. This was a group that could tell us a good bit about what was difficult, and what was straightforward, about implementing these tools. For balance, we also spoke with a few organizations that were not major users of new planning tools: one with a very simple supply chain, and another that felt it was cost effective to stop at only a minimal implementation of scheduling technology. We did not attempt to document the substantial benefits of advanced planning systems in this study; these benefits are well articulated elsewhere.

While the interviews included some industrial manufacturers, food and consumer products were the best-represented industries. All of the organizations that were interviewed both manufacture and physically distribute product. Most are primarily make-to-stock rather than make-to-order businesses. The range of activities discussed with them represents short- and medium-range data development and planning, generally covering some subset of:

- Sales forecasting
- Quantitative support for Sales & Operations Planning
- Integrated supply chain tactical planning
- Production requirements calculation from the distribution network requirements
- Master scheduling of production
- Detailed scheduling of production
- Inventory deployment planning in a distribution network
- Short-range transportation planning and load building

The next section describes the issues we discussed with them and basically what they told us. The final section in this chapter summarizes our conclusions.

Specific Challenges

The issue areas that we discussed with these early adopters were:

- Data availability
- System interfaces
- Complexity of planning
- Capability of current planning technology
- Resistance to centralized planning
- Traditional functional management versus integrated planning
- External collaborative supply chain planning
- Expense of planning processes and systems
- Measuring benefits and selling management

Data Availability

Getting complete, correct, and timely data to drive planning has been a problem at most of the organizations interviewed. Generally, no previous process or system had ever forced the organization to assemble complete and, even more critical, *consistent and timely* data. Some organizations had problems with inadequate transaction systems; more had poor procedures for entering and maintaining the consistency of data. One interviewee reported having new planning processes literally fail and finally having to abandon them because of data problems. In any case, planning with poor data reduces benefits and dramatically reduces the credibility of the plans and the planners.

A few of the interviewed organizations had implemented new transaction systems; others worked with their legacy systems. The majority went through difficult data cleanup exercises during initial implementation of their new planning processes. Somewhat surprisingly, virtually all of them now report having largely solved their data problems. For example,

- A very large food-processing firm that, ten years ago, was struggling with a legacy inventory system that delayed inventory status data by forty-eight to seventy-two hours now has a multilocation WMS that provides accurate, almost real-time inventory information.
- Another consumer goods manufacturer has, after trying to do sophisticated planning for a few years with poor transactional data, finally implemented a comprehensive ERP system and now reports no significant data issues.

The lesson to be drawn is that a high-quality, consistent, timely supply of data is a critical precursor to a reasonably smooth implementation of advanced planning processes. Organizations have achieved this data availability with new, comprehensive ERP systems, but also with minor upgrades to legacy systems or data management processes.

Must data be complete and correct *before* implementing planning processes? No. None of the firms interviewed waited until they had pristine data; they just jumped into new planning processes. And the new planning processes and software are themselves often the only practical way to identify some latent data inconsistency problems. But the organization that knows it has many problems with its operations-oriented data would be well advised to correct the biggest problems before attempting to implement sophisticated planning.

System Interfaces

While all the respondents in this study mentioned the need to build interfaces and the systems-driven aggravation and delays associated with building them, all found the investment justifiable and the finished interfaces acceptably functional. One manager noted enthusiastically that: "Interfacing is easy, compared with the other challenges." Another commented that the web of interfaces that had been created with multiple legacy systems and multiple planning tools is "very complex, too complex."

A few of the organizations interviewed believe in making the most of the interface needs, of "turning a lemon into lemonade" by constructing a data repository at each key interface, such as:

- A sales forecast database (created by forecasting, used by two or three different downstream planning functions)
- A distribution requirements planning (DRP)–oriented requirements and deployment database
- A production plan and schedule database

These are planning-oriented versions of the data-centered architecture discussed earlier in this chapter. By constructing these databases, they have not only met the need for interfacing, but created data structured in the way they wanted it for their organization, accessible on an ad hoc basis with the reporting tool(s) their organization prefers. They also have separated planning modules from execution software modules by this means, which permits them to replace individual planning software modules as they feel the need (and even to replace transaction systems without replacing planning modules).

Other organizations interviewed feel that these databases are too expensive to create and manage and have built the simplest interfaces possible, sought out planning software suites that are as preintegrated as possible, and eagerly expect to implement the planning modules from their ERP vendors.

Complexity of Planning

Implementing a planning system means building a mathematical model (usually multiple models) for a significant fraction of operations. Understanding the possibilities for structuring that model is quite an intellectual task. It requires staff training, help from the software vendor, and often help from a third-party implementer. Maintaining enough knowledge in the organization that the *model can be correctly updated by internal resources as the business changes* (or as planners get smarter about how to plan the business) is even more of a challenge. Self-sufficiency has value; one interviewee expressed considerable displeasure with the availability of support from his software supplier.

Let us discuss how the experienced organizations have met these challenges. First of all, in some cases they have selected software that made it easier to build models, to understand the models, and to maintain complex parametric or model-structure data. Some tools come with their mathematical models already largely structured; others require model building from elementary components. Prestructured tools are usually easier to implement, but typically less flexible.

Software friendliness varies widely, not only with respect to daily use, but also in ease of model building and maintenance. A truly graphical display of the model may help, for example, but even graphics vary greatly in their quality and usability.

The best tools give users a sense of how models are structured and how the solvers work, a sense of what is in the conceptual "black box" of planning algorithms, without forcing users to go very far inside that box very often. This insight is important so that users can understand whether a tool is performing correctly, can change the model when necessary, and can explain the models to their management.

Secondly, experienced users have figured out how to right-size the amount of planning complexity they really need. In planning, unlike many other parts of a business, one can choose simplicity or complexity. This trade-off balances many factors:

- How many variables must be considered simultaneously to propose a valid plan
- The budget available for initial software and process implementation
- The time and annoyance associated with maintaining parametric data, versus simply developing part of a plan manually
- The availability of a solver that solves the problem one really needs to solve
- Wait times for solver completion
- User preference for how much of a plan a solver should propose

One of the interviewed firms feels that planning simplicity is so important that it halted its implementation of advanced planning after implementing shop floor sequencing, from which it had successfully achieved considerable work-in-process inventory reduction. Another organization interviewed, with thirty SKUs, twenty-five customers, and excess production capacity, feels that any sort of advanced planning is too complex for its business. In a few cases, right-sizing planning has meant adopting a new, simpler tool or building new models that are less comprehensive, less complex than the ones they tried first.

The majority of our interviewees feel strongly that relatively sophisticated planning tools and approaches provide very high returns on the effort expended, through all the benefits of better plans. Generally, they have learned the lesson that with any given planning tool, one *starts with a relatively simple model and then adds complexity as use shows it is necessary.*

Thirdly, they have organized to support sophisticated planning. In some cases, this has meant creating a "super-user" position or a headquarters staff position that supports multiple users in multiple locations. It has meant a lot of training, both as part of initial implementation and to handle ongoing staff turnover. It has not, for our interviewees, meant hiring extremely specialized staff. Organizations have not been motivated to employ staff with a master's degree in operations research to perform routine planning or to maintain models.

They expect the tools to be sufficiently usable that that type of employee is not required.

Capability of Current Planning Technology

The majority of organizations interviewed had experience with multiple planning tools from multiple software vendors and in many cases were on their second- or third-generation tool to support a given function. A few of the organizations had begun with custom-built planning tools in the 1980s and then converted to packaged software as it became available. While their experiences with the quality of software varied, the feelings of most can be summarized as follows.

- Most had complaints about the overall usability of the first-generation custom or packaged tools they had implemented ten to twenty years ago. Most tools of that period did not have all the attributes necessary for a smooth implementation and usage experience.
- The majority of users felt good about the usability and effectiveness of their current software suite and expected evolutionary rather than revolutionary change in the near future.
- A few expressed frustration that their tools still could not propose good answers to certain planning problems they had, such as large-scale simultaneous multilocation master scheduling, varying quality of material supplies, or large-scale plants that needed detailed scheduling to be performed in a single-model instance. Solve times on large models are still annoyingly long with some tools, sometimes to the point of making those models essentially useless.
- There were occasional complaints about the quality of display screens, difficulty in interpreting output, lack of capability to add notes to schedules, reporting inflexibility, and limitations on ad hoc data retrieval. One concern was that the complexity of report generation prevented occasional users from being able to get the data they needed out of the system. One manager expressed frustration that his planning software suite was not sufficiently preintegrated in terms of internal data flow.
- A unique perspective came from a manager who had been involved with custom planning systems fifteen years ago and recently became reinvolved in looking at planning software. He was surprised that he had found no package today that could simply develop the "complete plan" in one grand optimization.
- Another very experienced manager stressed his organization's current push toward using daily time buckets with all planning modules, in-

cluding *forecasting*. Some of their current software is not up to that challenge.

Do these concerns mean one should wait for perfect tools? Again, most of these users feel their current tool set is very effective. There will be better software available in another ten years, but there are a lot of very powerful and refined tools available now that can add great value in most organizations. Most of us should work aggressively with today's technology, gaining the immediate benefits of better planning and taking our organizations up the planning learning curve.

Resistance to Centralized Planning

In most businesses, as advanced planning approaches are adopted, there is a push toward doing a significant amount of the planning centrally. Production planning and inventory deployment are, for example, often centralized. Detailed manufacturing scheduling is a notable exception; it stays at the plants in most sophisticated planning approaches. Centralized planning is often a difficult pill for field management and staff to swallow, as it means they have less autonomy and control over their own activities.

Our mature organizations have dealt with centralization issues in several ways. Many had adopted centralized planning years ago, prior to implementing advanced planning techniques, and felt that centralization was not a current issue. Others moved toward centralization as part of the new processes. Some of these simply forced it by management decree; others expended effort on explicit organizational change programs. Most of our interviewees expressed satisfaction with their approach, although a couple made comments like "It took a year for the field to adjust." No interviewee said that centralization issues had stopped adoption of advanced planning.

A few interviewees spoke of consciously moving their master scheduling activity to a plant (particularly if many products are produced at that plant only) to maintain the plant's motivation and commitment to customer service. This responsibility "helps the plant to take a whole supply chain perspective."

Traditional Functional Management Versus Integrated Planning

Many of the interviewed companies reported issues with traditional organization structures that resisted adoption of integrated planning, i.e., "siloed" managers avoiding cross-functional planning. But most interviewees said they had achieved progress and improved coordination across their organizations, facilitated by advanced planning processes.

Regardless of where planners sat in the organization, as one might expect, many said that:

- Manufacturing management still fought for longer production runs and low manufacturing cost
- Logistics fought for low inventories and optimized transportation
- Marketing was proliferating SKUs on a geographic basis to better fit local market preferences

Without exception, the planners we spoke with placed themselves above these issues intellectually and emotionally. And the way they described their recent experiences indicated that even the narrow interests in their organizations were no longer naïve to the impact of these variables on the overall economics of the business or unwilling to work on them. These organizations have come a long way in understanding integration issues, but they continue to manage their businesses with mostly traditional functional organizations and with traditional incentive programs.

While we did not explore the issue in depth, there appeared to be some subtle differences of opinion among our planners on the proper role for advanced planning processes. While some seem to favor truly comprehensive tools and plans that simultaneously trade off many variables in the enterprise, cutting across all internal organization boundaries, others seem content with processes that align more closely with traditional functions. Totally integrated planning is not shared universally as a goal by our interviewees. One manager expressed the feeling that: "We don't want our plant schedulers worrying about distribution issues."

External Collaborative Supply Chain Planning

What about the complete supply chain, the raw-materials-to-final-use-by-a-consumer chain? Planning the complete chain of operations as one — to operate an interorganizational value chain that is optimally efficient in cost, inventory, and fixed assets — is an idea whose time has come. It offers the ability to construct virtual businesses with hard-to-duplicate costs and hence long-term competitive advantages. Many planning software suppliers have added features to directly support interorganizational planning.

There was surprising similarity among our interviewees about where they stood on this topic and a great deal of interest in it. Most are performing vendor-managed inventory (VMI) processes with some of their customers and have the tools in place, such as EDI, to transact business that way. Most have not yet integrated their VMI systems with their mainstream planning processes. Many have experimented with pilot collaborative forecasting programs with customers, but do not have a general program in use. A couple reported episodes with customers that clearly indicated to them the customer's interest in, as one said, "pushing channel costs upstream, not in reducing overall supply chain cost." Many of the interviewed organizations also have programs to communicate time-phased material requirements to their suppliers well in advance of actual need.

With respect to supply chain fully integrated planning, none felt they had it in place or were close to having it, but most were interested in a longer term sense. Most felt that continuing to perfect planning within their organization was still their top priority.

Expense of Planning Processes and Systems

Do operations managers feel that sophisticated planning systems are too expensive? No one interviewed for this study felt that they were cheap, but all of the experienced users felt that they were worthwhile. Total expenditures in this group ranged from a few hundred thousand dollars for a one-location scheduling implementation to the several tens of millions of dollars a major food company had spent over the last twelve years on a combination of new technology and massive upgrades of legacy systems.

Most of our interviewees thought about the cost of implementation primarily in terms of their own staff time, related systems upgrades and interfaces, and consulting services in support of implementation. The license fees for packaged software were a smaller but significant part of the commitment, and the cost of computer hardware only a very small part. Those who had developed custom systems or made major investments in legacy systems had the greatest experience with massive commitment of funds. Unlike most planning processes that are performed by a relatively small staff, some DRP process implementations have involved training hundreds of users at great expense.

As discussed above under the complexity banner, a few of the organizations had downsized the complexity of their planning software and models. In doing this, they had also downsized some costs and felt very good about their cost reduction.

Measuring Benefits and Selling Management

Few organizations do a good job of measuring their performance quantitatively. Fewer still measure it before and after new planning processes/systems are implemented to specifically gauge benefits. Most organizations that measure benefits do so with some form of the classic metrics:

- Operating cost (procurement, manufacturing, logistics, other)
- Customer service in the form of fill rate in the promised delivery time (some combination of unit or case fill, line fill, order fill, and perfect orders)
- Inventory investment (materials, work in process, and/or finished goods)

Some organizations have measured benefits rather precisely. A prior study conducted at a food processor showed that a new master production scheduling tool reduced changeover frequency and severity by 20 percent (while almost exactly maintaining inventory and customer service), a savings worth $5.5 million per year. Several of the current interviewees reported quantitative benefits from their new planning processes, the most frequent being "letting us cut inventory while keeping service up and manufacturing cost down." But none of the current interviewees had numbers to offer off the tops of their heads, and most were not particularly concerned by that fact.

Why? In a couple of cases, these planners said they had already established the importance of effective planning with their management. Their organizations adopted sophisticated planning approaches the first time based mostly on faith, as predicting the business impact was essentially impossible. But once implemented and accepted and valued by the organization, there was no need to prove again that good planning was important, any more than company accountants routinely prove that they need financial systems or the customer service organization proves it needs an order management system. These planners said they were expected to manage prudently the cost of upgrades and new planning systems, but they did not have to make a quantitative case for their second-generation tools. Of course, not all companies feel that way. Some interviewees believe their management would invest further only in response to numbers.

Implications of the Advanced Planning Interviews

With any technological advance in industry, there are leaders and there are followers. We interviewed a relatively small set of leaders in advanced supply chain planning to see what they could tell us.

There was relative consistency of opinion on most subjects, although different users stressed different aspects. All but the two "minimal-technology" users felt that comprehensive advanced planning processes and systems were cost effective and well worth the trouble. However, a couple had retreated from the most advanced approaches toward simpler techniques.

Most combined manufacturing/distribution businesses of substantial size are complex enough to achieve net benefit from sophisticated planning, usually great benefit. But it does take a certain amount of organizational will and commitment to see their way through the implementation process:

- Master data and operations data need to be reasonably complete and clean to avoid considerable frustration.
- Software must be found or created that genuinely fits the key business issues and falls into an acceptable place on the power and complexity versus speed and simplicity curve.
- While out-of-pocket costs are usually not huge, there are several different types of expenditures that have to be planned for and cheerfully spent:
  - Data cleanup
  - Data interfaces/repositories
  - Software licenses, sometimes including systems software to go *under* applications
  - Consulting from the software provider and/or a third party
  - Staff upgrades in some cases
  - New computer and possibly communications hardware
  - Ongoing data maintenance
- Organization changes need to be made to have a structure appropriate for the new planning processes.
- A complex modeling exercise has to be performed as part of implementation (and ongoing maintenance), which is new to most organizations
- Priorities have to be established on what aspects of operations are most worthy of advanced planning

The firms interviewed feel they have navigated these waters successfully, although usually not via the most direct course. They are generally not distinguished as the largest company in their industry or having the most powerful staff resources, but they are special in having managers who had the vision and will, as early adopters of advanced planning, to pursue new technology and turn it into a success.

9

THE MOST SUCCESSFUL PLANNING APPROACHES: ELEGANT SIMPLICITY AND OTHER REASONABLE GOALS

Consultants and the software industry, as well as widespread circles in educational institutions, produce constant pressure for novelty — which should not be confused with innovation.

Paul Schonsleben[70]

Product flow planning approaches and technology have reached a certain level of maturity and stability here in the early twenty-first century. We can therefore make some generalizations about the most important factors in good system design. This chapter briefly draws those conclusions.

OUR PRINCIPLES ARE ESSENTIAL

The principles of good planning taught in this volume are the foundation of success. They are not, collectively, easy to live up to with real-world planning approaches. But coming as close to them as possible is a worthy goal for transforming planning in a business and for designing and developing systems that will support better planning. We will reiterate a few of them here and add a few refinements as well.

Developing a Comprehensive Vision of Planning

One of the first themes we introduced in Chapter 1 was the value of taking a comprehensive look at the operations of the enterprise (and a reasonable planning sphere for its supply network) and deciding how we can best plan the flow of product. We have labored over many aspects of that theme: the tools we have at our disposal (Chapter 2), some helpful planning structures (Chapter 4), the relationship between planning and some standard philosophies of operations management (Chapter 5), a methodology for comprehensively improving planning (Chapter 6), its use or neglect in various real-world cases (Chapter 7), and how we can best implement planning software (Chapter 8).

Elegant Simplicity

Simplicity may seem like a strange principle to mention in a book that is filled with complex diagrams that point out just how many dimensions must be dealt with to be able to produce great plans and actually operate the business based on them. And it might have been a misleading principle to introduce early in this volume when some readers might misinterpret the term as simply: "Don't do elaborate planning; just find a cheap rock-simple way to do it and go on to other issues."

But a good bit of what we teach here comes down to finding the most elegantly simple answer to complex problems. Where do we introduce sophistication; where do we, in fact, want to keep things rock simple? Can the right integrated plan be more useful than three separate plans? Can twelve planners in four locations successfully guide an enterprise, or do we need nineteen planners in seven locations? Can one planning process be good enough that it is quite effective for all seven product lines we distribute, rather than one process for four of the lines, a different one for two of them, and a unique one for a unique process?

We have seen several organizations license powerful software and design elaborate processes to gain the maximum benefit out of planning, only to see the processes fail to be executed because there was more work implied by the processes than staff available to execute it and because the staff that was there *failed to see the benefits* of those elaborate processes.

Supply chain planning is, in a sense, only one business problem. We make it more complex by breaking it up into many different problems, managed by different managers, often taught as different disciplines: inventory control, production control, distribution requirements planning. Learning to see it again as one problem, with one set of decisions that have to be made, and identifying the simplest way to make those decision well, is the first part of our challenge.

Robustness

One of the better insights into master production scheduling is that the great master scheduler does not just develop a schedule that meets planned demand most efficiently. He or she develops a schedule that simultaneously meets planned demand efficiently and protects the business to some degree from the one or two other possible futures that the scheduler does not really expect, but knows just might happen. If a planned sales promotion is like ones that have had mixed success in the past, the smart master scheduler may reserve production capacity *during the promotion to make the last 40 percent* of the special purple box product the promotion requires, rather than make it all up front as marketing might prefer. If a certain process line is known to be prone to catastrophic failure, he or she may maintain extra inventory of the product it makes, accepting the fact that the extra inventory damages the metrics (key performance indicators) for which he or she is responsible.

Analogously to that, as we design and modify planning approaches, we need to keep the future in mind. For all our preaching in this book about the need to continuously evolve planning processes, there is not going to be time and budget every quarter to make significant changes in the planning process. The less change we need to make to keep up with the changing business, the better. Elegant simplicity in our planning approach is half the battle. If we have built a single process and system strong enough to handle the current range of business needs every week of the year, it can probably handle some change in the current business as well. Conversely, if we design the complete planning process around one great planner and he or she goes on a two-week vacation, that may be dangerous for the enterprise.

Tolerance for volume growth is another dimension of robustness. If we are using a solver that suggests plans in two minutes of computer time, and product stockkeeping unit growth drives that to six minutes, we adjust and go on. If we have a solver that requires two hours of computer time, and product volume growth drives that to six hours, we have a significant process problem (we just cannot tolerate the extra four hours in our planning cycles).

Robustness is a simple concept, but requires us to think about risks and mitigation of those risks through good design of processes, systems, and organization. It is easy to keep a solid backup planner in the process so that vacations are not catastrophic (and it does not add cost, as planners spend a significant fraction of their time on special studies anyway). Future changes and problems, on the other hand, usually seem to come from a direction we were not expecting. Our bottom line: Great planning approaches are designed to create superb plans and not to be fragile.

Having the Right Amount of Inventory

One of the more confusing things that can happen to the planning function is to hear the demand from management that "inventory has to be reduced." Planning-driven decisions are the primary determinant of inventory levels in most organizations and hence it is an appropriate request of planners, but it can be confusing nonetheless. Let us think a little more carefully about inventory.

There is a "right amount" of product inventory for an enterprise to hold, based on:

- Decisions about business strategy and philosophy (operations excellence, customer intimacy, etc.) and what kind of service we need to provide
- The structure of the supply network; which players are expected to hold inventory at what levels
- The philosophy of operations and planning that has been adopted in the enterprise
- The supply–demand strategy the enterprise has adopted for a particular product line, and the customer order cycle and "decision point" that follow from that supply–demand strategy
- The investment the enterprise has made in processes and information technology systems for activity monitoring (e.g., real-time inventory visibility, supply chain event monitoring) and to support planning
- The planning processes themselves (e.g., are we re-evaluating inventory levels in our distribution centers on a daily basis or a weekly basis?)

So there is a right amount of inventory and right places to hold it based on these decisions. You can have too much inventory for the strategy and structure decisions you have made or too little. Determining the actual right quantities is, as we discussed earlier in this volume, quite difficult. We can attempt to do that with simulation, with inventory formulas, with benchmarking against other businesses we think are similar (and then making adjustments for all the elements we know are different), with incremental experimentation using the business itself, or by telling ourselves things like "Since we have been operating successfully with twenty-one days of supply, and we are making this planning change that should cut out the need for two of those days, we will now operate with nineteen days of supply."

If we believe that we should be able to provide a required level of customer service with a certain level of inventory and we are not able to do so, we have to re-examine whether our planning processes are working as planned, whether we are executing operations as we believe we should be able to, or whether we have simply accumulated too much unplanned inventory (sludge) through not managing excess and obsolescence effectively (or having financial management that is unwilling to take the accounting write-off of inventory that we have actually identified as excess or obsolete).

Returning to the demand that inventory be reduced, how we respond to that depends on our situation. If we have gotten sloppy with our planning and can meet the demand by simply planning better, then shame on us for our sloppiness and let us fix the problems immediately. If we have too much excess and obsolescence on the books, let us dispose of it. If we actually have the right amount of inventory for the decisions we made above, we can interpret the demand as a call to change some of those decisions and ask for the time to do that and to implement the new decisions with new supply–demand strategies and new planning processes. If we have the right amount but we must reduce it suddenly anyway, we need to make executives aware of the implications of doing that in terms of the service reduction (and possibly operating expense increase) consequences that will result and make sure that the business reasons for reducing it are valid. Some poorly managed enterprises create an oscillation around inventory: reduce it, suffer service failures, increase it to improve service, and so on.

Again, the demand to reduce inventory creates a confusing and complex situation. But we can understand our situation and make the right decisions to deal with it.

STAYING IN TOUCH WITH FUNDAMENTAL PLANNING CONCEPTS

As we first mentioned in Chapter 1, product flow planning is a conceptually slippery space. It is extremely easy to improve on a given concept and end up confusing the situation to the point of stopping progress. For example, the concept of a sales forecast seems simple enough, "what we expect to sell." But we have seen organizations twist it almost beyond recognition. If we cannot provide all the product we might sell, should we not produce a final forecast which is a "capacitated" sales forecast that reflects that constraint? Perhaps. Or maybe the forecast really ought to be the sales plan. If we also happen to be a make-to-order business, then can we not really combine the concept of forecast with production plan to create a "production forecast"? Not if we value our sanity.

Most organizations find that the concepts of forecast, production plan, master schedule, material supply plan, inventory deployment plan, available to promise, capable to promise, profitable to promise, and so on need to be guarded rather carefully. If they are not, there is no end to the confusion that is created. We advocate creative business-oriented approaches to planning in order to best serve the enterprise and potentially achieve competitive advantage. Sometimes that will involve novel ways of planning or combining traditional kinds of plans. But in doing this work we need to:

> **13. Be students of the body of planning knowledge that has been developed, and be rigorous in defining our approach in relation to the fundamental concepts.**

Admittedly, maintaining this degree of perspective on what we are doing, while also being creative, is not easy. Nor are we always helped by the vast literature on planning, which contains many techniques that are specialized for very specific types of business or that are just plain ill conceived. For example, a fundamental concept, such as the bill of material, can get stretched into more exotic and debatable ideas such as planning bills of material and super bills.

Sales & Operations Planning (S&OP) has also been misunderstood in some quarters. In recent years we have seen "S&OP" substituted for the production plan in the classic MRP II hierarchy diagram (the production plan concept still should generally be maintained, partly because it is needed to support the S&OP process). We have also seen the "S&OP Plan" term substituted for the complete tactical planning process that should go on in most organizations. These "popularizations" of S&OP are dangerous because they make it easy to forget what is special about S&OP: to gain commitment from functional management across the enterprise to a single integrated aggregate plan, which drives sales, financial, and human resources planning just as much as it drives manufacturing or distribution.

COMMON MISTAKES IN DESIGNING AND IMPLEMENTING PLANNING APPROACHES

1. **Believing that the "best practice" of the 1980s and 1990s is good enough**. Truly effective short- and medium-range product flow planning

is very difficult to achieve. As we at least implied in Chapters 2 and 5, none of the planning technologies or schools of operating philosophy, none of the orthodoxies, provides the perfect answer to all challenges. Designing, implementing, and evolving a planning approach that will give a unique enterprise and its supply chains a competitive advantage requires enormous ingenuity and persistence and probably some lessons from all of the schools. Stopping at what one school offers, be it a Class A MRP II implementation or an operating approach that seems acceptably Lean, virtually guarantees planning mediocrity.

2. **Believing that there is a silver bullet operating philosophy**. There is no one philosophical insight that will solve all problems. In fact, there are challenging planning and scheduling problems to solve under each of the philosophies. You or your organization may adopt a new philosophy and it may be a more powerful one for your business, but one reality is that it will lead to new planning challenges!

3. **Believing that there is silver bullet planning software**. Like the interviewee mentioned in Chapter 8 — who thought that "Gee, after all these years, isn't there software available to license that just solves all these planning problems seamlessly?" — it is tempting to hope that a definitive solution could be purchased. Planning software has come a long way in the last thirty years, and powerful algorithms and good user interfaces are broadly available, but in a sense the state of the art has not changed very much over this period. Then, as now, the challenge was to build planning models that accurately capture the essence of the problems, can be maintained with interfaces from other systems and an acceptable quantity of user maintenance effort, and then provide users with starting points from which to interactively, on a "man–machine" basis, develop great (re)plans. Truly automated planning — "the computer just does it" planning — remains extremely rare. We may see some successful examples of that during our professional lifetimes. For now, we can leave it that finding or creating the best interactive software to support its planning approach is a critical element for most enterprises and one of the most difficult. But with that done, there are a hundred other things that still have to be done well to really be effective planners.

4. **Believing that "siloed" functional groups are a relic of the past**. After a few decades of attacks on parochial organization structures, one might think that they would have virtually disappeared: manufacturing, sales, distribution, and so on. But they are so fundamental to the management process, including incentive programs that typically reinforce their power, that they easily carry on even in today's process-oriented business culture. While few managers want to talk about their influence, it is present,

ready to encourage narrow decisions that are suboptimal for the whole enterprise and ready to torpedo planning approaches that naively attempt to optimize across functional boundaries. But those boundaries have often been successfully breached, usually by planning and execution processes that make it powerfully obvious how product flow can be better managed with an integrating approach.

5. **Believing that the planning whole is as good as the sum of separate parts**. While any enterprise needs several plans to manage product flow, isolated plans that are individually good will seldom add up to an effective overall system. That is true even when each of the plans is a nice example of part of a classic planning paradigm, such as MRP II. Murphy will usually find the weaknesses at the boundaries of the plans: aggregate to detailed plans, material to manufacturing plans, the sales plan to the operations tactical plan, manufacturing to inventory plans, and so on — and raise havoc at those boundaries. An important job of planning management is to periodically review the complete set of planning processes, figure out where the gaps are, and design new processes that overcome the limitations.

6. **Believing that "implemented" planning software, with well-integrated data flows and well-trained users, is a completed project**. New systems for planning are a necessity, but getting them implemented in a mechanical sense is just the beginning of the fun. They must be stoked, stroked, and tuned; users must be taught and assisted and taught again how to produce top-quality plans with the new tools. Sometimes a new tool must ultimately be exposed as the wrong tool for the job and abandoned or heavily modified. The potential for great improvement in planning effectiveness is usually there, but it usually takes a special kind of persistence to deliver it.

PRIMARY PROCESSES AND SYSTEMS THAT MAINTAIN GREAT PLANS

This volume has repeatedly stressed the need for improving the enterprise planning approach by doing a great many things well: defining planning structure, working up- and downstream in our supply network, designing processes, finding software, managing data, building models, tuning and more tuning, keeping it simple, and keep improving. This view implies that improving planning is fairly prosaic; there are a lot of small things that must be done right. If done well, they produce excellent returns for the business.

While that view is generally true, we need to make one more point. If you are able to construct and execute primary planning processes and systems that deal well with all the appropriate decisions that must be made, planning becomes easier and the business runs very, very smoothly. Processes that get plans right the first time, that do not require days and weeks of iteration in the organization — that is a true breakthrough. The ideal planning approach is one in which straightforward primary processes, with no feedback loops, are able to quickly regenerate plans that take all significant current information into account, producing excellent plans on the first go-around: "Doing it right the first time."

To put it in the terms we discussed in Chapter 1, if we can accomplish this, we have built a planning approach that is truly adequate for the business we are trying to support; we have created a "brain" that is smart enough to actually deal with the life of the business "organism" we are directing. Having done this, we believe we mostly have solved the planning problem for our business. We believe there are no more big pots of money on the table that can be captured via better planning.

What do we mean by primary processes? We mean the primary flow of planning decision making, without feedback loops, without negotiations, without expediting, without collaborating in the specific sense we use that term in this volume. When we generate a master production schedule, it is the right master production schedule because it comprehends everything important to be known about demand, capacity, manufacturing economics, inventory, and material availability. We are unlikely to modify it today, because there is likely to be no compelling reason to modify it. We may modify it tomorrow, because the world may have changed significantly by then, and we may need to respond in a measured way — after all, planning is really replanning (Principle 6). When we regenerate our plan for tomorrow's replenishment of field inventory of finished goods (assuming that we use a supply–demand strategy that requires field inventory), we know it is the right plan because it comprehends everything to be known about demand, transportation and warehouse capacity, and inventory as of the close of business today. We will regenerate it again tomorrow because there will be much new information by then.

Have we reached nirvana if we have done this? No. The business we are planning is probably still a very tough, very competitive business. We have achieved, however, a very significant competitive advantage because our competitors have almost certainly not arrived at this level. And we have definitely gotten ourselves out of the business of firefighting. Several years ago, we interviewed a plant planner who had recently finished implementing a new planning system that was working extremely well. He was proud of it, but said he missed the firefighting because it "made him feel important." We were not sympathetic.

Achieving this level of planning excellence is a function of the complexity of our business, the resources we can bring to bear on planning. We have a lot better chance in a large but relatively simple business. For example, the half-billion-dollar bottling business reviewed in Chapter 7 could easily afford the incremental staff and planning tools to achieve a breakthrough and be very good at planning at least the filling and distribution portions of its operations. On the other hand, a large contract manufacturing business in the high-tech industry is too dynamic to really keep a handle on with any known technology.

Have we finished our work if we reach this level of planning? Of course not. The business will continue to change, probably dropping us out of this planning "adequacy" state if we cannot quickly figure out how to change with it. We may be ready to move to a different supply/demand strategy that promises a higher level of total performance, but also needs a different approach to planning. And our feeling of adequacy is probably based on some given level of correctness of information about demand in our supply chain and flexibility in our supply chain. We can probably imagine reaching a still higher plane of planning with more nearly perfect information about downstream demand and inventory, or with better forecasts, or with more responsive suppliers. Thus, we may need to turn most of our energy to these information collection and supply chain partner problems, the hardest nuts to crack in "planning": having truly good forecasts, truly good downstream information from ultimate consumers (which have likely resisted our efforts to date), and truly responsive suppliers.

If this planning breakthrough level exists, why would we set any goals other than that? Why would we not always "go for it" in our planning structure vision and plan to create whatever we have to create to optimize product flow? If we are able to confidently design a planning structure that will achieve this level, we probably should target that vision. However, it is likely that we do not have sufficient time and money to achieve that goal. If our business is complex, we may not even be able to generate a concrete design to plan optimally. The majority of efforts to create the ultimate, grand planning approach have been disappointing, at least to the degree of still leaving their architects with many obvious problems to solve. Thus, in many situations, there are reasons to aim for more modest goals.

CONCLUSION

And so we commend you to the world of operational entropy — a world of machine breakdowns, of corporate acquisitions, mergers, and spinoffs; a world of sudden decisions to move production to a manufacturer in China; a world where Wall Street just demands that we have a 70 percent sales spike at the end of the quarter; a world of violent weather and violent political activity ready to disrupt our activities.

You have the conceptual tools and the principles to make great improvements in product flow planning and hence in operational effectiveness, in the ability to provide the right amount of service with the least quantity of resources. You know where to find specific knowledge and skills when you need them.

There is no more fascinating problem in business than that posed by trying to plan and coordinate an enterprise's sphere of influence in a supply network so that product flows as smoothly as we know it could. Enjoy the multidimensional subtleties of the challenge you face.

Go forth and be insightful and rational. Go forth and be a pillar of confidence, knowledge, and leadership.

REFERENCES

1. Riezebos, Jan, *Design of a Period Batch Control Planning System for Cellular Manufacturing*, Dissertation, University of Groningen, Netherlands, 2001.
2. Hopp, Wallace J. and Spearman, Mark L., *Factory Physics,* 2nd ed., McGraw-Hill/ Irwin, Boston, 2000.
3. Anthony, R.N., *Planning and Control Systems: A Framework for Analysis*, Harvard University, Boston, 1965.
4. George, Michael L., *Lean Six Sigma: Combining Six Sigma Quality with Lean Production Speed*, McGraw-Hill, New York, 2002.
5. Muzumdar, Maha and Deise, Chuck, Available, capable, profitable: driving customer satisfaction and the top line, *APICS—The Performance Advantage*, 13(2), 54–58, 2003.
6. Goldratt, Eliyahu M., *What Is This Thing Called Theory of Constraints and How Should It Be Implemented?,* North River Press, Great Barrington, MA, 1990.
7. Shingo, Shigeo, *Non-Stock Production: The Shingo System for Continuous Improvement*, Productivity Press, Cambridge, MA, 1988.
8. A.T. Kearney, A.T. Kearney's Perspectives on Operations Excellence, 2001 GED Program Results, white paper.
9. Wagner, Harvey M., And then there were none, *Operations Research*, 50(1), 217–226, 2002.
10. Hadley, G. and Whitin, T.M., *Analysis of Inventory Systems*, Prentice-Hall, Englewood Cliffs, NJ, 1963.
11. Silver, E.A., Pyke, D.F., and Peterson, R., *Inventory Management and Production Planning and Scheduling*, 3rd ed., John Wiley & Sons, New York, 1998.
12. Clark, A. and Scarf, H., Optimal policies for a multi-echelon inventory problem, *Management Science*, 36, 1329–1338, 1960.
13. Plossl, George W., *Production and Inventory Control: Principles and Techniques,* 2nd ed., Prentice-Hall, Englewood Cliffs, NJ, 1985.
14. Martin, Andre J., *DRP: Distribution Resource Planning,* rev. ed., Oliver Wight Publications, Essex Junction, VT, 1993.

15. Womack, James P. and Jones, Daniel T., *Lean Thinking*, Simon & Schuster, New York, 1996.

16. Goldratt, Eliyahu M. and Cox, Jeff, *The Goal: A Process of Ongoing Improvement*, 2nd rev. ed., North River Press, Great Barrington, MA, 1992.

17. Schragenheim, Eli and Dettmer, H. William, *Manufacturing at Warp Speed*, St. Lucie Press, Boca Raton, FL, 2001.

18. Silver, E.A. and Meal, H.C., A heuristic for selecting lot size requirements for the case of deterministic time-varying demand rate and discrete opportunities for replenishment, *Production and Inventory Management*, 14(2), 64–74, 1973.

19. Manne, Alan S., Programming of economic lot sizes, *Management Science*, 4, 115–135, 1958.

20. Hillier, Frederick S. and Lieberman, Gerald J., *Introduction to Operations Research*, 7th ed., Holden-Day, Oakland, CA, 2000.

21. Lasdon, L.S. and Terjung, R.C., An efficient algorithm for multi-item scheduling, *Operations Research*, 19, 946–969, 1971.

22. King, R.H. and Love, R.R., Jr., Coordinating decisions for increased profits, *Interfaces*, 10(6), 4–19, 1980.

23. Glover, F., Jones, G., Carney, D., Klingman, D., and Mote, J., An integrated production, distribution, and inventory planning system, *Interfaces*, 9(5), 21–35, 1979.

24. Miller, Tan, *Hierarchical Operations and Supply Chain Planning*, Springer-Verlag, London, 2001.

25. Hax, Arnoldo C. and Candea, Dan, *Production and Inventory Management*, Prentice-Hall, Englewood Cliffs, NJ, 1984.

26. Johnson, Lynwood A. and Montgomery, Douglas C., *Operations Research in Production Planning, Scheduling, and Inventory Control*, John Wiley & Sons, New York, 1974.

27. Shapiro, Jeremy F., *Modeling the Supply Chain*, Duxbury, Pacific Grove, CA, 2001.

28. Graves, Stephen C., A review of production scheduling, *Operations Research*, 29(4), 646–675, 1981.

29. Tayur, S., Ganeshan, R., and Magazine, M., Eds., *Quantitative Models for Supply Chain Management*, Kluwer Academic, Norwell, MA, 1999.

30. Forrester, Jay W., *Industrial Dynamics*, The M.I.T. Press, Cambridge, MA, 1961.

31. Gordon, Geoffrey, *System Simulation*, Prentice-Hall, Englewood Cliffs, NJ, 1969.

32. Plate, Tony and Perrott, Dale, Complexity science as a new strategic tool, *Quarterly Strategy Review CGEY Strategy & Transformation Practice*, Cap Gemini Ernst & Young, April 2001, 6 p.

33. Murthy, Sesh, Akkiraju, Rama, Goodwin, Richard, Keskinocak, Pinar, Rachlin, John, Wu, Frederick, Yeh, James, Fuhrer, Robert, Kumaran, Santhosh, Aggarwal, Alok, Sturzenbecker, Martin, Jayaraman, Ranga, and Daigle, Robert, Cooperative multiobjective decision support for the paper industry, *Interfaces*, 29(5), 5–30, 1999.

34. Buffa, Elwood S. and Taubert, William H., *Production-Inventory Systems: Planning and Control*, rev. ed., Richard D. Irwin, Homewood, IL, 1972.

35. Glover, F., Tabu search: a tutorial, *Interfaces*, 20(4), 74–94, 1990.
36. Glover, F., Taillard, E., and DeWerra, D., A user's guide to tabu search, *Annals of Operations Research*, 41, 3–28, 1993.
37. Lloyd, Tom, When Swarm Intelligence Beats Brainpower, http:/money. telegraph.co.uk, June 25, 2001.
38. Ling, Richard C. and Goddard, Walter E., *Orchestrating Success: Improve Control of the Business with Sales & Operations Planning*, Oliver Wight Publications, Essex Junction, VT, 1988.
39. Viewlocity, Bridge the Chasm Between Planning and Execution with Supply Chain Event Management, Viewlocity white paper series, 2001.
40. Vollman, Thomas E., Berry, William L., and Whybark, D. Clay, *Manufacturing Planning and Control Systems,* 4th ed., McGraw-Hill/Irwin, Boston, 1997.
41. Cox, James F. and Blackstone, John H., Eds., *APICS Dictionary,* 9th ed., APICS— The Educational Society for Resource Management, Alexandria, VA, 1998.
42. Schrage, Michael, Worst practice, *CIO Magazine*, February 15, 2003.
43. March durable-goods orders fell, capital spending remained weak, *Wall Street Journal*, p. A3+, April 25, 2002.
44. Kahla, Paul, Inside Cisco's $2 billion blunder, *Business 2.0*, March 1, 2002.
45. Aeppel, Timothy, More plants go 24/7, and workers are left at sixes and sevens, *The Wall Street Journal*, p. A1, July 24, 2001.
46. Allen, David, *Getting Things Done: The Art of Stress-Free Productivity*, Viking Press, New York, 2001.
47. Treacy, Michael and Wiersema, Fred, *The Discipline of Market Leaders*, Perseus Books, Reading, MA, 1995.
48. Wallace, Thomas F., *Sales and Operations Planning: The How-to Handbook*, T.F. Wallace, Cincinnati, OH, 2000.
49. Oliver, Keith, Chung, Anne, and Samanich, Nick, Beyond Utopia: the realist's guide to Internet-enabled supply chain management, *Strategy + Business,* 23, Second Quarter, 2001.
50. Rosenthal, Beth Ellyn, Reverse Auctions Improve Quality, Price and Delivery of Custom Goods, www.OutsourcingSupplyChainManagement.com, October 2001.
51. Verga, Gillian, Reverse auctions, strategies and lessons learned from a successful implementation, *APICS—The Performance Advantage*, 12(1), 28–31, 2002.
52. Koch, Christopher, Motor City shakeup, *Darwin Magazine*, January 2002.
53. Landvater, Darryl V., *World Class Production and Inventory Management,* 2nd ed., John Wiley & Sons, New York, 1997.
54. Reeve, James M., The financial advantages of the lean supply chain, *Supply Chain Management Review*, p. 42, March/April 2002.
55. Hines, Peter, Lamming, Richard, Jones, Daniel, Cousins, Paul, and Rich, Nick, *Value Stream Management: Strategy and Excellence in the Supply Chain*, Pearson Education Limited, Harlow, UK, 2000.
56. Proud, John F., *Master Scheduling,* 2nd ed., John Wiley & Sons, New York, 1999.
57. Goldratt, Eliyahu M., *Critical Chain*, North River Press, Great Barrington, MA, 1997.

58. Project Management Institute, *A Guide to the Project Management Body of Knowledge (PMBOK® Guide)* — 2000 Edition, Project Management Institute, Newtown Square, PA, 2000.

59. Dennis, Pascal, *Lean Production Simplified: A Plain Language Guide to the World's Most Powerful Production System,* Productivity Press, New York, 2002.

60. Shingo, Shigeo, *The Shingo Production Management System: Improving Process Functions,* Productivity Press, Cambridge, MA, 1992.

61. Burbridge, John L., *Production Flow Analysis for Planning Group Technology,* Clarendon Press, Oxford, 1989.

62. Burbridge, John L., *Period Batch Control,* Clarendon Press, Oxford, 1996.

63. Taylor, S.G. and Bolander, S.F., *Process Flow Scheduling: A Scheduling Systems Framework for Flow Manufacturing,* American Production and Inventory Control Society, Falls Church, VA, 1994.

64. Bermudez, John, Does Your Management Structure Support Supply Chain Cost Reductions? Executive View column published by AMR Research at http://www.amrresearch.com/Content/view.asp?pmillid=14885&docid-8894, April 2, 2002.

65. Schrage, Michael, Good network, bad data, *Fortune,* p. 254, June 2001.

66. Adams, Jeff, Don't join the revolution, *iSource Business,* November, 25–26, 2001.

67. Lewis, Robert D., The value of a test drive, *InfoWorld,* 24(13), 48, 2002.

68. Smith, Howard and Fingar, Peter, Making business processes manageable, *Internet World,* pp. 21–24, April 2002.

69. Renner, Chris and Schutt, Jeff, Supply chain management, in *Evolving E-Markets: Building High Value B2B Exchanges with Staying Power,* ISI Publications, Pembroke, Bermuda, 2000.

70. Schönsleben, Paul, *Integral Logistics Management: Planning and Control of Comprehensive Business Processors,* St. Lucie Press, Boca Raton, FL, 2002.

INDEX

Bottom-up planning, 44
BPO, see Business process outsourcing
Brand management, 173
Budget, 58, 154, 160, 162, 187, 198, 220, 222
Buffer, 137
Build to order, 78
Business analytics, 52
Business case, 154, 170, 180, 193
Business philosophy, 75, 77
Business processes, 64
Business process outsourcing (BPO), 178, 179, 180
Business releases, 160
Business requirements, 202
Business rules, 42
Business strategy, 10–11, 75, 109, 150–151, 232
Business-to-business transactions, 105

C

Canned foods processor, 113–114
Capable to promise (CTP), 13, 46, 48–49, 139
Capacity, 12, 20, 37
Capacity requirements planning, 28
Capacity utilization, 8
Capital requirements, 17
Caps Logistics, 46
Carrier assignment, 46
Case studies, see Planning structure, transformation, cases in
Cells, 30, 81, 139
Central distribution center, 117
Central inventory control, 94
Centralization, 15, 96, 98–99, 174
Centralized planning, 98
  resistance to, 224
Central planning group, 158, 176, 188, 189, 191
Champion, 147, 149, 151, 191
Change, 65, 172–178
  resistance to, 167
Change management, 167
Changeover, 34, 70, 85, 184, 186
Channel, 31
Channel master, 217, 218

Chaos theory, 41
Charter, 150
Chesapeake Decision Systems, 46
Chilled period, 65, 66, 67
Cisco Systems, 68–69
Classroom training, 189
Cleveland Consulting Associates, 45
Collaboration, 11, 15, 85, 88, 108, 191
Collaborative forecast, 132, 226
Collaborative planning, 3, 53, 101, 103, 104, 105–108, 164, 194, 225–226
  architectures, 215–217, 218
Collaborative planning, forecasting, and replenishment (CPFR), 54, 216, 217
Collaborative scheduling, 186
Collaborative tools, 98
Communication, 12, 55, 67, 87, 175, 188, 212
Competing plans, 177
Competitive advantage, 14, 156, 237
Competitors, 5, 105
Complexity, 24, 95–98, 221–223
Complexity science, 41, 42
Complex planning logic, 120, 135
Comprehensive vision, 230
Computer-less operations, 13
Computers, 12, 197, 199, 212, 228, see also Data and systems; Information technology; Software
Conceptual training, 166
Conference room pilot, 164, 165, 195, 196, 204, 206
Configure to order (CTO), 111, 113–114, 116, 119, 120, 121, 128, 135, 152
Conservation of product flow, 61
Consignment, 32
Consistent data, 219, 220
Constraint, 28, 29, 33, 37, 45, 70, 84, 129, 137, 142, 184, 186, 193
Consultants, 158, 193, 210
Consumer, 6
Consumer goods, 28, 31
Consumer packaged goods (CPG), 23, 117, 133, 166, 173, 196, 198
Consumer products industry, 218, 220
Continuous improvement, 121, 209
Continuous replenishment, 31